AFRICANA COLLECTANEA

VOLUME XXVII

AFRICANA COLLECTANEA SERIES

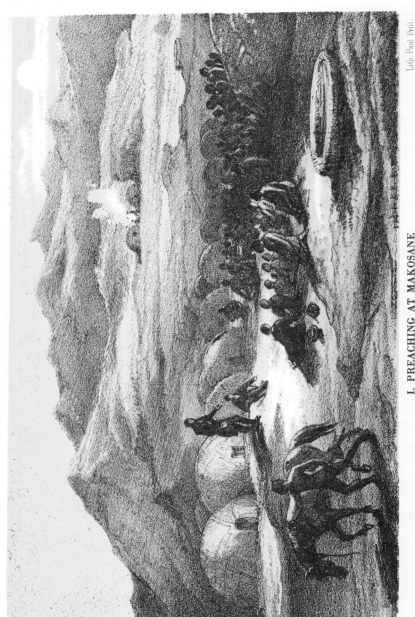

I. PREACHING AT MAKOSANE

Lith. Paul Petit.

NARRATIVE

OF

AN EXPLORATORY TOUR

To the North-East of the Colony

of the

CAPE OF GOOD HOPE

by

T. ARBOUSSET and F. DAUMAS

Facsimile Reprint

CAPE TOWN

C. STRUIK (PTY.) LTD.

1968

C. Struik (Pty.) Ltd.
Africana Specialist and Publisher

This edition is limited to 750 numbered copies.
Nos. 1–50 are specially bound in de luxe style.

This is No. 164

❧ PRINTED IN SOUTH AFRICA BY
THE RUSTICA PRESS, PTY., LTD., WYNBERG, CAPE

PUBLISHER'S NOTE

When we decided to reprint this book in our AFRICANA COLLECTANEA SERIES we learned that the original French edition was extremely well done but both English editions rather poorly. Therefore, we have chosen for our reprint the first English edition, published in Cape Town by A. S. Robertson in 1846, but included the beautiful illustrations of the French edition and the map of the second English edition.

C. STRUIK

LIST OF ILLUSTRATIONS

NARRATIVE

OF

AN EXPLORATORY TOUR

TO THE

NORTH-EAST OF THE COLONY

OF THE

CAPE OF GOOD HOPE.

BY THE REVS. T. ARBOUSSET AND F. DAUMAS,

OF THE PARIS MISSIONARY SOCIETY.

———

TRANSLATED FROM THE FRENCH OF THE REV. T. ARBOUSSET,

BY

JOHN CROUMBIE BROWN.

———

CAPE TOWN:

A. S. ROBERTSON, HEERENGRACHT,
SAUL SOLOMON & Co. ST. GEORGE'S-STREET.
1846.

Printed by
Saul Solomon & Co. "Gazette" Office,
St. George's-street, Cape Town.

ADVERTISEMENT.

_____

An interest in the Bechuana Tribes on the Frontier of the Colony having been excited in Cape Town by the visit of Mr. Arbousset and several relatives of Moshesh, the Chief of the Basutos, and a desire having been expressed by many for a translation of copious extracts from the following work, the author requested the translator to enable him to gratify his friends, promising, at the same time, to give every assistance in his power, in comparing the translation with the original. The extracts were accordingly made; but it soon appeared much more desirable that the whole work should be translated; and this also was accomplished under the immediate superintendence of the author, who hoped to have seen the work published before he left the Colony to return to his station. Circumstances, however, over which neither he nor the translator had any control, have prevented its publication until now.

J. C. B.

Cape Town, 25th August 1846.

PREFACE TO THE PARIS EDITION BY THE COMMITTEE OF THE PARIS MISSIONARY SOCIETY.

————

The exploratory tour to the north-east of the Cape of Good Hope, undertaken by Messrs. Arbousset and Daumas, was undertaken with a particular object in view; —it was altogether a missionary tour. To seek out unknown tribes, to open up communication with their chiefs, to mark out plans suitable for missionary stations, to extend the influence of christianity and civilization,—such are the duties which every missionary imposes upon himself when he travels, and such were the objects which the authors of the following narrative had specially in view. A missionary is not by his vocation either a naturalist or a philosopher; it is not in the service of science that he crosses the deep or traverses the desert; nobler objects are set before him, and higher interests engage his attention. At the same time the sacredness of his purpose forbids not that he should attend to other objects which are only indirectly connected with what is, strictly speaking, his mission. And if on his route, he finds himself in a position to note some observation, to verify some fact, to undertake some investigation in the domain of natural history, of geography, of statistics, there is nothing to induce him to decline a labor, which in such circumstances becomes a duty. It is in this way that, without cultivating science for its own sake, more than one christian missionary has enriched that branch of literature which embraces voyages and travels with valuable documents and researches, by which men of science would have considered themselves honored, had they gathered them as the fruit of close and protracted study. Crantz has thrown a great deal of light on the geography of Greenland ; Ellis, Williams, Tyerman, and Bennett have added much to our information in regard to Oceana ; Medhurst has written a work on China, rich in observations ; Bishop Heber has made us acquainted with the manners of India ; Jowett has explored the shores of the Mediterranean ; Gobat, Abyssynia ; Campbell and Philip, South Africa ; and, not to prolong the enumeration, Messrs. Arbousset and Daumas have made a tour through the country lying between the Orange River and the Namagari, which has not been unproductive of facts in regard to the geography and statistics of that part of South Africa through which they travelled.

To say nothing of the numerous native tribes which they have studied more closely, and described more carefully, than any had done before them, they have deserved well of science for two discoveries of great importance. They have revealed the fact previously unknown of the existence of cannibal tribes in the neighbourhood of the Malutis, and they have discovered the source of the principal rivers of South Africa, in a mount which crowns, on the north, the chain of the Blue Mountains. The Orange, the Caledon, the Namagari, the Letuele, and the Monuenu, have all one common source, and they make their escape in the south-west, south, north and north-east directions by the sides of one mountain, which, on this account, the missionaries have named the *Mont-aux-Sources*.

There is still much that is obscure in the knowledge which we have of the geography of South Africa ; but, thanks to the french missionaries, this part of the world will soon be better known. They have already prepared seven charts of districts previously unexplored, which have been published by the committee of the Société des Missions Evangéliques.*

* These charts will be found in the *Journal des Missions Evangéliques,* or they may be procured separately, at Delay's, No. 62, rue Basse-du-Rempart.

We may remark, in concluding this short preface, that
the author of this narrative of an exploratory tour to
the north-east of the Cape of Good Hope, M. Thomas
Arbousset, minister of the gospel, is settled at Moriah,
in the country of the Basutos, and that his fellow traveller,
M. François Daumas, also a minister of the gospel, is
settled at Mekuatling, amongst the Lighoyas. The missionary station of Moriah was founded in the year 1833 ;
that of Mekuatling, in the year 1837. At both of these
stations the effects of christianity and civilization are apparent.* The Société des Missions Evangéliques has
founded, and maintains, five other stations in South Africa,
namely, Motito, Beersheba, Bethulie, Thaba Bosio, and
Wagonmakers Valley.

M. Cassilis, missionary at Thaba Bosio, has prepared a
valuable work on the sechuana language, which the committee of the Société des Missions Evangéliques have
published under the title of *Etudes sur la Langue Sechuana.*
It contains a grammar, rules of syntax, and a collection of
the poetry of the Bechuanas, and may be procured at
the Office of the Society, or at Delay's, 62, rue Basse-
du-Rempart, Paris.

In the orthography adopted throughout the Narrative,
no silent letters are employed. The vowel sounds are as
follows : —

> a—as in *man.*
> e—as *ey* in *they.*
> i—as *ee* in *meet.*
> o—as in *open.*
> u—as in *put.*

* Details will be found in the *Journal des Missions Evangéliques,* published
monthly at the price of six francs per annum, by Delay, No. 62, rue Basse
du-Rempart, Paris.

CONTENTS.

CHAPTER XXIII.

NOTICES OF THE BUSHMEN AND THEIR LANGUAGE.

CHAPTER XXIV.

BECHUANA TRIBES, AND HISTORY OF MOTLUME.

CHAPTER XXV.

MOKONIANE AND MOSHESH.

CHAPTER XXVI.

SETTLEMENT OF MOSHESH AT THABA BOSIO.

CHAPTER XXVII.

SETTLEMENT OF MISSIONARIES.

APPENDIX.

CHAPTER I.

BEFORE entering upon our narration, it may be well to
give our readers some idea, however imperfect, of the
preparations we found necessary for a journey into the
unknown and barbarous regions we were about to visit.
Even in civilised countries, well provided with spacious
and well-kept roads, with canals, with rail-roads, and
with coaches and carriages of every description,—where
at every stage one meets with a town, a village, or at least
an inn,—a journey of some weeks cannot be undertaken
without considerable care and trouble. There is baggage
to arrange, there are trunks to pack, there are friends to
visit, there are a thousand little things to attend to,
many of which have been forgotten till the eve of
your departure,—and some, perhaps, are only remem-
bered as you are about to commence your journey,—
annoying yourself and your friends, and fully justifying
that expression of Madame de Stael, " *Voyager est un des
plus tristes plaisirs de la vie.*" What, then, must be the
case, when, instead of a civilised country provided with
every convenience for travellers, you have to traverse
savage and uncultivated deserts, where such conveniences
are unknown ? When, besides packing the trunks, carpet-
bags, and portmanteaus, with which the traveller must
provide himself in Africa as well as in Europe, it is necessary that he himself see to the getting ready of his vehicle,

and the collecting of his team, that he look out for
guides, and settle with them the terms of their engage-
ment, that he form some estimate of the provisions
likely to be required by the whole caravan, throughout a
journey which will occupy he knows not how many weeks,
collect these provisions, and stow them away in his enormous wagon, and that he provide himself, moreover,
with every thing requisite for encampment in the
wilderness? Let this be considered, and our readers
will not be astonished at the preparations of a missionary for an exploratory journey into regions almost
unknown to Europeans, and amongst savage tribes,
animated by feelings which, if not decidedly hostile,
were yet of a very questionable character, and some of
whom were known to be cannibals.

Our company consisted of nine individuals :—two Bas-
tards, at once good guides and good huntsmen, four
others, drivers or servants, one basuto herd, M. DAUMAS,
my fellow missionary, and myself. We had two wagons
and thirty draught oxen, some of which, however, were
destined for slaughter, when we should be unable in any
other way to procure food. We had also seven horses,
which were to be used with the saddle on any excursion
we might have to make by the way, but on which the
ox-wagon could not be employed. To enable us, moreover,
to retrace our steps, we took care to supply ourselves
with chronometers and with mariner's compasses.

On the 13th of March 1836, every thing was ready for
our commencing the journey. Feeling the necessity of
putting ourselves under the protection of God, and of
commending to his paternal care M. GOSSELLIN, our fel-
low-labourer, and the station at which we were about to
leave him,—we spent half-an-hour in prayer with our dear
brother. Many where the thoughts and feelings which
crowded upon us ; we knew not to what people, or into
what regions, the Lord was sending us ; we knew not
what trials we might be called to endure ; we knew not
how, or when, we should return, or what in the meanwhile

might befal the station of Moriah, and the friend we were leaving there. Prayer calmed our anxious spirits, and alleviated the anguish of our hearts ; we parted, trusting in our heavenly Father, relying on his wisdom and goodness. It was not self-interest, nor mere curiosity, which prompted our journey. The gospel in our hand, we were going forth to carry its divine light into the midst of tribes benighted by ignorance, and the grossest superstitions ; we were going forth to labor for the advancement of the Kingdom of Christ; we were going to save souls, and the sacredness of our purpose gave us a confident assurance that God would bless our feeble efforts.

Having travelled throughout the day, first in the direction of N.N.E., and afterwards in that of N.N.W., we pitched our tent, on the evening of the 13th of March, in a most picturesque spot, at the foot of two mountains standing near each other,—the one low, of a rounded shape and gentle slope, the other presenting an imposing appearance from its height and form.

It is steep, and of difficult ascent ; at some places the sides appear almost vertical ; its height from the base to the summit is about 1,300 feet, and its circumference must be twenty or four-and-twenty miles. The natives call it the K"eme, and speak of it as one of the highest mountains in the country. It is surmounted by an enormous rock, which presents the appearance of a tower, and which seems to be sustained there by some invisible power. Suspended on the brow of a mountain, it forms a prodigious projection, in the shade of which the Saule gently flows through a narrow passage between the two mountains which it has opened for itself.

This river,—which, in its meanderings, waters the base of these mountains,—is to the prairies which it traverses a source of fertility, but to the natives it is an object of dread. They call it the Putiatsana, of which designation we have received two different explanations from them. Some make it a derivation from the verb *puta,* to gather up,—saying, that at times when a great deal of

rain falls on the White Mountains, the river rises rapidly,
and engulphs and sweeps before it the weaker cattle
grazing on its banks; and that, therefore, they call it the
Putiatsana, or the Gatherer. Others, with less reason
perhaps, consider that it must have got its name from the
puti, an antelope fawn, which, from the description they
give of it, appears to be a kind of chamois (*antilope
rupricapra.*) It is about the height, they say, of a she-
goat of two years old; it is speckled with reddish-brown
spots, like the chamois; it has no beard, but it wants the
black stripe along the back, which is one of the characteristics of that animal; it has no tail; the male only has
horns, and these are small and short. The Basutos are
very fond of its flesh, but, contrary to their usual custom,
they give the entrails to their dogs. One circumstance
which rather tells against the supposition of those of the
natives who derive the name of the river from the name
of this animal is, that the *puta* does not live on the
banks of the Saule; its habits are those of the goat; like
it, it is never happy but on the mountain top, or in the
depths of the wood, and it seldom quits these retreats.

By some, the Saule is called the Little Caledon, from
the name of the river to which it is a tributary. It has
two sources; the principal one is about 30 miles to the
N.E. of Thaba Bosio,—the other is about 12 or 14
miles to the S.E. of that capital of the Basutos. The
waters of the Saule are pure and limpid, and in some
places deep. Where we crossed it, it rolls over a bed of
very hard black grit, or iron-stone. About a hundred
paces distant, the view is bounded by an eliptical semicircle of rocks, terminating in a narrow passage which
the Saule has opened for herself between the two hills
of which we have spoken. There she stealthily disap-
pears amongst the rocks, which seems determined, if possible, to prevent her escape. A little further on, finding a channel less encumbered, she flows on peacefully
for about five miles, and then mingles her waters with
those of the Caledon. We never tired looking on the

scene ; every thing around us was grand, magnificent, and life-like, contrasting strongly with many a gloomy monotonous scene which had wearied the eye on other journeys we had taken. That circus, girt about with rocks, the rough and rugged sides of which may be seen reflected in the waters below ;—that little wood, whose refreshing green does every thing possible to soften whatever may be too harsh in the outline of the landscape ;— every thing, in short, concurs to excite in the soul emotions of inexpressible delight. Never had we experienced a sweeter, or more extatic, joy than we did, when, with the Bible in our hands and with prayers on our lips, we turned towards the outlet from that mountain temple to gaze on the work of God, and the magnificent vestment with which he had there enrobed creation. Never before had the contemplation of his works excited such transports of grateful feeling, or such deep-toned devotion ; not that the Lord had at any time, or in any circumstances, left us without an assurance of his presence : but we have found that those scenes which elevate the soul, like those which soften the heart, deepen the feeling that the Lord is near, and render manifest to the eye, as it were, the wonders of his goodness and his power.

Before taking leave of the Saule, I must say a few words in regard to the inhabitants of its waters. The form of two species of these arrested my attention. One of them was a fish about 16 inches long ; the head and body were flat, the colour a uniform grey, the flesh white, and very delicate. The other was a little larger, with a cylindrical body, of a deep brown colour, and an elongated head. It is a species of barbel, having long barbels at the mouth. I shall afterwards have occasion to speak of the way in which the natives catch these fish.

If we may believe the natives, the Saule must also be inhabited by crocodiles, end these of two different species; one which the Basutos call the *Kuené,* and another

which they call *Lefitué*. The former is said to be about
the size of a young calf; the latter, so large that its
body forms a kind of bank when it lays itself across the
stream.   The Basutos have a great, and somewhat
superstitious dread of both.   We may relate a few of
their traditions, leaving our readers to attach to them
what importance they may think proper.

"When a man," say they, "walks on the banks of
the river, woe to him, if he happens to be seen by a
Kuené, or a Lefitué!   The crocodile has the power
of seizing the shadow of a man passing by, and by it
dragging him into the river, where it will certainly kill
him, though it will not eat a morsel of his flesh."
"How did you know that?" we one day asked some of
them who were speaking on the subject; "they take
cattle in the same way," was their reply.   "One of them,
in this way, caused a cow to fall into the river; when
she was pulled out again, she was found to be dead, but
in no way mangled; they opened her, but they found
neither blood in her heart, nor marrow in her bones;
without a doubt the crocodile had sucked away both!"
Another story which we had from the natives was this:—
"The *kuené* seized a man who was passing near the
Saule, and dragging him in to his dwelling, which was
dug obliquely upward from under the water, left him
there, and went to call the *lefitué*.   While it was away,
a ray of light coming through a chink in the earth,
the prisoner saw lying just at his hand some cop_
per bracelets some strings of beads, and a pickaxe.   He
took them, cut an opening with the axe, and escaped.
These things, say they, may have belonged to some former victim of the crocodile."   The Basutos have not the
least doubt of the truth of this story.   They believe also
that the glance of the *kuené* or *lefitué* may prove fatal.
"A year ago," said some of them to us one day, "two
young children were playing together on the banks of the
river; they amused themselves by dipping their heads like
ducks.   In the evening, their parents being alarmed at

not seeing them return, went to seek them, and found them drowned in a little shallow basin. A crocodile, cried they at once, has killed them by its glance."

The next day, the 14th of March, we left the banks of the Saule,—the Putiatsana, or *noka e bogale*, the *wicked river*, as the natives sometimes call it,—and continued our journey in a northerly direction, amongst groups of little hills, which were covered with excellent pasturage. Towards noon we came in sight of Bosio ; an hour after we were abreàst of Lisonein, another considerable basuto town; an hour later, we were on the banks of the Caledon; and before night we reached the Wesleyan missionary station of platberg.

The country slopes gradually, almost imperceptibly, from Moriah towards the Caledon. From the Caledon to Platberg it begins to rise.

CHAPTER II.

THE designation Platberg (flat mountain) was given originally to a dry and open spot of ground within the 28th degree of south latitude, and 26th degree of east longitude, lying on this side of the river Fal. There the Wesleyan missionaries laboured for about twelve years, endeavoring to raise the feeble body of Africans to the rank of active and intelligent christians. They aimed high, but with little success. There the name was descriptive of the locality; but towards the end of 1833, the inhabitants of old Platberg emigrated to a more fertile district, and they gave to their new location the name of their former residence. It would be difficult, however, to trace in new Platberg any resemblance to a flat mountain. Let one picture to himself, on the contrary, a very long hill, or narrow ridge of hills, inclining towards the S.W., and abutting on the Waterberg mountains towards the E. On the brow of the ridge stand the chapel and the parsonage; and in front of these stretches the little village in one long street of twenty-five or thirty houses. At the side are numerous kitchen gardens, which are watered by a pretty mountain stream, walled in by an immense bank of rocks, the towering and deeply indented crest of which commands the whole plain. On the south and the west the horizon stretches away to the distance of fifteen or sixteen miles. On the opposite sides. it is bounded by the Waterberg, the view of which in no way compensates for the loss of that of the White Mountains which it conceals.*

New Platberg numbers about 200 inhabitants, who, thanks to the strictness of Wesleyan discipline, and to the zeal and energy of their spiritual instructor, have made no small progress in the christian life. It presents a religious aspect much more satisfactory than many a village in Europe. The day of rest is, generally speaking, well observed; the attendance on the sanctuary is in general numerous, attentive, and devotional; the meetings for prayer on the sabbath, and in the course of the week, are well attended. Oftener than once have we been surprised and refreshed by hearing the more advanced members of the church speak of their spiritual feelings with that simplicity which is so characteristic of pagan converts:—" I am a dull fellow. I understand very little of the holy truths. I have only a little love to the Lord Jesus Christ." Such is the simple way in which they express themselves in conversation, whether with one another or with strangers. The schools, also, although organised on no particular plan, present a satisfactory appearance. They follow, as they can, the plan of mutual instruction. In the class, as in the house, the more advanced instruct the more backward; many read fluently, and begin to write; they can also repeat many portions of the sacred volume.

The inhabitants of Platberg are Bastaards,— a designation we can never use without a painful feeling. It speaks the depravity of man; and it reminds us that wherever Europeans have carried their civilization and their industry, there they have also carried their vices. South Africa has her Bastaards, and South America her Mètis. In every country colonised by Europeans we find a mixed race,—a living testimony to the sin of their fathers. But leaving such painful reflections, we shall endeavour to make our readers acquainted with these men,

* The history of the locality is given more fully in the " Journal des Missions Evangéliques" for 1834.—p. 50.

with whose designation they may be familiar, but of whose character, perhaps, they know little.

The Bastaards sprung from the intercourse of the dutch settlers with the Hottentots, who originally inhabited the district of the Cape. Very few of them are the fruit of legitimate marriage, although the law of the Cape prohibiting the marriage of settlers with natives, was not passed until 1804, and, if we mistake not, it has been long since repealed. It is, then, in the ordinary sense of the term that they, or their fathers, were first called Bastaards. When these unfortunate children of the Boers had so increased as to make the white man tremble for his safety, they were driven beyond the boundary of the colony, towards the interior of the country. The greater part of them then crossed the Orange River, and located themselves in the neighbourhood of the spot where Philippolis now stands; and spreading themselves thence to the north and to the east, they are now to be found as far as Platberg, in which district some thousands of them reside. Amongst themselves they take the designation Binnelanders,—*Inhabitants of the Interior*. They have continued the use of the dutch language, cherishing at the same time, however, inveterate hatred towards the colonists.

The Bastaard is of middling stature, and rather thin in his person; he is of a tawny complexion; his hair is less crisp than that of the negro; he has a flattened nose, sunken cheek, high cheekbone, small eye deeply set, and a flat forehead—the distinctive characteristics of the hottentot race. He has no beard; a little down grows upon his upper lip, but seldom on the cheek or the chin.

In moral character he inherits the phlegmatic temperament of the dutch colonist, and the idleness of the Hottentot. Anger alone can rouse him from his habitual sluggishness. But when that passion animates him, he is a true Hottentot,—treacherous, malicious, and passionate,—and he gives himself up to unrestrained rage and revenge.

His habits are, in general, gentle and peaceful. His

usual occupation is the rearing of cattle, or the cultivation of a narrow strip of corn, or of a small vegetable
garden, which, if it furnish little produce, requires little
care. Often out hunting, and often visiting his friends,
he is exempt from avarice and ambition ; and he gives
himself little trouble to acquire riches, or to lay up an
inheritance for his children. He has few wants, and he
only looks after the absolute necessaries of life for himself and his family. If he can procure milk, some heads
of indian corn, a sheep for slaughter from time to time,
and occasionally an antelope, and moreover an ox to
exchange with some travelling merchant from the colony
for tea, or tobacco, or a piece of damaged cotton print,
all his desires are satisfied. He has no further ambition.
He can live ; and he wants the energy necessary to lead
him to seek to better his circumstances.

During his leisure time, and of that he has abundance,
he finds a pleasure in lounging about the house of his
missionary, whither he goes,—sometimes with, but oftener
without, an object. It is seldom, if he be a pious man,
that he has not some spiritual malady of which to complain to his religious instructor :—" Oh, how my peace is
dried up ! Oh, how cold my heart is !" Or he speaks of
his debts and his loans, or oftener still of his horses and
his cattle. And, if at the moment the bell summon the
worshippers to the sanctuary, thither also he goes most
willingly,; for all possess a respect for religion, and all
are more or less acquainted with its doctrines and its
duties ; and some, though unhappily their number is
limited, love and practise these. But their habitual
nonchalance is carried into their piety,—preventing its
development, and paralysing its effects.

If such be the character and dispositions of those of
the Binnelanders who live at the missionary stations,
what can be expected of those who live on farms, or in
solitary dwelling places, far from the salutary influence
which these stations exert ? Rude and ignorant, having
little intercourse with their fellow-men, and subjecting

their conduct to no law but that of their own judgment, or their own caprice, they are as despotic and as depraved as were the dutch farmers of the colony. They are subject to their chief; but they yield to him a very stinted submission. They are nominally governed by law ; but their laws are obeyed neither by those for whom they were designed, nor by those who ought to see them enforced.

Those who are easy in their circumstances, and pique themselves on their civilisation, dress in european style; but many still wear the kaross, or cloak made of skins of the sheep or the jackall sewed together. The same incongruity is seen in the structure of their houses ; some build them of raw brick or of clay, on a plan which is simple, and not unhealthy though very incommodious ; but others content themselves with a narrow, low and smoky hut formed of mats, and into this the people and their household utensils are huddled together in the most disgusting confusion.

Brought to a state of semi-civilisation, the Bastaards are now stationary ; or their progress in farming and in the mechanical arts is at best so slow that it is almost imperceptible; so that we should not be astonished if the Bechuanas, who are as yet far behind them, should some half century hence overtake and outstrip them in the march.

In character the Bechuanas have greatly the advantage of them. They are more energetic, more resolute, more enterprising, and more persevering. There are bechuana tribes who already cultivate the ground better than do the Bastaards, and others among whom the people are more industrious than they. The bechuana female would by her diligence put the bastaard female to shame. The former is active and laborious, the latter is indolent in the extreme. The bechuana female undertakes, it may be said, the whole work of the house, the charge of the children, the cares of house keeping, and the cultivation of the ground. The bastaard female devolves the whole of these upon her bushman servants, who occupy a middle station betwixt that of slaves and that of domestics; she never leaves the house, and rarely quits the chair in which she lolls the live-long day; the utter inanity in which she passes her days does not prevent her from professing a sovereign contempt for her bechuana sister. We do not suspect her of having read Montesquieu, but, judging from her conduct, one would conclude that she had adopted as her maxim, the remark in " Les Lettres Persanes,"—*C'est sur des chaises que la noblesse s'acquiert.*

We have already stated that the station of Platberg is built on the western slope of the Waterberg;—Masite is situated on the other side of the hill, about a mile distant. On contemplating the numerous advantages enjoyed by the latter locality, we were suprised that the missionaries had not made choice of it for the location of their station; perhaps they were afraid to mingle the emigrant Bastaards with the Aborigines. The town of Masite consists of no less than seven basuto villages; they cover all the eastern side of Waterberg, which is a little lengthened link, separated from the great chain, forming an irregular table land, running from north to south, and covered with excellent grass and a few bushes. As places surrounded by mountains have usually many names, Masite is also and more commonly called Marisa, the *Pasture Ground.* This designation we consider preferable to the other, and shall accordingly adopt it, that the town may not be confounded with Masite, which lies opposite Moriah.

It is long since Marisa first arrested the attention of the brethren at Moriah. At the commencement of their labors, they hesitated for a considerable time in deciding betwixt these two places in making choice of a sphere of labor; and should the inhabitants of Platberg leave that village, as has been spoken of, the missionary society of Paris would immediately establish a basuto station at Marisa;—a place more advantageously situated for such a purpose could not be desired. Many of the inhabitants of Marisa recognised the writer of these pages when he visited the place, as they had seen him before in 1833. They said they were glad to see him again. He felt himself constrained to preach to them the gospel; they listened with attention, mingled with wonder. When he had finished his discourse, one of them cried out "Jehovah is very great. But can he make rain?" These poor people are still strangers to the fundamental truths of religion. The Wesleyan missionaries have not been able to visit them often; a multiplicity of duties connected with the internal affairs of their station, having hitherto hindered them from extending their labors to those who live beyond it.

Before leaving Marisa we went to visit a lovely little cascade in the neighbourhood, formed by a tiny brook which sends up a soothing murmur as it rolls over the crumbled rocks. At the side of it are some trees, and amongst these, the old trunk of the wild olive. They could not fail to arrest the attention for a few moments in a country where every object makes an impression, because new and unknown. We found growing on the banks of this cascade the black maidenhair (*asplenium adianthum nigrum*) to which the natives have given a name similar to that given by botanists. They call it *moriri u-letlapa*, (the hair of the rock.) This plant, rather rare in these parts, is much sought after by the natives. They delight in the aromatic odour given out by the leaves when burning, and this they inhale at once by the nose and the mouth. The ashes of the maidenhair mixed with the fat of the sheep, are applied to wounds as an astringent, and they are used as a tonic. The ashes of the root taken in a glass of warm water, acts gently on the placenta. We saw, also, in the same place a variety of the Venus' hair (*adianthum capillus Veneris.*) It had all the characteristics of that plant, excepting that it was divided into digital folioles, instead of having those of a cuniform shape. Endowed with the same medical properties as the other plant, it has received from the natives the name of *ma-o-*

ru-metsu (mater expulsans.) When it is used medicinally, the natives employ the juice which they express from the boiled root. This genus of plant is very common in the country of the Basutos. It grows in moist places, at springs, under the shade, and in the clefts of rocks. The natives add to the word *ma-o-rumetsu*, the adjective *amanianiane*, (small) to distinguish this plant from that which they call *ma-o-rumetsu a mangolu*, or the great *ma-o-rumetsu*. This is our male fern, differing from it in no respect. The Basutos attribute to it great aperient powers, as our physicians did formerly. They employ only the root.

On departing from Marisa, we entered on the route followed by the missionaries on their first journey to the country of the Basutos. After travelling two hours, which were fully occupied with meditations on the past, we halted for some minutes before a dome-shaped mountain peopled by baboons. This animal is common in South Africa, especially in the colony,—where it has given a name to a river—the Baviaans River— in the district of Somerset. The Basutos are not acquainted with any other kind of ape than what is found here. They call it Tsuéne, from the name of a bulb on which it feeds. The comparative magnitude of its facial angle, the length of its muzzle, the calosities on its buttocks, which the natives attribute to its manner of sitting on the rocks like a man, the appearance of its cheeks, the strength of its canine teeth, and the height of its stature—which is about four feet—are all the characteristics which it has in common with the baboon. The length of its tail seems to connect it with the varietyof the monkey, but its wicked and lascivious propensities are those of the baboon as described by BUFFON, and by SPARMANN in his travels in South Africa.

We shall bring these remarks to a conclusion by recording, in all their simplicity, the observations made to us by the natives in regard to this animal, leaving our readers to determine how much, and what, is to be ascribed to credulity, to ignorance, or to exaggeration. "The Tsuène," say they, "wicked animal! it does not work; it only knows to drag itself along by scrambling up the mountains, raising deceitful cries.   When you are in the fields watching your harvest during the night, it comes,—it makes havoc around you; and not content with all the corn which it has eaten, it takes an ear of wheat, lights it at the fire, and puts it on your face. You awake; *Ki'ng* (what is that?) The wicked beast grins in your face, and flees.   The Tsuéne, sometimes, when it is alone walks erect like the ourang-outange; he then carries a stick in his hand; if he sees any one, he throws away his stick, and flees on all fours. Sometimes the stick serves him as a weapon of defence, but his principal strength is in his teeth.   He fights with men—but very seldom—and sometimes he comes off conqueror. He can defend himself against three good dogs, and he will engage the hyæna in single combat. Alone he cannot contend against the tiger ; but if there be several of them together, they begin to set up doleful cries as if craving for mercy ; but soon they surround the common enemy, try to frighten him, rouse themselves for the combat, fall on him, and tare him in pieces.   At every snap of their teeth, they make a wound almost an inch deep, and bring away a round piece of flesh, as neatly cut as if done with a punch. They feed on roots, berries, lizards, and scorpions. Sometimes, when a young baboon has, with the assistance of his stick, dug out a root, a strong one will come and snatch it from him ; and even if he have got it swallowed, he will force him to give it up by suspending him by the hind legs, and shaking him furiously till he is glad to disgorge it. The female chastises her little ones ; and, in fleeing, she carries them on her back."

CHAPTER III.

THE first village to which we came on our journey was
Buchap, situated about twelve miles to the north of
Platberg. The site of the village is extensive, the land
is fertile, and the pasturage good; but as there is a deficiency of water, the population is by no means numerous:
there cannot be more than about fifty inhabitants. The
Wesleyan missionaries hoped, at one time, to attract
thither all the Griquas of Old Buchap, but Berend, their
chief, has now been for two years in Namaqualand,
wandering in the desert, hunting, and driving about his
flocks from place to place. Amongst nomadic tribes,
the missionary must lay his account with such trials. The
continual migration of such people presents a barrier to
their civilisation, which is almost insurmountable; and
the servant of Christ who is called to minister unto them,
requires great faith, and courage, and perseverance.
Look to the indefatigable Mr. SCHMELEN, who, though he
has labored thirty years for the conversion of a namaqua
tribe, has not yet got them to settle. He still follows
them in their migrations, pitching his tent in the desert,
and again striking it at the signal for removal.

The appearance of Buchap is sad and desolate. There
is no trace of cultivation—not a sound—scarcely a sign
of life. Some huts formed of mats, suspended from
poles, may be seen amongst the rocks,—some blackish

figures loitering about these wretched dwellings;—a little further, and in a retired spot, something like a cottage built in the european style, the ruined condition of which tells that it has long ago been abandoned;—with the exception of one room, in which some corn has been deposited, all the apartments are empty, and serve as a retreat to the swallow and the bat:—such is Buchap. The sight of this solitude and desolation grieved us to the heart. We prayed for our dear brother EDWARDS, the Wesleyan missionary, who erected the dwelling ; and we asked ourselves, whether we were prepared to endure a similar trial, if, at any time, it should please the Lord to appoint it.

Cut off from intercourse with others, as the inhabitants of Buchap may appear, they are not destitute of religion and religious ordinances. They have some knowledge of the truths of christianity, and some of them have received the truth in the love of it. They lived long with missionaries at Old Buchap; they improved the privileges they there enjoyed ; and they gladdened the heart of their pastor by the sincerity of their faith, and the regularity of their conduct. Now they are left alone, and they seem lost in the desert ;—but it is not exactly so. The brethren from Platberg come, from time to time, to preach the gospel at Buchap, which they look upon as an out-station, and their ministrations are enjoyed. The attendance at such times is small; but it is serious and attentive. We were particularly struck with this when we had the pleasure of preaching to them.

Before quitting Buchap, we may give our readers a short sketch of the tribe of the Griquas, which differs in but few particulars from that of the Bastaards. They were formerly known by this latter name; but, through the influence of Mr. CAMPBELL, this name was superseded by that of the Griquas, and their principal town, formerly called Klar Water, was called Griqua Town. The Griquas are a mixed race, having the same characteristics,

II. BASTARD

and almost the same manners, as the Bastaards,—speaking
the same language, and intermarrying with them. The
characteristics of the Hottentot predominate in the former;
those of the dutch race, in the latter. For what african
blood they have, the Bastaards are indebted entirely to
the aborigines of the Cape colony. The Griquas trace
theirs, in some measure, to the same source,—but also, in
part, to the hottentot tribes of the Namaquas and Korannas. The Griqua is less of the mongrel than the Bastaard; his features are better defined; his bearing is
more manly; his hair more crisp; and his complexion
more dark. Notwithstanding these physical differences,
the moral character is almost the same in both. Like
the Bastaards, the Griquas are indolent, apathetic, and
content with little. With a horse and a gun, a Griqua
is rich;—very rich if, in addition to these, he own a
wagon and a plough. Notwithstanding their natural
indolence, they have,—thanks to their religious instructors,—made considerable progress in civilisation and improvement. Thirty years ago, Mr. ANDERSON, to whom
they are indebted for their advancement, found them
poor, barbarian, and pagan, wandering about on the
banks of the Gariep, with a few flocks, knowing nothing
of Europeans, but their name and their vices. The kind
missionary offered himself to become their instructor,
followed them with his family through all the vicissitudes
of their nomadic life, and undertook their conversion and
civilisation. After five years of fatigue and toil, he succeeded in getting them to settle. The greater part
renounced their superstitions and their wandering mode
of life. They now live at Griqua Town and Campbell's
Dorp. They have given up their miserable huts for
houses more healthy, and more commodious; and their
sheepskin cloaks for european clothing. They are regular in their attendance at religious worship, and they
begin to enjoy the blessings of a partial civilisation
effected by christianity. Taste and skill in vocal music
is one, and not the least interesting, trait in their charac-

ter. Their voice is not deep-toned, but it is pretty flexible, and it is raised without difficulty to the higher notes. That of the women is particularly sweet and harmonious. In the evening, after the cattle have been brought back from the fields, they collect in groups before their houses, and by the light of the stars they sing some of the sweetest of England's sacred airs. Those of *New Sabbath*, and *Gloucester*, *Milburn*, *Auburn*, *Miles' Lane*, *Calcutta*, *Smyrna*, and *God save the King*, are familiar to them. Happily ignorant of all profane song, they know nothing of music but its moral and religious influence. They sing only the praises of God,—such as have been left to them in simple and beautiful dutch verse by the pious Dr. VAN DER KEMP, or composed by their missionaries.

The Griquas are at present governed by WATERBOER, a man of remarkable firmness and intelligence. He uses all his influence to maintain peace between the Griquas and the Bastaards, who are opposed to one another, and who are both of very vindictive dispositions. And he has entered into treaty with the government of the colony, engaging to do every thing in his power to secure for the english authorities, the esteem and friendship of the natives.

We shall conclude this short and imperfect notice of the Griquas and the Bastaards, with the transcript of a letter received from a missionary who resided a long time in the midst of them. "The Griquas," says this correspondent, "are a people of very recent origin, their history scarcely extending further back than forty years. A slave, called ADAM KOK, the great grandfather of ADAM KOK, who is at present the reigning chief at Philippolis, collected, by dint of industry and labor, a sufficient sum wherewith to purchase his freedom, and he subsequently procured a farm amongst the colonists of the Cape. Many of the Hottentots and people of color gathered around him. He sold his little domain, and emigrated into the country of the Namaquas, where his subjects were increased by the addition of a considerable number of the

natives. Mr. ANDERSON, the missionary, led ADAM KOK
and his followers still further to the north, and, with the
assistance of Mr. CAMPBELL, he gave to the new people
a brief code of written laws. The people were declared
independent; they took the name of Griquas, and they
agreed to acknowledge KOK and his descendants as their
legitimate sovereigns. But after some years, a powerful
and ambitious man called WATERBOER, gathered some
partisans, and got himself acknowledged as chief by a
part of the tribe. KOK, followed by his family, and all
who remained faithful to him, removed towards the
south, and established themselves at Philippolis. This
new colony increased, little by little, by emigrants of
mixed blood from the colony; and the inhabitants have
taken the names of Bastaards, of Overlams, and of
Binnelanders;—designations which, strictly speaking,
belong to the Griquas as well as to them.

"The word Griqua appears to be an abbreviation of
Cherigriquois, the name of a tribe living to the south of
the Little Namaquas. It is believed, that after the first
immigration of ADAM KOK, many of the Cherigriquois, in
the neighbourhood of whom he lived, connected themselves with him; and that, in this way, the designation
came to be ultimately adopted by the people. The word
quas is the termination of the names of all the old
hottentot tribes,—as the Hersaquas, Lusaquas, Dunaquas,
—which leads me to think, that in the Namaqua language it signifies nation or people."

CHAPTER IV.

A considerable part of the day of March 16th, was lost in seeking our oxen, which during the night had wandered to a distance from the camp, seeking for water. We were thus detained till about half-past twelve o'clock. We then travelled till evening without halting. From Platberg to Buchap, we had travelled along a narrow valley betwixt two unbroken chains of high hills; but on leaving Buchap, as we advanced to the north, the hills began to recede from each other; the country opened up; the woods and streams became more rare; the ground less black, and more sandy. About half-past four we came in sight of the point where the chain of White Mountains abandons the north-easterly direction to run E.N.E. It is from this point that they receive from the dutch, the name of Blaauw Bergen, or Blue Mountains. After having traversed a plain about two miles and a half long, through which flows a stream which empties itself into the Caledon,—we arrived, towards evening, at Umpukani, where we found a resting place under the peaceful roof of Mr. and Mrs. JENKINS, of the Wesleyan society.

Umpukani, or—as it is more commonly called in that country—*Tlotlolane*, is a hill of considerable magnitude, in the form of a tongue; the summit of which is towards the west, and the inclination towards the east. On the

brow of the hill stand two european houses; to the
right is a kraal of about two hundred and fifty koranna
huts; to the left is a pretty fountain, which can be turned
in to water the garden of the mission house when necessary. In the neighbourhood are detached hills, inhabited by peaceful Bechuanas. On the east side, the horizon
stretches away about a hundred miles, where it is ter-
minated by the peaks of the Blue Mountains.

Mr. and Mrs. JENKINS, who formerly resided at Old
Buchap, founded the station of Umpukani, about three
years before our visit. In the choice of a locality, as
well as in the construction of the houses of the station,
they have manifested a prudence and an industry which
might well serve as models for all missionaries in South
Africa placed in similar circumstances. They have
erected, at little expense, a dwelling, which is at once
simple and commodious, and is not altogether devoid of
elegance. The house is built of raw bricks; and the erection, serving for chapel and for school, is formed of reeds,
and is covered within and without with a coat of clay. The
garden, although very plain, is well cultivated, and produces the principal vegetables of the country. In one
corner of this little enclosure, stands Mr. JENKINS' study.
In Mr. JENKINS there is united—and that in a high
degree—all the necessary qualifications for a missionary
appointed to labor in a country where every thing is yet to
be done. He can turn his hand to any thing,—and he can
do it. After having preached the gospel to the heathen
around him—sometimes under the shadow of a rock—
sometimes by the light of the stars—sometimes in the
midst of an imposing solitude—sometimes in the midst
of the noise and confusion of a hottentot kraal—he does
not consider it beneath him to engage in the most menial
occupation, which is forthwith elevated and ennobled by
the christian principle which is the motive and the guide
of all that he does. By turns he labors as a mason, as a
carpenter, as a cabinet-maker; he puts his tools to rights,
or he makes a shoe; he forges a ploughshare, or he

sharpens on his anvil the hoe of one of his parishioners; he directs the construction of a water-course, or the erection of an enclosure for cattle. The calls upon his obliging disposition are incessant. How painful is it to add that his services are but too often repaid with ingratitude!

Umpukani is inhabited by Bastaards and by Korannas. It is to the latter that Mr. JENKINS has chiefly devoted his time. They have now heard the gospel for many years, and they begin to appreciate it, and to experience its power. Twelve of them are members of the church. The interpreter, amongst others, is a pious and zealous man. One of these Korannas was asked, "How goes it with your soul?" He answered,—"I find myself like a man born in a wicked kraal, and under a wicked chief. I have abandoned my former master to choose a better one; but my old chief says to me continually, 'Ah, will you not return to us? Have you left us altogether?' While a voice within me on the other hand says, 'No, it is much better to serve Christ;'—thus my poor soul is attacked on both sides."

HANTO, the chief of the tribe, seemed also to have a pretty correct acquaintance with the truth of christianity. "What is faith?" we asked him. "It consists of keeping a firm hold of the promises of God, deep down in the heart." "Where does it end?" "In heaven." "How so?" "Because there one sees, and possesses the promised blessing." "Do you love the Lord Jesus?" "My heart seeks him, and desires to love him."

He who spake thus had then only a few days to live. He was shortly after mortally wounded by a lion. When dying, he strongly urged upon his people the practice of piety; and his last words were—"All is well." He was about thirty-one years of age, and was succeeded by his son KOPIE, a lad of about eighteen years of age, remarkable for his intelligence and gentle disposition.

HANTO was, in every respect, the most interesting Koranna we have known. He was of great stature, and well proportioned. He had fine black eyebrows, lively eyes, of a fine oval. He was endowed with a quick apprehension and retentive memory, and was considered well acquainted with the history of his tribe. To him we are indebted for the greater part of the information which follows.

" In the neighbourhood of the Cape of Good Hope, there lived, some eight generations back, a hottentot chief called KORA, whose name originated the name of the tribe. It was with him that the Europeans who first settled there, entered into treaty. According to an old tradition, they besought KORA to grant them as much land as they could surround with an ox-hide, cut into thongs. This appeared to KORA a very moderate request, and he granted it with the greatest readiness. But soon the strangers began to encroach upon the lands of the natives, and war was the consequence. KORA was then alive. It is not known whether, or no, he was slain in battle; but it is known that he died young. He left, as his successor, a son called EIKOMO. He also had to defend his territory against the daily encroachments of the colonists. He could not long resist them, and he was ultimately driven back to the river Braak. Going from that place further to the north, he arrived amongst a numerous tribe of Hottentots wandering on the banks of the Gariep, and called Baroas (the hottentot bushmen.) He entered into treaty with them, and settled in that country, not far from the place where Griqua Town now stands. In that country lived and died Kuebib, Kongap, Kuenonkeip, Makabuté, and Kaup, the successors of EIKOMO."

On comparing these traditions with the history of the Cape colony, we find some interesting coincidences. It was in 1652, that is about eight generations back, that VAN RIEBECK founded the colony. In 1659, VAN RIE-BECK having made a distribution of lands amongst the dutch colonists, the Hottentots and they were involved in war. In 1669, peace was concluded with the aborigines, and the dutch were permitted to occupy a piece of land, stretching three miles along the shore. And in 1673, they were again at war with the Hottentots. But let us return to the Korannas.

The Korannas, superior to the other Hottentots in stature and muscular strength, are greatly inferior to them in moral character. Excessively vain and impudent, they have a great deal more of effrontery than of true bravery. They are almost always at war with their nighbours,— not that they delight in war, but they like the pillage by which it is attended.* From the time of their emigration to the banks of the Gariep, no tribe in the neighbourhood has enjoyed a moment of repose. Furnished with fire arms, and mounted on good horses, they have pillaged all the tribes around them in succession. With the exception of HANTO, to whom reference has already been made, and perhaps one or two others, their chiefs have filled all their neighbours with terror. They speak of them as *wolves*. We may mention as amongst the most formidable of them, PIET-WITTE-VOET, SARLES, and VOORTOOW.

To a love of plunder the Korannas join an excessive idleness. All the work is done by the women, or by the bechuana servants, who are never paid. While the Bechuanas lead their herds to pasture, and construct enclosures for them of stone or of palisades, cultivate their gardens, and till their fields—the Korannas leave their cattle to find pasture where they may, construct no folds for them, and plant only tobacco. The following is the description of their mode of life, given by a missionary who lived a long time amongst them. " Before the day has begun to dawn, the Koranna raises his head from his pillow, lights his pipe, and again goes to sleep. At nine o'clock he wakes to smoke again; he drinks some cups of new milk, and again lies down. At eleven o'clock, after having smoked, he amuses himself sometimes with making a wooden bowl with his knife, sometimes with fashioning a bone into a tobacco pipe. Two o'clock comes round; he takes a hearty meal, smokes his pipe for the fourth

* "The Bechuanas," say they, "are the cows and we are the calves; it is for us that they fatten their flocks."

time, and again to bed. Towards evening he rises to smoke and drink his milk, and then lays himself down till the morrow."

Capricious and insubordinate, the Korannas tolerate their chiefs rather than obey them, each recognising his own will as his only law. They are irreconcileable in their hatreds, and if any one fall into disgrace with his tribe, there is nothing for it, but to separate himself from it for ever. Inclined to a nomadic life, and passionately fond of the chase, they have no local attachments, and they leave without regret, never to revisit more, the place in which the want of game prevents them from enjoying their favorite pursuit. The koranna women are as indolent as the men, and no less vain. Like the most civilised Europeans, they find food for their vanity in the change of fashions, and in the display of their coarse adornments. Fashion required formerly that their hair should be disposed in circles rising one above another in the form of a cone; now it requires that it should be cut quite close all round the head. Their bodies are loaded with beads, they wear them on their necks, their arms, their loins, and their ancles. Their dress consists of an apron of small cords, which descends to their feet, and a kaross, made from the skins of the sheep, or of some other animal, sewed together. They anoint their bodies with sheep-tail fat, mixed with a reddish-colored ochre. Consuming a great part of the day in smoking, and leaving their children covered with vermin, and their houses in a state of the most disgusting filth, like the men they reserve all their activity and vigour for the *sukeis*, or *pot dance*. When the moon enters her first quarter, all the kraal assemble on some favorite elevation; then they dance, to the sound of the tangtang, all the night long, and sometimes for eight nights in succession. In this amusement the Korannas place no control on their passions, and abandon themselves to excesses of which it would be a shame even to speak.

From what we have said, it may be gathered that the

Korannas are amongst the most depraved of the african tribes. True, there are to be found at some of the missionary stations, a few on whom the gospel has exerted its power,—but they are few indeed; and itis no less true, that although they have made some progress in civilisation, the tribe of the Korannas, of all other hottentot tribes, is that which tries most severely the patience of the missionary who labors amongst them.

CHAPTER V.

MERABING AND THE MANTATEES.

On the 18th of March, we left the peaceful dwelling of Mr. JENKINS, to travel towards the capital of the Mantatees, situated about thirty miles to the north-east of Umpukani. The further we advanced to the north, the more open did the country become, and it assumed more the appearance of an extensive table land, without the aspect of it becoming on that account, the less monotonous. It was all, as before, chains of hills, broken in upon by some mountain, on the dull and frowning front of which, the traveller looks in vain for some object to relieve his eye, and dispel his ennui. After a journey, which was rendered exceedingly painful by bad roads and a sultry heat of 122 degrees Fahr., we arrived, about two o'clock, on the banks of a little river rolling away to the Caledon. Our guides outspanned,—we made hastily some cups of tea, and laid ourselves down under the wagons, to enjoy, in this partial shade, some hours of repose. In the evening we inspanned again, and as we were very desirous of arriving at Merabing that evening, that we might there pass the sabbath, we, with the whip, urged on the tardy steps of the oxen. After having gone over what seemed an interminable hill, and through a dangerous defile, where we expected every moment to see our conveyance dashed to pieces, we arrived at Umparane, a fertile spot, and delightfully situated,—the neighbour-

hood of which is inhabited by Caffers and Mantatees.
" Strangers," cried one of them from the top of the hill,
"don't destroy our corn! It is late. Where are you going
through the darkness which covers the ground? Will you
find the way which leads to the dwelling of the white man?"
" Perhaps not,'" we answered, " but let one of you come
and guide us!" " What will you give me?" " Tobacco.'"
The young Caffer immediately came down the mountain,
but he only conducted us to the end of his field of corn,
about which he seemed to be much more concerned than
about us; and I had to lead the way on horseback as I
best could.

After toiling on for a considerable time in darkness, and
not without some anxiety, we perceived in the distance a
glimmering light, the sight of which made us forget, in a
moment, all the fatigues of the day. This light, visible
through the openings of the shutters, let us know that we
were drawing near to the dwelling of Mr. ALLISON, the
Wesleyan missionary. I arrived first; I knocked gently
at the door. Mr. ALLISON was engaged at the moment
in reading to his wife, while she was teaching some little
girls to sew. They welcomed me with some anxiety,
being startled to hear one knock at their door in european
fashion,—a very uncommon event in their domestic life.
The rest of the party, with the wagon, soon arrived, and
received a most cordial welcome. After a long and
delightful evening, enlivened with the charms of frater-
nal intercourse and closed with prayer, we retired to
rest.

The next day was the sabbath. I preached on the
destruction of Sodom and Gomorrah; and in the evening,
Mr. DAUMAS spoke from those words of the apostle
John—" God is love." It was harvest time. The women
and the children were engaged in getting in the corn,
while the men were keeping one of their national feasts;
and the attendance, in consequence, was small. We
could not but rejoice, however, in the marked attention
and devotional feeling of the people. We had amongst

our hearers the principal chief of the tribe. The superior of the rest of the Mantatees by birth, he may be, but certainly not by intelligence. He said to us on coming out of the church, as if he had been addressing one of his barokas, or rainmakers,—" Oh ! but the truths heard to-day are beautiful! These words must have come from God! Can you not also obtain for us five days' rain ?"

SEKONIELA is the name of this chief; he is the son of the late king MOKOTCHO. He is tall, and of great muscular strength ; he has a broad, flattened nose, a dull eye, a gruff voice ; he appears to be about the age of thirty. Of a sullen and unsociable disposition,—he inspires his subjects with more of fear than of love. To judge by his vulgar and unmeaning countenance, one would be disposed to conclude that he was a simpleton ; but under this appearance of simplicity, there is concealed a marked propensity to cheating.

The queen MANTETIS, his mother, is a woman of great intelligence, and has a sweet and agreeable expression of countenance. The women of this tribe, subjected from their tenderest years to the rude labors of the field and to the toil of domestic duties, are in general shrivelled and deformed before they reach the age of twenty; but Mantetis has retained both a regular countenance and an elegant figure. Her dress consists of a thick apron of small cords, plaited by herself, and a cloak made of a large ox hide, softened and prepared by her sons. She has for ornaments, rings of copper on her two arms, and a collar of the same metal round her neck. Following the fashion of the country, she is always bare headed. She enjoys great consideration amongst the Bechuanas. She has been a widow for fifteen years. During the minority of her son, she acted as regent, and she now shares his authority. It is under her guidance that her subjects have emigrated from the north-east to the country which they now inhabit, and have there sustained some difficult sieges. They were formerly called Batlokuas ; from regard to her, they have taken the name of Mantetis.

The Mantetis, numbering about fourteen thousand, are spread over a country measuring about eighty or a hundred square miles. Like the Basutos, whose language they speak, and from whom they differ in but few respects, they live chiefly in the mountains where they feel themselves more secure.

Without entering into details relative to the history of the Mantetis, to which we shall afterwards have occasion to refer, we shall simply state, that they appear to have come from the neighbourhood of Delagoa Bay, about forty years ago, and that they appear to have been both numerous and powerful. After having resided for some time upon the territory of the Matebele tribe, they were driven before two formidable foes toward the west, where they committed fearful ravages. After having brought down upon several bechuana tribes all those evils which are the inevitable consequences of invasion, they have had for not more than twelve years, the free possession of the country they now inhabit. Reduced to a tenth of their original number by the many offensive and defensive wars in which they have been engaged, they live in perpetual fear, ever ready to act on the defensive. They greatly dread the attacks of Dingaan and Moshesh, and other neighbouring chiefs. while their thirst for conquest, and love of plunder, make them the terror and detestation of the weaker tribes.

Their capital, Merabing, is built on the summit of a mountain, about a mile long, and narrow in proportion to its length. From the base to the summit is about one hundred and thirty feet. It is flat on the top, but higher at the two ends. The sides are almost perpendicular. This stronghold is approached by two openings on the western side, which are very appropriately called Likorobetloa, or the hewn gates. These are narrow passages defended on both sides by strong walls of stones in the form of ramparts. By this simple defence, added to the work of nature, the inhabitants of Merabing have been enabled to sustain many protracted sieges. In time of peace the town numbers thirteen or fourteen hundred inhabitants ; but in time of war it affords protection to a far greater number, who flee thither from the neighbouring kraals. The dwellings, instead of being close to each other, are scattered in groups of twenty, thirty, or forty huts, as if to show that there is little sociality, or mutual confidence, amongst those who have been induced only by a regard to their own safety to live in the same locality.

The tribe of the Mantetis being shut up within a limited territory, their villages are not far from one another. Three miles south of Merabing is Umparani, which Sekoniela considers a second capital of his little kingdom. Makosane, situated about twenty miles to the east of Umparani, is governed by Mota, the youngest brother of Sekoniela. Towards the north, where the population is more dense, there is Rabochabane, the town of Moshew, the queen's brother. Nine or ten miles distant from Merabing is Mautsi, which may be considered the central town of the tribe, and around which lie a great many little villages. The chief of this town is ENGHATLA, the bravest of the nation. After having re- sisted long the attacks of his inveterate enemies, the Matébéles, he was at last overcome. Although he is now very much enfeebled, his name is not the less popular amongst the Mantetis, who are always speaking with admiration of his prudence, his bravery, and his physical strength. He has given one of his daughters in marriage to Sekoniela, to whom he considers himself a tributary, but not a subject, and for whom he has, in fact, very little respect. To render the enumeration of the towns of the Mantetis complete, we may mention also Morabing, Ramorisa, and Matining. This last, situated about thirty miles from the capital, marks the northern limit of the tribe.

The dominion of Sekoniela embraces also two or three thousand Caffers, or matebele refugees, the greater part of whom dwell on the mountains of Mekeling, opposite

Umpurane. Their principal chiefs are Mosete and
Maitlo-a-magolu, or *Great Eyes*. The Marimos, a bechuana tribe,—who were formerly cannibals, although
belonging to the tribes which were settled in the country
long before the Mantetis—are, nevertheless, considered
as a part of these. Lipetung, one of their villages, is
not far from Merabing. The chief residing there has
got the nickname of Mokuenaniana, or the *little crocodile*. Some allege that it was he who devoured the
grandfather of the present king of the Basutos ; others,
with more reason, attribute this deed to a man called
Racotsuané.

It is of importance to geographical science, but still
more so to the cause of religion, that the state of heathen
countries at the time of the introduction of christianity
should be ascertained with precision ; for in every country
in which the gospel has been proclaimed, it has, without
fail, altered the aspect both of the land and of its inhabitants. Our descriptions, though true to-day, will not hold
true forty years hence, excepting as descriptions of what
has been. If it be now said, that some of these people are
reduced to the necessity of eating one another to avoid
dying of hunger, it is neither the excess of population nor
the sterility of the soil which has occasioned the famine, and
the atrocities which have followed it ; for there are scarcely
sixteen or seventeen thousand people in a country which
might sustain more than a hundred and fifty thousand.
Their interminable wars and their love of plunder have
done it. These, leading them to neglect the cultivation
of their lands, or carrying devastation into newly sown
fields, or fields almost ripe for the harvest, cut off their
supplies and drive them to the horrible expedient of
devouring their fellow-men. And, if by the introduction
and spread of christianity, the cause cease to exist, the
effects will cease with it. The people will return to
gentler manners, and cannibalism will disappear.

The Mantetis are less indolent and inactive than the
greater part of the tribes around them. Enjoying a

Lith Paul Petit

III. KORANNA

Head shorn, with a wisp of hair left all round — copper ear-rings — powder horn — pouch in the front — clumsy shoes of native making — small Koranna saddle covered with a sheepskin.

healthy climate, which is exempt from long and excessive heats, and which is sometimes bitterly cold,—spurred
on by the necessity of providing against famine,—and
kept ever on the alert by the fear of attack,—they have
acquired a kind of superiority above the neighbouring
people ; and, placed in circumstances similar to those of
the Basutos, they have acquired some skill in the cultivation of the ground. The Mantetis and the Basutos
are now better agriculturists than they were before ; and
in this respect they are superior also to the Barolongs,
the Batlapis, and the greater part of the bechuana
tribes.

In the month of August, or to speak in the language
of the country, *two moons after harvest*, the men and the
women shoulder their *mogumas*. These are hoes of
native manufacture ; the blade is of an oval shape, about
ten inches long and seven broad ; it terminates behind in
either one or two prongs, driven, when red hot, through
the *tlogo*, a large head left at the end of the handle.

In the morning, as soon as the cows have been milked,
the natives go out to the fields, generally singing ; they
go on laboring till two or three o'clock in the afternoon.
The women—who frequently dig, keeping time—do as
much work as the men, if not more ; but both the one
and the other do it badly. They give themselves little
trouble to secure anything like a regular appearance
in their fields. They dig a little bit here, a little bit
there, making the most confused patch-work imagin-
able ; the earth however is turned up and it produces
abundance of millet and maize, the stalks of which
reach sometimes the height of seven or eight feet; it
yields also the sweet reed, pumpkins, beans, one or two
kinds of native melons, and even potatoes, which have
been introduced by the missionaries. Some of the natives begin also to sow wheat.

The millet is the principal support of the Caffers and
the Bechuanas, and of almost all the african tribes. In
that country it is generally called caffer corn, but its

proper name is indian or african millet. The cultivation of this plant requires a great deal of attention, and it keeps the natives occupied three quarters of the year. Not that it does not grow easily, and that even without being watered, in those districts which are in any way adapted to its production, but, betwixt the seasons of sowing and for reaping, it must be weeded two or three times, it must be hoed, it must be thinned, it must be pruned, it must be protected for six months from the cattle and from the numerous flocks of birds, and, while it is yet young, from the locusts, which only eat it when it is of a certain height. The Bechuanas have two kinds of this millet; they call the one *mabele-a-masheu,* white corn, and the other *mabele-a-mafuberu,* red corn. The latter scarcely attains to half the height of the other, and is not so highly valued. The qualities of the two are the same, both grains furnish a flour cooling and nutritious; but it contains no gluten, and it coagulates with difficulty. To remedy this inconvenience, the natives mix with the dough a certain proportion of milk, or, if milk be scarce, they substitute for it a few slices of fresh pumpkin. Like the Bechuanas, the Mantetis eat their grain baked with water or with milk, or in the form of a coarse bread, which they call *bogobé.*

As to the moral character of the Mantetis and the Basutos, we may say of them, as a traveller said of the Jolofs,—"They are generous, but it is amongst themselves." They are ready to oblige any one who may be able at some future time to return the kindness to them; they undertake, with their whole heart, works for the benefit of the kraal; such as leading the cattle to pasturage by turns, or constructing a stone enclosure for the herd, or they will assist to soften the skin of an ox, or an antelope intended for a cloak. But these good qualities, in themselves rather equivocal, are darkened by many moral defects,—such as falsehood, theft, and adultery. The national propensity to indulge in these, finds no sufficient check in the existing laws. These can neither suppress the propensity, nor prevent the crime. The law punishes

the regicide with death, but the ordinary murderer often
escapes by paying some compensation to the family of his
victim, of which compensation the local judicatory retains
a tenth. This is a deviation from the law of retaliation
which is as old as the world. The abduction of the
wife or daughter of a man in authority, brings in its
train a capital punishment; but in other circumstances,
the seducer escapes on making some reparation to the
offended party. If it is a husband, he gives him one
or two horned cattle; if it is a father, he agrees upon
a dowry and marries the daughter. For theft they
exact restitution or compensation. If the thin stolen
be of little value, or if he who suffers by the robbery
have abundance, the matter is passed by, or the thief
is made the but of jest and ridicule.

Notwithstanding this appearance of indifference, the
Bechuanas are as uncompromising in the maintenance of
their rights as other people. It is only when they consider that it will be better for them that they submit to an
infringement on them. The law of retaliation may not
be always carried out in practice, but it is nevertheless
considered a right upon which every man may insist. It
is recognised by the Bechuanas, the Basutos, the Mantetis, and by almost all the tribes of Africa. The right
may not be always exacted, but it is not abandoned, and
every one is at liberty to insist upon its execution. At
my own station, a Basuto whose son had been wounded
on the head with a staff, came to entreat me to deliver up
the offender,—" With the same staff, and on the same spot
where my son was beaten, will I give a blow on the head
of the man who did it." The prosecution is conducted,
and publicly decided at the door of the chief of the kraal
in which the crime has been committed, or at that of the
chief of the tribe, according as the one or the other may
have been chosen as arbiter betwixt the parties. These
speak by turns, and are allowed full liberty of speech in
pleading the case.

With these tribes, as with all the blacks, the marriages
are bargains in which the women are purchased. Two

or three cows with their calves, together with some sheep
or goats, is the price which the lover, if poor, must pay
over to the father or the nearest relatives of the betrothed.
If rich, he pays ten, twenty, thirty, or even forty head
of cattle. I know a basuto chief who very recently gave
a hundred oxen, and who, by this princely magnificence,
procured for himself the nickname of the *prodigal child*.
A man is at liberty to have as many wives as he can purchase and support. As for him who is poor, he must
live in celibacy, unless he choose to become the serf of
some powerful chief, who may give him one of his concubines. This custom of buying wives has prevailed
amongst all the nations of antiquity. Jacob gave seven
years' service for Rachel. The prophet Hosea purchased
his wife for fifteen pieces of silver, and an homer and a
half of barley. Amongst the Babylonians, according to
Herodotus, the marriageable virgins were sold by the
public crier to the highest bidder. The Greeks, the
Indians, and the Germans, caused a dowry to be paid for
their daughters. The Romans, amongst other kinds of
marriage, had the marriage of coemption. To this day
the Tartars, the Turks, and the Negroes of Senegambia
purchase their wives. Amongst the Bechuanas the
daughter is considered the property of the father, and if
he sells her, it is to set up his sons, or to provide for his
own future wants in old age, if he should then find himself forsaken by his family. Like Laban, and like the
Hindoos, the father does not marry the second daughter
before the elder. If the elder die after marriage, leaving no children, the husband has a right to demand her
sister, or to have back his dowry. If he dies first, his
brother succeeds him. In that case, he makes to his
father-in-law a small present, and slaughters an ox, with
the gall of which, he and his betrothed sprinkle themselves as a sign of purification; but there is not, strictly
speaking, any celebration of marriage. A man is not
compelled to take in marriage the widow of his brother.
In the event of his refusal, she is at liberty to return to
her father, or to take another husband.

They practise circumcision on the children of both sexes, at the age of twelve or thirteen, but they do not associate any religious idea with this rite. They have scarcely retained the idea of a Supreme Being. The more enlightened admit that there is a *Morena* in heaven, whom they call the *powerful master of things*, but the multitude deny that there is, and even this name of *morena* is the same as they give to the lowest of their chiefs. All the blacks whom I have known are atheists, but it would not be difficult to find amongst them some theists. Their atheism, however, does not prevent their being extremely superstitious, or from rendering a kind of worship to their ancestors, whom they call *barimos*, or in the singular *morimo*. Before leaving the Mantetis let us glance at the history of the mission to these people.

Towards the end of 1833 Sekoniela became acquainted with some labourers sent to the Basutos by the Paris Society for Evangelical Missions. He entreated them to instruct him in the Christian faith, and establish themselves in the capital of his little kingdom. One of his subjects, it was said, some moons before had dreamed new dreams. He had seen strangers arrive in the country, who brought it peace, and a large increase of the flocks, and fair and good words. This dream, which had produced some agitation in the minds of the people, was not forgotten when, eight months afterwards, in August 1834, the Mantetis saw Mr. ALLISON, a Wesleyan missionary, arrive at Merabing. He declared himself ready to preach the gospel to them, and he established himself amongst them. The natives received him warmly, and could not be tired of seeing and hearing a white man, a *Moruti*, sent by *Morena*, who came to speak to them of God, and to depict Him under new colours. They burdened him with questions about the news which he brought them. But the instructions of the missionary were too foreign to their previous ideas to be comprehended ; and the doctrines of original corruption and the necessity of a Saviour, were too humbling to their pride to be

received.   They would have upset all their ideas on the
origin of evil; for their idea is, that if man suffers, or is
subject to death, it is not on him that the blame is to be
laid, but on the power of sorcerers, or the wicked spells
of the *Barimos* (spirits of the dead.) So the old men,
when once their first curiosity was satisfied, showed themselves very indifferent, and scarcely accessible to the
efforts of Mr. ALLISON. "Why," asked the Queen, "if
what you preach be true, did not the Lord reveal it
sooner to the nation?   How can it be that our ancestors
should have died in entire ignorance of all these things?
And why have I myself heard them only in the decline
of life, when the taste for novelty has already quitted
me?" Sekoniela has not ceased to attend the instructions
which a considerable part of the people still receive, but
he affects not to understand anything of them.   His son,
on the contrary, scarcely 12 years old, receives with
docility and profit the lessons of Mr. ALLISON. " I assure
you," writes that missionary to us, "that it does my
soul good to see the good dispositions of Seto; you would
be delighted to hear him pray for the missionaries.   He
is really converted to God, and appears to take great
pleasure in directing sinners to Christ.   The boy has lived
for some time in our house, and I have more than once
seen tears run down his cheeks while we were speaking
to him of his soul."

This youth is not the only one who appears to have
received serious impressions; there are several of the
natives who repay the care of their missionary, and
whose zeal consoles him for the indifference and obduracy
of too great a number of their countrymen.   And we
may, nevertheless, hope that this state of spiritual torpor
will not continue long; for whoever knows the love
and devotion of Mr. ALLISON cannot help thinking
that he will at length see the fruits of them.   The
young people, in particular, give him hope as they
engage his time.   Mr. and Mrs. ALLISON devote a great
portion of their time and their resources to the teaching

of elementary schools, and to the training of some children whom they have received under their roof, where they feed them, clothe them, and bring them up at their own expense. The simplicity of their manners, their activity, and their devotedness, speak to the heart of the savages far more eloquently than could their discourse. Heathen people, indeed, can scarcely form any idea of christianity but from the conduct of their instructors, and we can well affirm, that the conduct of Mr. ALLISON embodies much useful and valuable instruction for the savage.

CHAPTER VI.

WHILST resting at Merabing, it occurred to us that it would be well, as we were there, to visit the Blue Mountains,—mountains, which so far as known, no European foot had yet trode. Their high hills, peopled by numerous bechuana tribes to whom the gospel was unknown, presented to christian travellers an interesting field to explore; and it was important to us to ascertain how far these people were prepared to receive the word of life, and what probability of success awaited the labors of missionaries. Mr. ALLISON confirmed us in our resolution, and himself agreed to accompany us for the first few days of our tour; Mrs. ALLISON helped us in making arrangements for our journey; and on the 20th March we took our leave of her, after having committed ourselves to the protection of the Lord.

Our hottentot guides, for whom a tour was a treat, could scarcely contain their joy, or restrain themselves in giving expressions to it in shouts and bravos. It was amusing to witness the somewhat disorderly haste with which they saddled the horses, collected the dogs, and prepared the guns. Monaile, the most experienced of our guides, and the one in whom we could place most confidence, alone was calm. He had no sympathy with his companions in their joyous and boisterous mirth, for he knew better than they the dangers to which we were likely to be exposed.

" The Malutis," said he to us, " are infested with hyænas,
tigers, lions, and even cannibals; there is no beaten
track ; I may lose my way, and we shall all run the risk
of perishing from hunger !" "Go on, you coward," was
the ready answer of his companions, "this gun can kill
any thing,—and these horses, what can they not clear ?"

Directing our course at first to the south of Merabing,
we rode on horseback for six hours across high hills,
over elevated flats, and through fissures and fens which
are always found about the approach to mountains ; and
before sun-set we arrived at the foot of the chain, where
we made our first encampment. Kuening, for that is the
name of the place, was formerly inhabited by tribes of
Bechuana-Bakuenas. In the neighbourhood there is a
number of deserted kraals, and, everywhere around, the
ground is covered with human bones, and skulls, and
broken pots, and such like remains. " Look at the work
of the Matebeles," said Monaile, "they kill the Bechuanas as we would kill dogs. It is well that you men of
peace have arrived in the country ; but for you we had
been all dead men; this is what was being done with the
black nation."

Kuening, both from its fertility and its agreeable and
commanding situation, is admirably adapted for a missionary station. The winter, indeed, is very severe, but
this is of little consequence there. The former inhabitants will return with joy to cultivate these fertile valleys,
from which war has driven them for a time. They will
return with eagerness to localities to which they have
given names expressive of the abundance in which they
lived. One of their rivers they have named Atana (*where
the cattle multiply,*) and another Khomokuanu (*where
the cows love to feed ;*) these two small rivers are among
the number of streams which feed the Caledon.

The first object which attracted our attention at Kuening, was a rock about a hundred feet high, and four
hundred and fifty long. It is composed of a soft but
fine sandstone, the colour of which is a dull yellow. It

is disposed in regular, horizontal beds. The front of this giant of the desert overshadows a little wood, through which winds the limpid Atana. At its base is an excavation in the form of a grotto, which served us for a lodging, as it usually does to the native travellers who go from Thaba-Bosio to Dingaan's, and to the king of the Basutos himself, when he goes to hunt antelopes in those quarters.

Our hottentot guides had no sooner caught sight of this grotto, than with high spirits they set about their little preparations for passing the night. With some stones and some dried grass, they made themselves a bed, upon which, after smoking their pipes, they were soon wrapped in a deep sleep. With us it was otherwise. Accustomed to a somewhat less primitive couch, we slept very little and very badly, notwithstanding the fatigue which oppressed us. My sleep was a prolonged nightmare, during which my cries and interrupted exclamations more than once disturbed Mr. ALLISON's repose. The next day, after a night which had rather increased than diminished our fatigue, we had to begin climbing the rough and steep sides of the mountain chain under which we had encamped. There appeared to be nothing before us but a world of mountains piled one above another in strange confusion, which seemed to rise and recede from us as we approached. When we thought we were ascending, we were only going round a peak, or laboriously winding about so as to pass a link of the chain. We were ever reaching new ridges, new precipices, new defiles; there seemed to be no end to them. Add to this the fatigue, the discouragement, and the hunger we were suffering, and it will not be surprising that we had already spoken of giving up the journey, when an incident occurred, than which nothing could be more à propos, to divert the sadness of our thoughts.

Our huntsmen succeeded in bringing to the ground a young elan, which they had run down in the course of the morning. Every one pressed round this capture, as if,

with the sight of it, to compensate himself for his fatigue.
Our Hottentots dispatched it with wonderful dexterity;
they gathered some brambles, struck a light, and made
a fire; they cut large slices from the animal, and hastily
broiled and devoured them. We followed their example,
and like them we swallowed these pieces of flesh half
raw, and still quivering with life. After this repast,
stretching ourselves on the grass, we enjoyed a repose of
some hours. This slumber ended, our guides proceeded
to cut up the elan, the different quarters of which they tied
to our saddles; and they dragged the remainder of their
booty to the side of a pool, where they buried it
under the water, with a view of preserving it for themselves, or for any other hungry traveller who might pass
that way.

The elan of this country, known by the name of *antelope
canna*, is common in all parts of South Africa, excepting in the Cape colony, where, even in 1806, BARROW
complained that the dutch farmers had almost destroyed
the species by their inconsiderate (meaning too frequent)
hunts. It is also a fact that this animal flees from men,
as these increase in their neighbourhood. We ourselves
have seen it disappear within these few years before the
tribes of Basutos, and seek refuge in the mountains, for
which it has a decided preference. There, although liable
to become the prey of lions, tigers, hyænas, and other
ferocious animals, it feeds more peaceably than in the
plain.

The natives say that it eats bitter and poisonous plants,
which communicate to its entrails a nauseous and sometimes a poisonous odour; and they refuse to eat them. The
flesh of the canna is good, and almost equal in quality to
beef; it has a slight taste of venison. The flesh of the
male is preferable to that of the female, because it is
generally fatter. The hide of the male is also more
esteemed for its strength and its thickness; lashes, bridles,
harness, saddles, native cloaks, and shields are made of
it. Its long slender horns serve the Bechuanas and
Caffers for pipes. The step of the canna is a kind of

nimble and sustained trot, which it can maintain for half a day when it is pursued by the huntsman. It does gallop, however, when it finds itself hard pressed; but that pace does not suit it, and it is soon abandoned. I have often seen herds of these animals in the spring season. When they saw me, they quickly filed off, with the male at their head. When they were at the distance of a gunshot, they stopped an instant, panting and foaming at the mouth ; and they uttered plaintive cries of *he !* *he !* which betrayed their trouble and disquietude. The canna does not attain its full growth till near its fifth year. It may then be nine or ten feet in length, and about five feet in height. The one we killed was three years old ; it was eight feet long, five feet high, four feet and a half from the tip of the horns to the mouth. The horns alone were two feet long. When young, these animals are of a reddish brown, which becomes darker as they grow old.

The Basutos, who always mingle with their real knowledge a little of the marvellous, give to the herds of these animals an imaginary shepherd, whom they call Unko-nagnana (*little nose.*) He lives in the Malutis, and is never seen by human eye. They also pretend that the canna has, between the two horns, and hid in its hair, a very dangerous yellow viper, which they call *kuane.* For this reason, when the canna is brought to the ground, they strike it with a stick with heavy blows on the top of the head, before stabbing it to the heart. They purify themselves before eating the flesh, because of the venomous juices with which they believe it to be charged.

There is in the memory of the Basutos a traditional song, which, with a good deal of originality, takes up their notions of the canna. We may therefore insert it here, with a literal translation :

LITOKO TSA POFU.

" Mathlethla a tokuana mamalema a leuti ga e ka ea leka ea ka letlakure khomo pata namane malibogong khomo a bonkuananiana ea leuti thloro thloro einchueng

linaka e ka ki litsiba tse thlana khomo a isu ga maluma
a motu khomo e yile thlare se le botluku khomo ga e
thlethe o leletse fèla khomo e nioretse metsi mabalule ki
etella pele marumo ki makhua matlaba liulu makeku a
mo loeletsa lilata."

THE PRAISES OF THE CANNA.

Brown-colored Trotter!
Sprout of the mountains!
It cannot gallop ;
It goes as its sides go.
It is a cow that conceals its calf in the unknown fords of the rivers;
It is the cow of Unkonagnana.
The heigho! of the mountain,
The heigho! amongst the rocks.
Its two horns,
Perhaps they are two reddish feathers!
An ox which one presents as food to his uncle or his aunt
Although it has eaten a woful plant.
Let fly!—It trots no more!
It has stopt to weep!
Or is it that the leader of the herd thirsts for delicious waters?
These weapons, they are the darts!
The piercers of the white ant hills!
—Already the old men at the kraal are sharpening their knives!

As our readers are not likely to be in a position to
appreciate the beauties of sechuana poetry, they must
receive on our testimony the assurance that there is here a
combination of originality, of action, and of naïveté, which
is not altogether devoid of elegance. But we must avoid
attempting to elicit its beauties by a commentary longer
than the text; we shall, therefore, confine ourselves to
some explanation of the details.

The sechuana word *litoko* has a more extended signification than the word *praises,* by which we have translated
it. It embraces all that is worthy to be narrated on the
subject of the song,—every thing remarkable that is
known; and in this narration the above piece answers to
its title. It takes up all the notions of the Bechuanas on
the elan, with an economy of words indispensable to a
people who have no other means than memory for preserving their traditions. The word *mathlethla* (trotters), in

which the *th* is pronounced as in English, is a beautiful
ontomatopy which well expresses the clumsy movements
of the elan, when it is large and fat.   The words *thloro
thloro einchueng,* imperfectly translated by *heigho ! heigho !*
represent so admirably the sigh of the animal in laboriously clambering up the steep rocks when it is
pursued by the huntsmen, that they always excite in
the Bechuanas a noisy cheerfulness.   This phrase,
" Those weapons they are the darts ! the piercers of the
white ant hills," will not be understood without explanation ; it implies that the assagaies of the Bechuanas are
going to pierce the elan, as they pierce the hills of white
ants :—hills, which rising sometimes to the height of three
feet, frequently serve the Bechuanas for a mark when
they practise throwing the assegai.

In pursuing our route beyond Kuening, we remarked
numerous indications of the soil containing porphyry. We
should not be surprised if there were, in the neighbourhood of Kuening, a quarry of marble.   The fine-grained
blue granite is very common there.   We picked up a
small lump of porphyry, containing beautiful rock crystals, and bits of quartz of all colors.

After having gone thirteen leagues in a northerly
direction, we arrived at Macosane, a town under the
government of Mota, younger brother of Sekoniela.   This
town is composed of different groups of houses on a wide-
spread, elevated table land ; the view is bounded in the
distance by a chain of mountains arranged in the form
of an amphitheatre.   At the foot of the table land flows
the Tlotse, there a rapid stream, which may be regarded
as the second source of the Caledon.   On all sides, the
eye rests on rich and fertile valleys, fields of millet and
maize, and numerous herds of oxen and sheep which
are tended by young shepherds.   It would be an excellent place for a missionary station.   Its population is
concentrated, and the environs of the town alone present a sufficient field for the activity of two or three
missionaries.   Add to this, they would have no oppo-

sition on the part of the chief to apprehend. Mota
is a gentle and benevolent man, much beloved by the
Bechuanas, who rally round him with eagerness; indeed,
we should not be at all surprised if he happened to supplant Sekoniela in the government of the tribe.

Mota had sometimes attended the preaching of the gospel at Merabing; but to his subjects our evening worship
was a novelty. They gathered in a wide circle around
us, and listened to us with profound silence and the
greatest attention. It was under the vault of heaven,
and by the light of the moon, that we met for worship.
Service was opened with singing and prayer; after which
those beautiful words of the royal prophet were read and
expounded :—" Jehovah, our Lord, how excellent is thy
name in all the earth! When I consider thy heavens,
the work of thy fingers, the moon and the stars which
thou hast ordained; What is man, that thou art
mindful of him; or the son of man, that thou
visitest him? For thou hast made him a little lower
than the angels, and hast crowned him with glory and
honor! Thou madest him to have dominion over the
works of thy hands; thou hast put all things under his
feet; all sheep and oxen, yea, and the beasts of the field;
the fowl of the air, and the fish of the sea. Jehovah, our
Lord! how excellent is thy name in all the earth!"—
Psa. viii. The discourse was concluded by some reflections
on the work of Redemption, and the ministry of the Son of
Man, whom God made for a time a little lower than the
angels, and whom he has also crowned with glory and
honor.

On the morrow, seeing us depart, the chief Mota and
his people expressed grief at not having amongst them a
child of Jehovah to instruct them in the christian faith.
Mota gave us a guide, who was joined by some natives,
with the view of beating for the spring-boks and caamas
which abound in that region. While pursuing our journey
we caught sight of a chlamidophore of a grey colour; but
it glided so quickly into its burrow that our dogs were
unable to catch it.

The journey from Macosane to Buta-Bute, across deep valleys, or over flats interrupted by numerous ravines, is effected with difficulty. This country was once occupied by the Basutos, whose dwellings are still to be seen in ruins. It is now almost deserted ; but to all appearance it would not take long to re-people it, and it would prove an important missionary station. One might search all the country over in vain, for a more fertile soil and finer waters than the territory of Buta-Bute, and the springs which water it. The rigour of the winter, the bad state of the roads, and the scarcity of wood, are the only inconveniences attached to the locality. But these inconveniences would not prevent the natives from settling there; they naturally prefer the elevated regions, where they are more secure than in the plain.

Notwithstanding the advantages of its position, Buta-Bute is one of the most sadly celebrated towns in the country of the Basutos, for in that town they sustained, in 1823 and 1824, against the queen of the Mantetis, two sieges, the recollection of which still makes them cower with terror. Mokachane, it is said, lived in peace and abundance at Leinchuanng, near the sources of the Tlotse, on the spot which had seen the birth of himself, his children, and his grand-children. One of these, Moshesh, was the first who left his father to go and found Buta-Bute. He had scarcely been gone two years when he was attacked, almost unexpectedly, by a hostile horde with a woman at their head. Moshesh, and his Basutos, were sacked, pillaged, and ruined. They went afterwards to settle at Thaba-Bosio, which became the capital of their kingdom.

These wars, the principal events of which we shall relate in the historical part of this work, were bloody. The recollection of them is by no means effaced from the minds of the natives ; and the subjects of Sekoniela, in their daily dealings with those of Moshesh, continually entreat them to forget the atrocities of Buta-Bute. The two nations are still mutual objects of defiance and dread.

This is perhaps the proper place to speak of a mine of

platinum, which is to be found in the vicinity of Lein-
chuaning, but we can only do so from hearsay, as we
have not ourselves seen it. The metal is common in the
country. It abounds in the neighbourhood of 'Umpukani,
and also about Rachosane, in the district of Thaba-
Bosio. That which is found near the latter place,
appears to be of an inferior quality. The most esteemed
is to be got at Intluana-Chuana, on the surface of the
ground, in a small ravine. We there picked up some frag-
ments, which we sent to the museum of the Society for
Evangelical Missions at Paris. The Bechuanas grind it
between two very hard stones; they mix it with powdered
charcoal, and with fat, and smear it over their hair.
They give it the name of *secama*, which has also become
the name of Intluana-Chuana, the place where they get
it. That little village is built in the hollow of an immense
rock, which at a distance resembles a dwelling house,
and it is this circumstance in its position which has
obtained it the name of Intluana-Chuana. It is inhabited
by some Bechuanas, once cannibals. These fled at our
approach, driving before them their herds of goats and
sheep. Reassured at last by our friendly demonstrations,
they returned to us, and treated us hospitably. They
brought us for our supper some boiled pumpkin; and as
they could not lodge us, we past the night in the open
air, at the foot of the rock. In return for their hospitality, we preached to them the gospel, which they had
never before heard, and to which they listened with
attention mingled with fear. It was at Intluana-Chuana
that we parted with Mr. ALLISON, who was desirous of
returning to his post. Having selected the two best horses
from among those we had brought, and taken as a guide
Monaile, who would not leave us,—we proposed to
penetrate further into the Blue Mountains, by taking an
easterly direction instead of advancing to the north-east as
we had been doing.

CHAPTER VII.

THE MARIMOS AND THE MAKATLAS.

AFTER a toilsome journey of an hour and a quarter, we discovered a mine of iron at the bottom of a valley near the Caledon. It would be easy to work this mine, but the natives take no interest in it. Continuing our journey, we soon found ourselves near the tribe of the Marimos, or bechuana cannibals, of whom we had often heard accounts which made us look forward with some anxiety to the kind of reception we might receive at their hands. The sight of these blacks, of whose sanguinary habits we were not ignorant, was not at all calculated to inspire us with confidence. Their wild and ferocious looks,—their loud vociferations upon seeing us approach, —the sullen silence which followed these cries,—the instruments of death, such as clubs, hatchets, assagais, and knives with which they were armed,—all these inspired us with misgivings and fears, which it would be childish to try to conceal. Our guide, Monaile, after having more than once, in a low voice told me that they were cannibals, announced my arrival by crying, whilst we were yet at some distance from them,—" Lekhoa la Moshesh,"—" the white man of Moshesh !" The name of this formidable chief was to us a valuable recommendation. At once they changed their dispositions toward us, supposing these to have been hostile, which, however, we do not know to have been the case; and God did not permit them to do us any harm. By degrees I regained a little confidence, and announced to these formidable Marimos that I was the bearer of good news. "Do we know them?" said some of them between themselves. I asked them if they would be seated on the ground until they should hear them. "Why so?" said they, though at the same time they consented. When I saw them ranged in a semicircle around me, I placed myself near my guide, and with my horse's bridle in my hand ready to mount on the least sign of hostility, I began, with trembling I confess, to announce to them the glorious gospel. Sometimes interrupted by the observations which the savages made to each other, I availed myself of these intervals to raise my heart in prayer to God,—to strengthen my courage by the recollection that He watched over me, and to collect my ideas in a situation any thing but favorable to an extemporaneous address. I concluded my address with a few verses of a hymn which the savages repeated after me, and by a prayer in the sesuto idiom. When I had finished, I heard the savages say to each other,—"Oa re boletla go Morena oa legorimo,"—"he has talked to us of the chief of heaven." When I asked them if they would like to have a missionary like the neighbouring nations, they answered "Yes." "But when?" asked I. "You know, you know yourself," replied they all, with loud bursts of laughter.

I think that a mission might be established amongst them with the probability of its proving successful. The conduct of the neighbouring tribes which have already received the gospel, has in some measure prepared them for it. The Bechuanas are naturally imitative, and whatever is done by one tribe, that the others wish to do also. This disposition of the people, there can be no doubt, has greatly facilitated in some places the labors of the missionaries amongst them.

The country inhabited by the bechuana cannibals is fertile and well watered, and the climate is good. From the place at which I stopped in travelling through it,

I saw three villages very near each other. They were built on the side of a high mountain, at the foot of which were fine fields of caffer corn all around. Satisfied as I now am in regard to the disposition of the people, I would have no hesitation to go, and found there a missionary settlement, believing that eventually it would prove one of no small importance. From the time of the arrival of the missionaries among the Mantetis and the Basutos, the population of the country began to increase, through their endeavors to put an end to cannibalism, one of the most active causes of depopulation. The tribe of the Marimos consists of more than four thousand individuals, inhabiting about a dozen of villages,* The largest of these is Leribe, at the source of the river Futane. Formerly they led a wandering life on the Blue Mountains, where they made themselves dreaded by travellers. But their manners have improved within the last eight or nine years, in the course of which they have betaken themselves to agricultural and pastoral pursuits, and begun to form connections with the neighbouring tribes. Some of them already own small flocks of sheep and goats ; they also engage in hunting, and it is only in secret that they indulge their taste for human flesh. In illustration of this :—Subsequently to our visit to them in 1836, they devoured one of their own tribe, called Ramanchane ; but they took care to spread a report that it was an elan that they had slain. This word elan, like the english word venison or game, is rather equivocal in their mouth, they apply it pretty frequently to prey, or capture, of every description. And thus they call in the aid of artifice to bury in oblivion their horrible feasts; and when any one comes to enquire after a relative or a friend who has been devoured, they pretend that they have sent him to the woods or to the chase, that he was destroyed by some wild beast, or that he has changed his abode.

* The writer has since ascertained that they amount to a much greater number.

The chief of this tribe is called Mabala. He is about forty years of age, robust and tall, and is considered a good warrior. His subjects are known by the name of Marimos, or Maya-batu, *men-eaters*. The term *marimo* comes from the caffer *amalemo*, by suppressing the prefix *a*, which is foreign to the sechuana, and by the common change of the *l* into *r*, and the *e* into *i*. The singular of *marimo* is *lerimo*. Some caffer or matabele tribes say also *amalemo* (cannibals.)

The Marimos originally formed a very numerous, rich, and powerful people, inhabiting the north of the country in which they at present reside. They were known by the name of Bafukings. Kolumi, the most ancient chief whose history we can trace, died at a very advanced age, in the country situated beyond the junction of the Namagari and the Lekua. He left, for his successor, Kolukuane, who removed with his subjects to Buta-Bute, where he afterwards died in misery. His son Engabi was still more unfortunate than he. It was his lot to see his tribe stripped and ruined by a celebrated conqueror from the east, called Pacarita. It was then that the Bafukings, reduced to destitution, gradually became from necessity, both robbers and cannibals. The chief Engabi could not survive so many misfortunes ; he died of hunger, saying,—" I am old and withered ; there remains but few days for me to live ; let me die ; for by Kolukuane, I never will touch human flesh." Mabala, his successor, was, like him, exposed to the attacks of the Caffres, and to those also of a basuto chief who is still alive ; but, above all, to the fury of the queen Mantetis, who, in 1822, besieged Leribe, his principal city, massacred or dispersed its inhabitants, and laid waste the corn fields, the only resource of the people. From this moment, the fury of the Marimos knew no bounds. Urged by famine, they began to attack travellers in open day, to lay snares for them in the night, to throw themselves upon them as on their prey, and to devour them to assuage the gnawings of hunger. I shall here relate what

Mokapakapa, one of the inhabitants of the station of Moriah told me on this subject. " During four years," said he, " I was myself a cannibal, and it was in the following way I became one. Obliged to fly with my family from an enemy who followed hard after me, I set out during the night for fear of being perceived by the Marimos, I was not, however, able to avoid the snares which are laid for travellers. Two Marimos concealed in our road, quickly laid their fatal plaited rushes to catch our feet. Hardly had we fallen,—I, my three wives, my children, and my servants,—when a furious troop threw themselves upon us, tied us with leather thongs and conducted us to the kraal, loading us with blows, and crying *Ua! Ua!* like shepherds driving their sheep before them. Arrived at the kraal, we were received by the ferocious exclamation of *game! game!* In their language, in which irony and cruelty are blended, they called my children two pretty lambs, their mothers they denominated three cows, my servants three oxen, and myself an elan. These words were our death-warrant. My mother, my wives, my children, and my servants, were killed before my eyes, cut into pieces, cooked in dishes or roasted on the coals, until the last morsel of them was devoured. It was to my leanness I owed my life, and perhaps a little to my quality as chief. They sent me to watch the corn fields, and woe to me if at any time the locusts ravaged them. I was bound with thick cords, and nearly murdered with the lash, for my want of vigilance." Thus, as we have said, it was cruel famine that, by little and little, drove the Marimos to these horrible extremities. But that which was at first the offspring of necessity, afterwards became a strong passion ; they began to relish these odious repasts, and ultimately became greedy for human flesh, and even epicures in regard to this horrid food,—rejecting all the lean, and giving a preference to the flesh of children. As soon as they have seized upon a victim, they cut off his third finger, and allow the blood to flow from the wound until life is extinct ; they then tear off the hands and the feet ; they empty the scull and make a cup of it ; they fill the bladder with wind, and attach it as a trophy to their heads, or suspend it against the walls of their dwellings. Night and day they are on the watch for the passer-by, and when they espy one on the plain, they throw themselves upon him from the top of their retreat, seize him, bind him and conduct him to their kraal. If his resistance be troublesome, they cut him down on the spot, and carry him away in pieces. After having devoured his flesh, they melt the fat by the sun or by the heat of a fire, and either drink it or anoint their hair with it. If no other victims can be found, they eat their own wives and children, and exchange them with each other. The following is a specimen of the death-song which they chant at the commencement of their bloody sacrifices : " Re Marimo, re ya batu ; re ka gu ya, re ya batu. Re ya bokuana ba eincha, le ba nguana a monyenyane ; re ya menoana a batu ; re ya senyabela sa motu ; mosuu soa nyana oa Marimo u mokatlakutsoana pchanpchan taka tsa ame !" " We are cannibals; we eat men ; we can eat thee; we eat the brains of the dog ; we eat the brains of the infant; we eat the fingers and the fat of men. Poor play things for the Marimos. You will tickle our palates. Come along ! To the work my comrades !" The Marimos do not invariably employ violence to force travellers into their retreats. Sometimes they have recourse to stratagem. When they have reason to expect resistance on the part of their victims, they endeavour to conceal their intentions. " Follow us," say they, " we will be kind to you, you shall watch our fields, and go in search of wood for us." Or they will say, " Who told you that we were devourers of our kind ? It is false ; we only endeavour to strengthen ourselves against our enemies. You have as many enemies as we; let us join together to fight them ; remain then in our village." We have indisputable testimony, that in these different ways they have destroyed, in the space of a few years, many thousands of individuals.

Proceeding along the chain of the Malutis, at the distance of about six or eight miles to the south of Kuening, we find another tribe of cannibals, called the Makatlas. Rakotsuane, their principal chief, governs twenty-five or twenty-six kraals, the most considerable of which is Sefika. They are tributary to Moshesh, who has entrusted some flocks to their care, on condition that they will occupy themselves with the cultivation of the land, and cease to devour his subjects, the cannibals of the neighbourhood of Intluana-Chuana. They have confidence in Moshesh, but they dread Sekionela and his cruel mother Mantetis.

The Marimos do not differ in physical character from the other Bechuanas of the mountains. They are, in general, robust and well proportioned. They have nothing of the hideous leanness of the cannibals of New Zealand. They live in a delightful climate ; and since they began to live on human flesh, their supplies of this odious food have never failed them. Cannibalism apart, they have the same manners, the same customs, the same superstitions as the other bechuana tribes. We find, moreover, amongst them, the practice of human sacrifices on the occasion of a ceremony which they call *meseletso oa mabele*, or *the boiling of the corn*. They generally select for this sacrifice a young man, stout, but of small stature. They secure him, it may be by violence, or it may be by intoxicating him with *yoala*. They then lead him into the fields, and sacrifice him in the midst of the fields, according to their own expression, *for seed*. His blood, after having been coagulated by the rays of the sun, is burned along with the frontal bone, the flesh attached to it, and the brain. The ashes are then scattered over the lands to fertilise them, and the remainder of the body is eaten.

The other Bechuanas have also their *meseletso* ; but, in place of burning the blood and the bones of a man, they burn, on their lands, plants of a mysterious virtue, gathered and prepared by the most skilful *engaka* of the tribe. Some make the kidneys of the elan, or the dung

of the sheep, serve their purpose. When the smoke rises
and covers the corn, it prognosticates an abundant harvest;
and whenever the harvest is good, they say they must
have had a good *meseletso*, or, more frequently, that their
fields have been blessed by their *merimos*, that is, by their
gods, or the manes of their ancestors.

We cannot leave this subject without giving our
readers some idea of the literature of the tribes inhabiting these mountains, if one may apply the designation
literature, to the old wives' stories with which the mothers
put their little ones to sleep, and inculcate betimes the
first principles of bechuana morality,—that is to say, sub
mission to parental authority, and dread of the Marimos.
From amongst these tales,—which are the bechuana sub-
stitutes for those of Blue Beard and Tom Thumb at home,
—we may select that of Tselane.

A Mochuana had a daughter whom he tenderly loved·
One day having determined, like his countrymen, to
emigrate to new pastures with his family and flocks, he
said to his wife, To-morrow we set out; and to his daughter, My child, you will go with us. Next day he drove his
cattle out of the fold; his wife gathered the household utensils, which she packed in baskets, and put on her own head
and the heads of her servants, and she said to Tselane,
Follow us, my child. But Tselane replied, No, my mother,
I will not follow you; our house is decked with white and
red beads, it is too pretty for me to leave it. In the fields,
oh mother, it is cold by night and hot by day, and there are
tigers and lions, and hyenas and panthers there. I will not
quit the house. Her mother answered, My child, since
you are so naughty, you may remain here by yourself;
but shut yourself well in, Tselane, for fear you should be
eaten by the Marimos; so she set out. But some days
after she returned to see her daughter and bring her
food; and calling to her, she said, Tselane, my child, Tselane, my child, take this bread and eat it. To which the
little girl answered, I hear, my mother, I hear; my
mother speaks just like the *ataga* bird, and like the *tsuere*

which comes out of the thicket. For a long time her
mother continued to bring her food. At length she said,
My child, be no longer obstinate; your father has built a
pretty house, follow me, make my heart glad by your
obedience. But Tselane's heart grew harder every day;
she would neither be moved by the entreaties of her mother,
nor by the fine descriptions of her father's new house, nor
by fear of the Marimos.

One day she heard a rough voice calling to her,
*Tselane, my child, Tselane, my child, take this bread and
eat.* But she answered, with a scornful laugh, That
rough voice is not my mother's; get along, you wicked
Marimo; the door of my house opens on a precipice, you
cannot force it? Away went the Marimo, and lighting
a great fire, he made the iron of a hoe red hot, and
swallowed it to clear his voice; on which he returned to
Tselane, and tried again to deceive her, but his voice was
not yet sweet enough. So he heated and swallowed
another hoe-iron, and coming back said, Tselane, my
child, take this bread and eat. Thinking she recognised her mother's voice now, she opened the door to the
Marimo, who seized her, put her into a leathern sack, and
carried her off towards his dwelling. Being thirsty by the
way, he entrusted his burden to a troop of young girls, and
went to ask for beer in a neighbouring village, and went
to the very house where Tselane's aunt lived, and where
her mother happened to be at that moment. During his
absence the girls peeped into the sack through a little
hole, and saw a finger. Whose finger is this? they
asked; Mine, replied a stifled voice, I am Tselane. Off
they ran to Tselane's mother, and brought her secretly
out of the house. She instantly drew her daughter from
the sack, and having put in her place a dog, some scorpions, vipers, poisonous insects, bits of broken pots and
stones, she shut it up, and fled with Tselane and her
young friends. The Marimo, stupified by the beer, and
mumbling to himself, returned for his sack, and carried it
home; there he bade his wife make a great fire, put on

a pot full of water and fasten the door. His wife obeyed, and the Marimo went to open his sack. *Uch! Uch! King? King?* Och! Och! What's that! what's that! The dog and the vipers bit him, and the scorpions stung him, and the stones and the potsherds cruelly bruised him. Wife, wife, he roared, open the door! But his wife heard nothing; so seeing a little hole in the roof, he sprung out of it, rushed like a madman through the village, and flung himself on a heap of mud, where he was metamorphosed into a tree, in whose bark the wild bees make their honey; and the girls of the country repair to it in the spring, to gather *makapetla a linotsi,* the honeycomb dropping with honey.

CHAPTER VIII.

One of the principal objects of our excursion was, as we have remarked, to ascend to the summit of the Blue Mountains. We attempted in vain to do so from the side next Kuening; but we were more successful when we took our departure from Leribe, situated in one of the upper vallies of that chain. A small, and scarcely perceptible, pathway, which leads from Bosio to Mococutluse, the residence of DINGAN, served us as a conducting thread through the labyrinth of mountains. It was not until after a painful journey of a whole day, during which we more than once lost our way going up the western bank of the Caledon, that we reached the banks of the Namagari, about five miles beyond the summit of the principal chain. The natives, in travelling by this route, generally take two days to this journey, which fatigues more by its length than by the difficulty of the ascent ; for, with the exception of some places where we had to climb up rocks almost perpendicular, the ascent is not, in general, very steep. The slope is towards the north, and gives a passage to the Caledon, as it proceeds in little cascades in a hollow between two semicircles of mountains, which encase it from its source to the bottom of the chain. We had not penetrated far into the mountains, when we discovered on our right hand a chain of rocks of the second formation, so perpendicular and so regu-

larly cut, that, seen from a distance, they seemed like a
fortification. A little further on, rocks rose here and
there like so many natural towers ; in another place, in
the middle of a circular enclosure, a rock, slender and
straight as an obelisk, was all that remained of a conical
mountain, the sides of which had been so washed away
by rains, and stripped by the hand of time, as to leave only
the most hard and indestructible portion still standing.
Further on, rocks, known by their whitish and broken
fronts, bore upon their sides evident marks of the ravages
of lightning in deep furrows. The rock Lefiking, which
rises almost perpendicularly to a great height, and whose
sides present an immense cavity in which travellers often
seek an asylum, struck me above all the others by its
grand and imposing appearance. Here every thing
around conspires to plunge the soul into deep thought
and dreams of the past. The profound silence of the solitude is scarcely disturbed by the murmur of the river,
along which the swallow and the martinet skim lightly
in their rapid flight, or by the cooing of the ringdove
and the turtle nestling in the clefts of the mountain. In
the state of mind into which the contemplation of this
scenery had thrown me, little was wanting to bring my
emotion to a height, and to burst the flood gates which
pent up the feelings rising in my heart. And this was effected at once by the unexpected sight of a tomb amidst the
rocks,—the tomb of a traveller who had perished,—it may
be from hunger or from fatigue,—on the very spot were I
then stood. My guide, frightened at every thing that could
recal the thought of death, turned away his looks, passed
by, and contented himself with crying from a distance,
"The tomb of a traveller of my nation, who lies buried
there." These simple words,—reaching my ears at a time
when, like this poor traveller, I was overwhelmed with
fatigue and hunger, presenting to my imagination the
possibility of a death like his,—were not calculated to
change the course of the melancholy ideas with which my
mind was filled ; and trying enough as our situation was

in regard to the present, I was by no means free from anxiety in regard to the future. We had been employed the whole day in the laborious work of climbing the mountain, in order that we might gain its summit before the setting of the sun. We had taken no nourishment but a morsel of game, cooked upon the embers the preceding evening, and already had we began to feel the cruel gnawings of hunger.

Monaile, my young guide,—although more inured than I to the fatigues and privations of savage life, wearied and exhausted, with shoulder galled and bloody from carrying his musket,—walked on a few steps before me in profound silence. As for myself, scarcely able to sit on horseback, and too weak to walk, I was in a state of complete exhaustion, my eyes watered and became dim, my head reeled, and every thing seemed to swim around me. To complete our misery, we had lost our way. Having arrived about eight o'clock on the banks of the river Namagari, we knew not on which side to seek an asylum for the night. We suspected that we were not far from some kraal of the Bamakakanas, a cannibal nation. The thought of such a people in the vicinity was not calculated to inspire us with confidence. Monaile, still more frightened than I, had regained speech so far as to cry every minute, " My heart ! my heart! I think I hear dogs!" or to tell me again that the Bamakakanas eat the travellers they find straying in the fields. Finding it impossible to proceed further, we stopped on the banks of the Namagari, and determined to pass the night there. Fearing lest our horses should stray, we tied their legs together. We afterwards tried to make a fire with some thorns, but without success; and, perhaps, we may congratulate ourselves upon this, for the light of the flame might have discovered our resting place to the Bamakakanas, from whom we were little more than a mile distant. Enveloped by a thick fog, we squatted on the ground near our bundle of thorn, and thus passed the night, benumbed with cold and overcome with hunger and fatigue. We arose in the morning more dead than alive, mounted our horses and pursued our journey in the Blue Mountains ; but as our tour presents no remarkable incident, we shall not trouble our readers to follow us through it, but simply give a summary of the results of our observations.

The range of mountains which we then visited, is called by the natives Malutis, or Peaks, many of their summits presenting this form, in which respect they are unlike the other mountains in South Africa, which, in general, assume the flat or tabular shape. In going from the flats, the ground traversed before coming to what geographers denominate the *rameaux* of the second order, presents to the eye a succession of undulations gradually rising in elevation as they approach the lower range of hills, which are covered with fertility, and bordered with valleys of the richest green. The higher vallies are crossed in all directions by eminences,—sometimes isolated, sometimes in groups, but generally of a gentle declivity, and terminating, at no great height, in a level plateau. These elevations are composed of a hard sandstone of a yellowish color, disposed in horizontal strata, with a rugged surface covered with black mould, consisting principally of decayed vegetable matter mixed on the surface with a small quantity of sand ; but at the depth of two or three feet, we find all kinds of loam and marl, heaps of pebbles and gravel, intermixed with clay. Some geological characteristics of this alluvial soil, intimate the probable existence of iron ore in the vicinity. The long grass and herbage which cover these vallies, and which suggest the idea of a sea of pasturage, shelter and support a multitude of animals, such as the springbok, the grimme, the rietbok, the klipspringer, and the canna, surpassing all the others in beauty, and moving amongst them like a king. These animals multiply there, and they never migrate, although they are constantly exposed to the snares of the natives, and the attacks of lions, hyænas, and panthers. The woods supply shelter to innumerable tribes of the smaller birds; while the eagle, the vulture, the kite, and the sparrowhawk hover about in the higher regions. The climate of these vallies is salubrious, although keen and even cold in some parts; the streams are limpid and abundant; mineral or brackish springs are rare. In all our journey, we remarked but two hot sulphurous springs.

This country, the appearance of which more than once recalled to me that of the *Basses-Cévennes*, contains a population much inferior to what it might support. The tribes of Bechuanas, which have by turns occupied it, have never ceased there to keep up an exterminating war. There are now to be found but a few weak remains of these tribes, while the number of destroyed or abandoned kraals greatly surpasses those which are inhabited. From Mokoto to the Orange river, that is, in a zone of three degrees, the western district of the Malutis scarcely numbers forty-five thousand inhabitants (1836). The middle region of the chain, into which we enter on quitting the lower vallies, is of a different character. The rocks present themselves in close continuous groups of a steep acclivity, and almost inaccessible. At this height we found fine sandstone, flint, crystals, and some appearances of marble. The temperature is lower; vegetation, although still beautiful, becomes less vigorous. In the highest region, granite still constitutes the foundation of the ravines; but the top of the mountains is formed of a rough-grained stone, coarse, brittle, and of a deep-grey colour, which gives to this ridge that bluish tint which has secured for it the name of Blaw-Bergen or Blue Mountains. Although this name applies particularly to the northern part, and is less general than that of the white mountains, it has been preserved in the map accompanying the original. In this part of the chain, the beds of stone assume a much more decided inclination than in the vallies at the bottom of the mountains; this inclination in some places approaches the vertical, and we no longer find those crumbled stones,—those remains which cover the sides of the lower vallies. Here are to be seen only one mass of smaller links heaped one upon the other, or closely associated together, carpeted with a strong perennial grass of two or three feet in height, with a few shrubs here and there interspersed. In the southern part of this range vegetation is richer and more varied. The eastern side of the Blue Mountains presents a multitude of terraces which, gradually descending, terminate in the shores of the Indian Ocean.

During four months of the year, viz: from May till August, the summit of the Malutis is covered with snow ; from the beginning of October to the end of March, it is deluged with rains; and during the two following months, it is exposed to violent winds, or to fearful waterspouts, which render it uninhabitable. In winter, the climate is sometimes so rigorous, that cattle, and even shepherds, have been known to perish with cold. At Moriah, we have every year a little snow, and ice of about a quarter of an inch in thickness ; and in the neighbourhood, it has been found even three or four inches thick. The rain falls in torrents, and the hailstones are occasionally so large, and fall with such violence, that lambs have been killed in the fields by them. Sometimes, in less than five minutes, all the windows of our dwelling have been broken ; often, too, has the hail come through the glass, leaving behind it a hole as neat and round as that made by a musket ball.

The eastern aspect of the ridge, from its exposure, enjoys a climate more mild, and a vegetation more vigorous and varied. We find, however, to the west of the crest of the ridge some magnificent trees, among which we may mention, as one of the most common, a variety of the *cunonia Capensis,* the trunk of which is no less than from twenty-two to thirty feet in height; it is a white beech, and has a very loose fibre. It is found within the colony of the Cape also. There, however, it scarcely attains the height of ten or twelve feet. On both sides of the chain of the Malutis flourish the *olea Capensis*, the *euclea racemosa*, a variety of the *quer-cus Africana*, differing from the latter and from other kinds belonging to temperate climates, in its colour being white. Both the eastern and western regions are stocked with numerous troops of antelopes, among which we shall specify only the antelope-canna, the antelope-euchore, the gnu, the blue gnu, and the caama. There are many other kinds belonging to the sub-division of gazelles, both new and known. We may add to these, the *hirax Ca-pensis* of Desmarets, the flesh of which, though a little tough, is much relished by the natives, particularly by the Marimos, who also make excellent furs of its skin. The elephant, the buffalo, the giraffe, and the two-horned rhi-noceros, inhabit only the eastern side. It is only in that quarter also that we find a little noxious insect, annoying both to man and beast, the *acarus sanguisugus*, which Dr. CLARKE supposes to be the kind of louse which, of old, plagued the Egyptians. The dutch colonists of the Cape call it the *bosch-luis*, or wood louse. Rather larger than a common fly, it is of a smooth and almost round form. In Caffraria, where these insects have multiplied prodigiously, they appear from June to September, and torment the animals grievously. They bury their heads in the necks of the horses and oxen, and in the sides and groins of the sheep. When they wish to come out again the head remains in the wound; there is then formed in the ulcerated part a small tumour, which eventually dries and falls off. Besides men and cattle, these insects attack dogs, rats, and, it is said, even tortoises. They prefer, however, the weak and languishing of the flock, and thus cause a very great mortality among the feebler cattle. And if they do not really kill the fat ones, they make them poor and lean. The cows lose their milk, and sometimes even their teats, which become shrivelled, and fall off. As these *tigues* or *acarides* seek chiefly for bad humour and purulent matter in sick animals, they disappear when the cattle are in good condition. Cattle are sometimes protected from them by rubbing the part

they attack with fat, with tar, or with tobacco juice ; sometimes, also, the ravens free the cattle from them with their
bills. A variety of the wood louse, which the colonists
call *petit-bleu*, attach themselves, like the others, to
sheep and horned animals ; but they do not attack men,
and they are generally considered to be less dangerous.

CHAPTER IX.

BESIDES visiting the savage tribes which inhabit the Blue Mountains, and publishing the gospel to them, one of the objects of our tour was to trace the upper streams of some of the principal rivers of South Africa. It was known before, that the Caledon, the Orange River, and the Namagari, took their rise in the Blue Mountains; but this was the extent of the knowledge of geographers on a point which may be considered as not unimportant to the progress of science. No european traveller had yet penetrated to the sources of these rivers, and consequently their exact situation had not been ascertained. We have had the satisfaction to explore some of these sources ourselves; and with regard to the others, we have gathered so many particulars in our interviews with the natives, as to warrant us in offering to geographical science a small tribute of information, calculated to settle some questions, which, till now, have remained unsolved. Short and imperfect as our investigation may have been, we have satisfied ourselves, that the rivers of which we are about to speak, the Caledon, the Orange River, the Namagari, and some other streams of less note, take their rise in a mountain which the natives call Pofung,* because there they have frequent elan hunts; but which we have designated in

* The elan.

our map by the name of "*Mont aux Sources.*" This
mountain, which runs from east to west, is situated
near the 29th degree of south latitude, and about
the 30th degree of east longitude, at the extreme
north of the chain of Blue Mountains, of which it
constitutes one of the culminating points. It is about fourteen hundred feet above the level of the surrounding
soil, and may be about twenty miles in circumference at
the base; as to its height above the level of the sea, we
were not able to take the exact measurement, but it
cannot be less than ten thousand english feet. The summit of this mountain is in the form of a plateau, or table
land, and is clothed with the richest verdure. On the
west side of the mountain rises the river, which the
Europeans call Caledon, from the name of Lord Caledon, formerly governor of the Cape, but which the
natives name Mogokare,* because it flows through the
country of the Mantetis and Basutos. The Caledon,
which near its source is a stream of a few feet of water,
enlarges considerably in proportion as it approaches the
secondary vallies, and it is dangerous to cross it when
swollen by the fall of rains, and the melting of snow. At
Merabing it receives the Tlotse, which rises, like it, on the
west of the Blue Mountains, and now a river sixty feet wide,
it carries with it, as does also the Caledon, a blue gravel,
speckled with particles of mica. Opposite Thaba Bosio,
the waters of the Caledon are augmented by those of
the Saule, which rises in the Blue Mountains, and flows
nearly due east. The Caledon is every where confined
and rapid; in the summer, its waters being prodigiously
swollen, flow nearly on a level with the banks, and have
a depth of not less than twenty feet, with a width of
nearly three hundred. Notwithstanding its depth, and
the steepness of its banks, the Caledon might, in certain places, be led and employed to irrigate and fertilise
the soil.

Both rivers are bordered by willows, which generally

* By the middle.

rise to twenty-eight or thirty feet in height; and which,
besides the shade they afford to the traveller, furnish the
natives and missionaries with good fire wood and timber,
very valuable in a country where there would be great
difficulty in procuring any from other quarters. Rafters,
joists, and beams may be got, some of which are not less
than twenty feet long, and two feet in diameter; also planks,
door and window frames, boards, &c. The fresh leaves
of this willow furnish the cattle with a food, of which
they are very fond. The Caledon,—which, throughout
its course, can be forded in many places during the dry
season,—cannot be crossed without difficulty, and even
danger, when it has been swollen by the rains. At the
fords, which a little before might have been crossed with
a firm footing, nothing can be found but a deep quick-
sand, on which it is dangerous to venture. When the
ford is no longer passable, the river is crossed on the
trunk of a tree, which the hardy swimmer propels to the
opposite bank ; or on a triangular raft, hastily formed of
some pieces of wood rough-hewn, clumsily put together,
and covered with underwood and briers. It is to that frail
machine, dragged over by rope and dint of labour, that
the traveller successively confides himself, his family,
his wagon, and his baggage. The bed of the Caledon,
wherever it is not sandy, is formed of masses of stones
composed of clay, sand, mica, and oxide of iron, mixed
in different proportions in different places. This stone,
which the english call *iron-stone*, is common in the Malutis and the adjacent countries. The colour varies from
a dull yellow to a very deep brown ; but near streams it
acquires, by the action of the water and the sun, a tint of
glossy black. In all the sources of the Caledon may also
be found plenty of onyx and sardine stone. Agates in
the greatest variety of form and colour, plain or striated,
clouded with a bright yellow or a deep brown, are also
abundant here, as elsewhere are quartz and silex. Here
also may be found variolettes, a species of agates speckled
with white and glossy grains, and so strongly embedded

in the surrounding mass that they cannot be separated from it without difficulty. The more precious stones, such as opals, calcedonies, cornelians, although less common, are not entirely awanting in the Caledon, and some very regular crystals are occasionally found in its bed.

The Orange River, the principal stream in South Africa, rises on the south side of the Mont aux Sources. The water comes gushing from the earth, and soon contracts a dark colour, which has obtained for this river the sechuana name of *noca unchu*, the *black river*. To begin at it source :—It flows for a distance of about forty leagues through a valley formed by the two chains of the Blue Mountains, the direction being from north-east to south-west. In that part of its course, its waters are increased by a number of small tributaries, which descend from both chains of the Malutis. One of these tributaries, named the Makaling, or the river of Aloes, rises in the neighbourhood of Moriah, and flows from north to south, following the western bend of the Malutis.

After crossing the thirtieth parallel of south latitude, the Orange River issues by a narrow pass from the valley in which it has hitherto flowed, and takes a westerly direction, but gradually turns again towards the north. This part of its course, between the end of the valley, and the place where it receives the waters of the Caledon, has received from the natives the name of *Sinku*, which is also the name of the largest shield of the Matebeles. The dutch farmers named it the Great River, and Colonel GORDON gave it the name of the Orange River, from the colour of its waters. The willows, the mimosas, and the olive trees, which shade the banks of this river, the transparency and delicious freshness of its waters, the masses of brilliant rock which border its course, the cascades, and the verdant islets scattered upon its surface, present the most agreeable contrast to the arid, rough, and uncultivated aspect of the neighbouring plains, which are desert, sandy, and rugged, with here and there rocky eminences of a yellowish color. The bed of the river, very much confined towards its source, gradually widens as it proceeds; it is similar to that of the Caledon, and at certain places there is collected a sand spangled with mica, of the colour of gold and of silver. Its width, in the neighbourhood of Bethulie, is nine hundred and thirty feet, its depth, about two feet and a half, and the height of its banks, from twenty-four to twenty-five feet.

The Orange River, like the Caledon, is subject to periodical risings. These occur three or four times between the end of November and the middle of April; the first ˙ rising generally lasts from ten to twelve days, the others continue five or six weeks. These risings frequently delay travellers who require to cross the river, and sometimes they overtake those who are attempting to ford it.

Without stopping to notice the pretended medicinal virtues which the dutch settlers and the Griquas ascribe to the waters of this river, we may briefly mention, that a fine hot spring on the right bank of the stream, in the Buffalo Vley, flows into the Orange river, and that this spring is not the only one to be found in the neighbourhood of the river. The banks of the Orange were once frequented by the buffalo and the hippopotamus; but the numerous hunts of the colonists and of the natives, have driven these animals away, and they have sought a quieter and safer retreat towards the Black River.

The river Namagari, or the Fal, the most considerable tributary of the Orange, also rises in the same mountain, but on the north side. Four miles from its source, it is about eight feet wide, and brings down a bluish˙ gravel. Its direction at first is towards the north; it then turns, with an immense sweep, towards the west; and, completing its course in a direction from north-east to south-west, it comes and empties itself into the Orange

River, to the south of Campbell's Dorp, not far from the 29th parallel of south latitude, and the 24th degree of east longitude.

Among the streams which descend from the east side of the Malutis and fall into the Indian ocean, the Letuele is one of the most considerable. Rising in the eastern prolongation of the Mont aux Sources, it flows to the north-east, passes not far from Mococutlufe, and forming a *delta*, is lost in the Indian ocean. The Matebeles name it *molampo o mokolu*, the *Great River*, and agree in representing it as being as large as the Sinku. The native travellers tell us that it winds, with difficulty and many meanderings, across a country of high table lands. The bed of this river is deep and confined; the current rapid; the banks fringed with willows and mimosas. It shelters hippopatami and crocodiles, some of which are from ten to eleven feet long.

To complete what we have to communicate in regard to the rivers that rise in the Mont aux Sources, we must mention also the Monuenu, flowing parallel to the Letuele, about forty or fifty miles further to the south, and, like it, losing itself in the Indian Ocean.

The northern part of the Malutis, that over which we have travelled, is inhabited by two principal tribes, the Bamakakanas and the Matlapatlapas. The former dwell on the east side of the Malutis; the latter live about five and twenty or thirty miles further to the east. These two nations sought and found in the mountain heights, a retreat from their common enemies, the most formidable of whom is Dingan, king of Mococutlufe. Formerly his tributaries, they have withdrawn themselves from his bad treatment and pillage, taking refuge on the mountains, beyond the southern limits of his territory. Their population is increased daily by Caffre-Matebeles, who, like them, desire to withdraw themselves from the despotic authority of their king. In token of their emancipation, they no longer wear the *mokoko*,—a tuft of hair disposed on the forehead in the form of a circle, and

kept up by an inner support of pack-thread, or flexible
rush ; and they no longer wear the hair shaved like the
Chacas, but begin to let it grow, and to daub it with
grease, after the manner of the people with whom they
wish to be confounded. They may, nevertheless, be always
recognised by the round holes in their ears, from which
the Caffre-Matebeles suspend bits of reed, thin pieces of
iron, or ornaments of copper or brass. They resemble
the subjects of Dingan, moreover, in language, in manners, and in the identity of the physical characteristics of
the caffre race. Like all the Caffres, they are tall, well-
made, robust, of an active and turbulent spirit, and
always ready for attack or for defence. We have at Moriah
a refugee Matlapatlapa, named Mumpo; he stands six feet
high, has a black skin, quick projecting eyes, a little beard,
and a forehead set off with a magnificent scar, occasioned
by the stroke of a stone thrown by the hand of an
enemy. It is from him we derive the following details
of the history of his tribe.

When, tired of the oppressive power of the Chacas, many
Matebeles revolted, and sought a refuge in the high vallies of the Malutis. They had at their head a chief,
called Matlapatlapa, who has given the name to the tribe.
This chief, who was devoured by a horde of cannibals,
was succeeded by Mokokatue, who fell in battle a little
after. His son, Palule, still lived in the same place as
his predecessors, when, in 1836, we became acquainted
with his tribe. He was obliged, fifteen months after, to
take refuge among the Mantetis, and six months ago he
accompanied their chief Sekoniela in a military expedition against Dingan. After the return of Sekoniela,
Dingan reeked his vengeance on Palule, massacred a
part of his subjects, and dispersed the rest. Very few
of the Matlapatlapas are left in their country ; there
may be seven or eight thousand in all, wandering in the
mountains, a day's journey from Letuele, not far from
Enkalane, their former capital. They lead a very miserable life, subsisting by pillage, and watching for oppor-

tunities to revenge on their enemies the flesh and blood of
their kinsmen.

The Bamakakanas have not been less unfortunate than
their allies. Fifteen years ago, subject to the chief whose
name they still bear, possessing valuable flocks, and believing themselves to be secure in their mountains, they
were assailed and pillaged by a hostile horde. Sepeka,
chief of a party of the Matebeles, who had become formidable by acts of plunder, fell upon them unawares,
massacred their king and part of his people, drove away
their cattle, set fire to their habitations, and retired laden
with booty. Those who remained had then no resource
but cannibalism, as a means of escape from famine. The
Bamakakanas have now only ten villages left, of which
the principal are Sekubu, Mokhai, Makuele, and Moe-
seua. These, as well as a small caffre tribe known under the name of Matsetse, are subject to the son of their
former chief. He is a young man, thirty years of age,
called by some *Sekolume,* and by others, *Seketane.* The
Bamakakanas sometimes come and barter with the Basutos, whose manners and external habits they affect in
their travels.

All his subjects, as well as those of Palule, who
have not abandoned their lands, have become cannibals,
or *Amalemos.* More cruel than the Marimo-Bechu-
anas themselves, they make exchanges of their relatives
to be devoured ; for the same purpose they fatten the
sick old men. These horrible feasts are not, however,
sufficient to preserve this people from famine, which is
diminishing their number daily. Some emigrate to the
neighbouring districts, although, in their double character
of Matebeles and Amalemos, almost every where they
meet with foes. Among these refugees, those who obtain
the best reception, are those who go now and then to sell
hoes and tobacco to the Mantetis and the Basutos. The
Matlapatlapas and the Bamakakanas are not devoid of
industry and activity. They extract the iron from the
mountains near the sources of the Monuenu, the Letuele

and the Taka, and make of it hatchets and hoes   Others
cultivate large fields of tobacco in the fertile vallies on the
eastern side of the Malutis, which are well adapted to
the culture of this plant.   Besides these articles of barter,
for which they find a ready market, they also trade in
goats, sheep, and antelope skins.

There can be no doubt that these two nations would abandon their cannibal habits, if they could enjoy in peace the
fruits of their industry, and of the culture of their fields ;
but their crops of millet, sweet reed, maize, and pumpkins,
are scarcely ripe, when they fall a prey to some hostile
horde, who reap that which they have not sown, laying
violent hands at once on the fruits of the earth, and on
the small cattle of the kraal.   As for the unfortunate
inhabitants, despoiled of their resources, some lose their
lives in endeavouring to rescue their property ; and others
scatter themselves over the mountains, where they die of
hunger, or become the prey of wild beasts, or they are
devoured by their companions.

In time of peace, the Amalemos give themselves with
ardour to hunting the antelope and the gazelle, the buffalo and the kudu, animals unknown on the west of the
Malutis, but very common in the vallies on the eastern
side.   The scarcity of subsistence has made them overcome the horror which all the african tribes feel for the
flesh of the porcupine and the wild boar.   The serpent,
though eaten by the cannibal Bechuanas, is, with the
Amalemos, an object of superstitious dread, and is the
only animal from which they abstain.   The Marimos, as
well as the Amalemos, greedily seek for the Cape coney,
the engakana, a species of marten, and the brown otter.
And when these animals begin to fail them, they are reduced to eat the flesh of the jackal, the lion, the leopard, earth worms, young scorpions, and other reptiles
not less disgusting, and, perhaps, more venomous.

Fishing, which they practise with much skill, opens
up for them another, and that a valuable resource.   To
catch the fish they employ nooses of flexible reeds, with

a narrow opening named *littatla*. In the evening they lay these in some retired place in the river, with the opening turned towards the stream, and with some large stones laid on them for ballast. They then poison the water with the milky juice of some poisonous plants, which they carefully bruise between two stones. During the night, the fish, stupified by this juice, seek a retreat in their accustomed haunts, and numbers fall into the nooses, which the Amalemos come and draw out the following day.

CHAPTER X.

WHEN we returned from our excursion amongst the
Malutis, to the missionary station of Merabing, we found
our team recovered from their fatigue, and in excellent
condition to continue the journey. In this respect we
were much more fortunate than many travellers in
Southern Africa, who frequently, on returning from a short
tour, have found their camp in the greatest disorder,
some of their cattle injured or dead, others astray, and
the guides themselves indulging in every species of
vice; with us,—and for this we desire to be grateful—it
was far otherwise. All had been left in the hands of
true friends who had taken the greatest care of our
goods. Our horses alone were fatigued, and we gave
them a few days' rest; but the time was not lost. We
availed ourselves of this leisure to attend to several
things, and amongst others, we added to our stock of
provisions a fat ox, which was killed and salted in a
manner remarkable enough to warrant our attempting a description of it. It was led opposite the gate,
according to the custom of the country, and, by a blow
with a gun between the horns, it was knocked down
as game is by the huntsman. The natives then gathered
together from all quarters, frisking about with great glee,
to finish the work; a number of rippers at once cast off
their garments, and began by cutting off the head of the

animal, while it was still bellowing, and in a few minutes the carcase was flayed. The four quarters were carefully separated, and given to us; and the remainder, which was not a little, was put immediately under the coals. Every one thought himself warranted to take from it his share; heaps of wood, or fern-bushes, were piled up in several places and lit, the crowd gathered around them in regular circles, and nothing was heard but chattering, laughter and confusion.

In this sketch of a feast amongst a barbarous people, it may be mentioned, to complete the history of our ox, that the poor animal was salted in his own hide; as we had no other means of preserving the flesh, necessity, the mother of invention, made us have recourse to this. The skin cleaned of all matters adhering to it, was powdered with alum, half dried, and softened by friction. It was then made into a large leathern bottle or bag in which to carry our provisions. It would have been very imprudent to have taken with us a number of cattle or sheep, as these would only have proved a bait for the lions and hyænas in a country inhabited more by wild beasts than by men. The plan adopted saved us the trouble; and to our friends at Merabing, it appeared so simple and convenient that they constrained us to accept one of their own oxen to be killed and prepared in a similar way, should we be in want of provisions during our journey.

It was very kind in them; nor was this the only mark of attention that we received from them. They loaded us with kindness, and Mr. ALLISON procured for us several opportunities of preaching the gospel to the members of his own congregation, and to others in the neighbourhood, to whom he introduced us. I shall not forget, among other days, the first Sunday in April, a day which we passed among the Mantetis.

Early in the morning the church—plain, but decently constructed of willow stakes and reeds—was for that day furnished with a communion table of an oblong shape and white as snow; the natives were called to prayers

and they assembled in a crowd. Their astonishment
broke forth in whispering to one another, when, on entering the house of the Lord, they discovered there an object
which until then they had never seen, and the use of
which they could not imagine. By degrees they became
quiet; they pressed against each other, and squatting, or
kneeling down, their attention was fixed upon the object
of general wonder. Then the preacher appeared, and the
most perfect silence was observed. Not less affected than
the celebrated orator called to deliver a funeral oration
amongst the tombs of kings,—to adopt an expression of
MARMONTEL, the missionary affectionately looked upon
his audience for a moment; nothing appeared to him at
the time more humble and solemn than a temple reared
by the hands of the minister himself in the heart of a
barbarous country. He fixed his eyes for a moment on
the table upon which were placed the two sacred memo-
rials of our redemption ; then addressing the sons of
Ham in their own language, he said,—Men and brethren,
here is the table of the Lord Jesus. The assembled
pagans then listened to the history of the suffering and
expiatory death of the Saviour. Their attention was
very great, and every one was deeply affected when,
towards the close of the service, four missionaries, followed
by an african brother, approached the table ; they sang
there a hymn relating to the Lamb that was slain ; spoke
with feeling of the infinite love of Christ, of his watch-
fulness over his own; vowed with his assistance to live to
him more faithfully than in times that were past; and
partook of the supper in the sight of a multitude of
astonished Bechuanas. I cannot describe all that to
me was sublime and touching in this scene, occurring
as it did many thousands of miles from my native land,
nor can I tell how indelibly are imprinted on my soul,
the comforting words of the Master which were the subject of the sermon, "Seek ye first the kingdom of God
and his righteousness, and all these things shall be
added unto you."

IV. BASUTO

Lith. Paul Petit.

On the head a *kula* or jackal tail, scraped and dried—in the ear lobe a brass wire—
hanging round the neck a *lebeko* which serves to wipe off the sweat and to clean
the nostrils—over the shoulder a *moguma* or hoe—wrist covered with a piece of
quagga skin—in the right hand a horn filled with seed—rush belt on which is
hanging a *koma* or small round calabash serving as snuff-box—around the loins a
flexible sheepskin, called *setsiba*.

On the evening of the day on which, for the first time, the christian passover was celebrated among the Mantetis, a most edifying conversation took place in the house of the missionary. One of the natives, on being asked what it was to love God, replied,—that it was to do what he commanded us. And can you say that you love him? continued the interrogator. No, replied the person questioned, we must not tell a lie, amongst us there is only Chika who sincerely loves the Lord, and the truths that have been told to us.

This Chika was the convert who had the happiness of approaching the Lord's table with us. The first fruits of the mission, he causes his pastor to rejoice; he is a light in the midst of his countrymen, and promises to become, with the blessing from on high, very useful as an interpreter, and in many other respects. How precious to him must have been the testimony borne to the sincerity of his conversion by his countryman, and this testimony was unanimous. We know God a little, said some; but Chika knows him well. Others said, Many love God with the lips,—Chika loves him with the heart. After having heard many good remarks upon the topic of our conversation, I turned toward a little child, and asked him, "My little one, how is it that men do not love God? It is because they have bad hearts, he replied. Bad like what? Like stone. You would say, that it is very hard; is it not so? And how must it become? It must become softer. Soft! and like what? Like flesh." Every one smiled on hearing these correct answers of the child.

CHAPTER XI.

On Monday, April 4th, we again set out in a northerly direction, and commenced, in some measure, a new journey,—so distinct and peculiar had been the excursion in the Malutis. Our route was as follows : one hour N.W., one hour and thirty minutes N.E., three hours and five minutes N., one hour W., one hour and five minutes N. The number of turnings we were obliged to make, on account of the country being intersected by hills in every direction, would be almost incredible. Five miles from Merabing, a village was pointed out to us, inhabited by Bechuanas that were formerly cannibals. It is built upon a steep mountain, about six hundred feet in height. In front of it rose, opposite to each other, two immense granite rocks of such shape as to appear like an arch. Not far from thence was seen the town of Rabuchabane, built in a regular circle, upon the brow of a table hill; it is surmounted by a peak of considerable elevation, which, from its peculiar shape, has been called by the missionaries the Chimney. The eye, as far as it could see, could discover nothing but mountains, with fields of millet and of indian corn, and small clouds of smoke rising into the air from many different points, betokening kraals in every direction. The Mantetis appeared to us to be collected in the neighbourhood of their capital, probably as much for safety as for the beauty and the enchanting aspect of the country. We met a goodly number of natives, shepherds as well as laborers, and some among them were travellers like ourselves. They saluted us in a friendly manner, and appeared especially glad to see among our number their *moruti*, who had expressed a great desire to accompany us some twenty or thirty miles. But after having passed a great many villages during the day, and having met with numbers of persons of whom our time did no more than permit us to ask a few questions, it was our lot to encamp in the evening quite alone in an uninhabited place. However, as it was the first Monday in the month, our party did not forget to assemble together to present those petitions which christians in almost every land are accustomed, on that day, to present on behalf of heathen nations.

A hymn, in the spirit of the 65th Psalm, was first sung in bechuana, to the same air to which the words

O Dieu c'est dans tu Sion sainte
Que tu seras loue

are sung in the reformed churches of France. Then followed the prayer; after which our brother from Merabing read in his english bible the 49th chapter of Isaiah,— "Listen, O isles, unto me, and hearken ye people from far." Some of the passages of this prophecy arrested our attention in an especial manner, as for example the sixth verse, "It is a light thing that thou shouldest be my servant to raise up the tribes of Jacob, and to restore the preserved of Israel. I will also give thee for a light to the gentiles, that thou mayest be my salvation to the ends of the earth." Taken in a spiritual sense, that is to say, applied to the slavery of sin, the following words also became the subject of serious consideration for our servants, "That thou mayest say to the prisoners go forth : to them that are in darkness show yourselves." The answers of one of the guides to the questions suggested by this verse—and, indeed, his whole history—afforded a striking proof of the truth, that the conversion of the heart is the work of

God,—that it is the call of his love, the blame being ours if we neglect to profit by the means of grace which are supplied to us.

The night betwixt the 4th and the 5th of April was very rainy, but in the morning the sky was clear, and our friend from Merabing, after having bidden us adieu, returned to his home. Our people went to hunt, and killed three quaggas. They cut them in pieces upon the spot, but the flesh was brought to the camp, cut into slices, exposed upon the rocks and bushes, and so dried in the rays of the sun, and it was then salted and locked up in one of the wagons as provisions for the journey. It was not that we were then in want of it; but the Africans allow nothing to slip past them, and it would not be difficult to convince any one that our guides were no exception to the rule. As to the quaggas which were killed, they were grazing among a great number of others, but there did not appear to be a single zebra in the whole herd; it is the fact, moreover, that the zebra is not found either among the Basutos or the Mantetis, while the quagga is very common in their district,—a new and conclusive proof that the latter is not the female of the former, as was for a long time believed.

The difference that exists between these two kinds of asses, and their respective characteristics, are known to naturalists. Our own experience has convinced us that quaggas are docile, and easily tamed; the zebras are said to be much more untractable. It would not be right, however, to affirm, as Buffon does, that the inhabitants of the Cape colony use quaggas to draw their cars. The case is not common; it may have occurred, as for example, when some years since a team of eight or ten of these animals was publicly sold in Cape Town, during the government of Sir G. L. Cole, who was, according to report, one of the highest bidders. But these beasts had been tamed by an Englishman, at considerable expense both of money and of time. A dutch farmer would probably have no taste for such an undertaking.

Many colonists are to be found who have reared a quagga for fancy, but we have never heard of any who have taken the necessary care and trouble to break them in to labor; though this, we believe, would be found both practicable and useful; for the quaggas are very abundant in the whole of South Africa, they have no great vices, they are satisfied with little food, and they are more handsome than mules, and not less strong. What then is to prevent their being employed in the same service? Barrow, whose work may be consulted on this subject, is of opinion that they might be so employed.

Two distinct species of quaggas are found on this side of the Orange River, that which the dutch colonists call brown quagga,* with ash colored belly, very common also among the Amakosas; and the speckled quagga† which is a little larger than the former, and marked with brighter spots; it is similar to the zebra or wild horse‡ of Namaqualand.

The second species of quagga is not to be found, it would appear, in the Cape, in Caffraria, or among the Basutos. We only met with it in the district of the Yellow River. The Baperis have assured us that it is the more common of the two kinds in their country; ‖ and they gave us to understand that the brown quagga inhabits the south, and the speckled, the north of Southern Africa.

About one hour and a half from our encampment, toward the west, lay Racebatane, one of the principal villages of the tribe of the Lighoyas. We proceeded thither on horseback, to see it, and there to preach the gospel should the people receive us. This place is situated upon the declivity of a high hill terminating in a plain, it was the same spot that we had formerly called by the well-known name of Thaba-Cheu, or Mont-Blanc, from its bald appearance. About 130 dwellings huddled together among crumbled rocks, composed the whole of

---

* Blaauw-Kwagga.   † Bonte-Kwagga.   ‡ Wilde-Paarde.
‖ They call it *pitsi e tuluri*, *striped ass*, and the brown quagga, simply *pitse*.

the village, of which the population could not be less
than 400 souls according to our mode of computation,
that is by calculating three persons to a hut. The pasturage appeared to us good, but water scarce, as likewise
wood. However, this little village is furnished with two
fountains which supply the wants of the place; one of
these is reserved for the inhabitants, the other for the
cattle. The first fountain the natives say never fails;
but whatever may happen, a better one is to be found a
little further on. If we enter minutely into these matters, it is because Racebatane, or its environs, appears to
us, from geographical position and other advantages,
likely to become some day the site of a missionary station. The population in the immediate neighbourhood is
considerable; we observed, in particular, at a distance of
two or three miles to the west, a kraal as large as that
at which we then were. It is called Thaba Marimo, or
Mountain of Cannibals; it is situated in the centre of
three other villages, which all acknowledge as their chief
a Lighoya named Lessia.

As to the little village of Racebatane, it is governed
by Rantsane, an old man much respected. He was
very active for his age. I observed in his looks the
remains of youthful fire, and the whole of his physi-
ognomy pleased me. As we approached his dwelling,
I was recognised by a black man who assured me,
that he had seen me in the Cape colony; he received
us joyfully, and introduced us to his master, saying,
" my father, I bring these whites to you; here is among
the rest the white man of Mokachane." The old man
was squatting upon the skin of an antelope, near a
hearth without fire, unless one chose to give this name
to such a cloud of smoke as may be produced by
a handfull of green rushes in wet and cold weather.
Many persons had gathered around their *morena* for
some important business, but the debates ceased upon
our approach. Every body stared,—astonished and surprised. After a little time nothing was to be heard,

but cries of *peh! eoh!* and noisy outbursts of laughter, until the chief ordered silence. He, in his turn, fixed his eyes upon us for a couple of minutes, and then cried out, " Behold then, these whites! Oh! my brethren, are these indeed the white men?" We said yes, and asked him how it was that he had not yet gone to Merabing to see the white men, and to enquire after the truths which they preached ; to which Rantsane replied, that his feet were no longer good, and that his great age moreover would not admit of his travelling as much as he had done in his younger days. There followed then an animated conver-sation between him and the strangers, " What then," asked they, " is it only to-day that Rantsane sees the Ba-rutis ?" The Barutis," he replied, " I had simply believed to see white men. What do you announce?" " The words of the Chief of Heaven." " The chief of heaven? (*laughter*) Is there in truth a master in heaven ?" "Yes, Rantsane." "And what does He say ?" " He says that men have all strayed like lost sheep ;"—a counsellor repeated the words, "he says that men are all lost sheep." The missionaries continued, " We are all children of the master who is in heaven." Upon which a savage interrupted them, crying out : You whites, you are all the sons of heaven?" We continued, " All men, white as well as black, are children of heaven; but all men have forgotten Him who created them at first in his own likeness; all men are like lost sheep. Rantsane, and you, creatures of God, when will you learn to know Him?" "Strangers," replied Rantsane, " how can we know Him, inasmuch as we are left alone in these deserts ? They say that your hands engrave words that go and speak *far, far away.* Trace then this my word :—say, Rantsane is already bent under the duties of the day, and cannot repair to the white man of Moka-chane, to lend his ear to the wonders of the white man's mouth ; but he writes to a Moruti that he come quickly to instruct Rantsane and his people."

One of us, after some moments' silence and medi-tation, during which a great number of people col-

lected together, began to address them. He took for
the introduction of his discourse the request of Rantsane; and, as he could not but promise to write, he
besought the audience to attend, and told them the
substance of these *wholesome truths* would then be
told to them. His sentences were repeated one by
one, by the natives, with remarkable seriousness, and
with great wonder. We sung also some verses of a
hymn, and prayed twice; after which we wished to retire,
leaving the people under the influence of the good impressions which appeared to have been made, but Rantsane entreated us to remain. He had brought us some
sweet reeds, which he wished us to taste in his presence;
he then gave us four of his subjects to conduct us all
round his mountains, to prove to us that it possessed more
water than we had yet seen; and his last words to us were,
" if these waters are found, will the white man be
sent?"

Our return to the wagons was thus made rather cir-
cuitous. One of the men assured us, during our progress,
that Rantsane was formerly a powerful chief, but that he
had been very much weakened by the attacks of his enemies Matuane and Pacarita, who had carried away all
his cattle. Therefore it was that he had but a few
sheep, and not a single ox or cow. Metsing and Moli-
betsane, two of our most interesting young men at Moriah,
came originally from Racebatane; and one of the wives of
Moshesh came from Kolile, a neighbouring town, of
which the chief is Mosifa.

On our return to the wagons, we found our guides had
been feasting at the expense of the wild asses of the
day before. These good people had prepared us some
slices of their game, which we ate with no little relish,
although the meat appeared to us all to be very insipid and
very tough. When the quaggas are fat, the flesh is more
tender and better eating. Not all the Bechuanas, however, will eat it even then, for many of them say
that the fat of these beasts has a disagreeable smell; but

to the Griquas, this is a matter of indifference. They greatly relish the flesh of the quagga when fresh, and hunger makes them like it even when dry, although then it may be as hard as leather. And it must be allowed that an animal of the same nature as the ass, could scarcely be put to a greater variety of uses than is done by that poor people. Its skin, however ill adapted it may be for the purpose, is employed as lashings with which to fasten the frame work of their roofs, or it is converted into bags to preserve corn, or it is made into milk bottles, or into head pieces or caps, as we have seen done by more than one of the natives.

On the 7th April our journey was short, but interesting in regard to topography. For three quarters of an hour we travelled N.N.W., for an hour N., and then for a quarter of an hour N.N.W.

CHAPTER XII.

THE COUNTRY AND TRIBE OF THE BAMOLIBERIS.

At ten minutes past four in the afternoon we passed through a deserted village (Litsikela,) and about a quarter-past six, through another, which had also been abandoned. In both were found heaps of human bones,—to say nothing of rubbish, old sheep-folds, and other ruins obstructing the progress of travellers. Both places belonged, fifteen years ago, to a prince of the Bamoliberis, a tribe of Bechuanas now extinct, or nearly so. This chief was called Lekoro, and the country he inhabited retains his name, from which we infer that his power must have been considerable. Some persons of his tribe showed us five or six larger villages, once containing a great number of inhabitants, but there is now scarcely a soul to be found. And the worst is, that these misfortunes, the details of which are buried in oblivion, were, in all probability, brought upon his tribe by himself. Lekoro left behind him the repute of having done much evil. He has been called *the man of noise** and also *the man with hard jaws*† by which it is intimated that he never ceased quarrelling. We need not, therefore, be surprised to learn that he died young, according to the remark of the psalmist,—Bloody and deceitful men shall not live out half their days. As the petty king of the Bamoliberis became daily worse, many of his own nation declared themselves

---

* *Motu a lerata.*   † *Motu a lithlaga lithata.*

his enemies. A part of the rebels, commanded by Rachosane, a chief still living, but who has joined the Basutos, went and besieged him at Litsikela, his residence
took him prisoner, and kept him till he had given up all
his flocks for his ransom. But after that,—impoverished,
rather than corrected,—Lekoro was desirous of following
his system of robbery, and, accordingly, undertook a
military expedition to the Tambuqui country, from which
he never returned,—he, and the greater part of his
troops, having been killed there. The country, which
he left nearly depopulated, as we have just remarked,
and to which no one has succeeded, deserves a special
notice, for the benefit of those who may be studying the
geography of the country.

It is a fine country, and contains some excellent pasturage. It is situated in the neighbourhood of the Malutis, upon the western extremity of those mountains, but
so far removed from the hills, that the inhabitants of it
were formerly called the inhabitants of the plain. The
climate is temperate, it hails there every winter, but
snow is rarely seen, though about forty miles distant in
the upper country, it is often half a foot deep with ice
from four to five inches thick.

As to the nature of the soil, it differs from any we had
previously met with. Instead of a black mould containing
a great deal of clay, one now meets with a soil which is
much less stiff and firm ; it is lighter and more sandy, and
in many respects better adapted to tender plants. Great
quantities of small bushes grow there, and on these the
goats and sheep often browse. We every where observed
wild thyme, mint, and a kind of sage,—used, in the form
of a decoction, with good effect for the healing of ery-
sipelas,—and among the flowers, bright wall flowers, not
less beautiful than those which are cultivated in our
gardens, and very pretty violet-colored convolvolus. On
the other hand vegetation is not so vigorous as toward the
south, and lofty trees are altogether unknown.

We travelled over a magnificent land, extending from

Umpukani to Merabing, and thence to Racebatane. Leaving this latter place, the traveller begins to descend towards the north, all the streams flowing in that direction, or rather to the north-west, whereas, till that point, they flow south and south-west, so that he finds he has passed from the district of one river to that of another, from that of the Caledon to that of the Fal or Namagari.

We regretted much that our scientific information was so limited as we were now treading upon ground favorable to interesting researches. The place of our encampment, especially, appeared to us very remarkable. It was a high brow of shattered rocks, which had formerly been a mountain separated from the rest, the base of which is still seen. The sandstone rocks of which it was composed, at present lie scattered all around, and from the great disorder apparent, one naturally supposes that some extraordinary inundation, if not an earthquake, with or without explosion, must have been the cause of all this confusion. The former of these hypotheses becomes almost established when it is considered, that in the same district, upon the source of the Tiku, there is to be found, upon a level with the ground, a mine of coal tinted with copper, proving the existence of ancient forests in a country where the eye can scarcely now discover a small tree.

Again :—Not far from Monuanu, about four miles distant from the place first mentioned, and upon the same line, running from south to north, I saw a small hill, which presented appearances analogous to those I have just described. I suppose that it had formerly a flat shape, but by the catastrophe referred to above, traces of which are apparent, the centre has now become hollow—the cavity being about eight feet deep, about one hundred and fifty feet in circumference, and of an elliptical form. In the middle of this circle I collected some quartz, mixed with calcareous substances, also gypsum and red ochre, and in the neighbourhood small black stones, porous and so light that I took them for pumice stone.

The village of Monuanu contains no more than fifteen huts, so well concealed amongst the rocks as scarcely to be perceived at thirty paces distant. There must have been formerly a great many more, but the Caffres and Korannas, who have taken away the flocks, have destroyed also many of the people. The few who live there are kept in a state of constant anxiety. They fled when they perceived two horsemen in the plain, myself and my guide. The latter called to a woman who had concealed herself in the millet fields,—" Why are you afraid? We do not want to kill you! We only wish you to show us the road to the Motsi." She heard us, but did not dare to show us. We passed on towards a very tall and robust man, having a beard. He, in his turn, looked at us for a moment, and then running precipitately, withdrew to a short distance, but he stopped when he perceived that we were without arms. I assured him that I had good intentions, and endeavoured to remove his doubts by shaking hands with him, a mark of kindness which determined him to lead us to the village; but his trembling voice could scarcely articulate some broken sentences, such as the following, " My lungs are swollen. I am frightened. That woman there below is probably afraid of the horses; I, of the guns. Tell me, do you really mean what you say, and have I no evil to fear? Is there no person behind you? Arrived at the clan, we had in like manner to satisfy all present, that our hearts were as white as snow,—to follow the hyperbolical and figurative mode of speaking common among the natives.

It was not until after a great deal of explanation, that they consented to listen to our news, that is to say, to the gospel. Not a single female appeared at prayers, they all went away, dragging their children after them, in a way we had never seen before. The chief Ramofana, when once he was satisfied, told me that I had been taken for an emissary of Piet-Witte-Voet, which grieved me exceedingly. I offered him some tobacco in token of friendship, and accepted also some sweet reeds with which he presented me. When we were about to leave, this Ramofana, whose mild and gentle air pleased me much, took the reins of my horse, and conducted me himself for about ten minutes, until he had put me in the path we were to follow. Before bidding us adieu, he pointed to the west, to a spot situated at the end of a vast plain, where was a village of Lighoyas as considerable as Racebatane. It is called Tsekuaning, the name of the chief is Motlegnane. In the neighbourhood, there is another spot no less populous, which is called Makuabane, and which is peopled entirely by Lighoyas. At three or four hours' distance towards the south, I passed close to a mount in the shape of a dome, where the Mantetis at first established themselves before they chose Merabing for their capital. The country is very beautiful in that direction, but open; running waters are there very scarce, stagnant ponds more common. The name of the place is Sebopi—*an oven.* I question if a designation more appropriate could be found.

CHAPTER XIII.

CONTINUING our journey, we reached Kalasuane, where we again had the misfortune to frighten the natives. An old woman, amongst others, who met us in the fields, shrieked loudly at our approach, and began to cry like a child, making signs to us to pass on,—she allowing us, at the same time, to see her face only in profile. A little further on, a young woman, of whom we were obliged to ask our road, directed us wrong; but I perceived that she was trying to deceive us, so she did not succeed. She continued to cast side looks at us, while her voice continually failed her, and her countenance was suffused with perspiration. *U tsab'ang*, said I to her in her own language, with a view to remove her fears,—" What do you fear ? I am a man of peace ; my words are good." After that, I took up a loaf that she was baking, and put some morsels to my mouth, but nothing could give her confidence. Fortunately, the chief of the clan soon arrived, and, walking before the horses, he conducted us to the village. " I know," said he while walking, " that you are not wicked men, for your wagons have just arrived at my place, and your drivers have told me that you *love* people." Thus did we rejoin the wagons, around which were gathered a crowd of people, to whom we preached the glad tidings of salvation through Jesus Christ. When retiring, several of the natives said to

one another, *Kayenu re rutiloe,*—we have been instructed
to-day.

Kalasuane is a Lighoyas town, situated in the midst of
three or four others, acknowledging, for their chief,
Ngatu, of whom mention has just been made. It is
built upon the brow of a mountain which forms part of
a small chain, and it is defended by deep pits, formed
naturally by the rain in reddish earth, which is very
sandy, and broken up in all directions. The whole population of these different places does not exceed five or six
hundred souls, and they might, we think, be evangelised
from Racebatane, if an active and zealous missionary
were settled there.

We left the subjects of Ngatu some articles of european manufacture, for which they paid us in kind,
—that is to say, with millet, pumpkins, and maize.
They exchanged also, for salt and tobacco, a few articles of curiosity, as for example, a battle axe, copper
bracelets, and two or three *lebekos*, a kind of small iron
spoon *sui generis*, used to clean the nose and body, also
a *cheketse* (digger) somewhat resembling a pike, and
which is chiefly used to dig holes in the earth for catching
the game.

These holes, measuring from five to six feet in depth by
three in diameter, are shaped like a tumbler, in order
that the animal falling into it may be bent together, and
so rendered unable to extricate itself. The native name
for these holes is *mamena* or twistings. By working hard,
a man may make eight of these holes in a day; it is a
work to which the Lighoya is trained from his youth.
Armed with the cheketse, which he clenches firmly with
both hands, he kneels down, and digs away with the
sweat on his brow, knowing that his existence depends
in a great measure upon his exertions. His mamenas
finished, he covers them carefully in with reed and brushwood, and retires. They are situated near pools of water,
and consequently in the way of the gnus and quaggas
that come to graze there: and these animals, coming

V. ANTELOPE CANNA
(called 'eland' by the Cape farmers)

bounding along, tumble in, and are fixed at the bottom of the trap. The following morning, the savages kill them by thrusting at them with the pike and the lance, then dragging them from the pit, they carry off their prey to feast the kraal. Sometimes, however, they have to dispute their prey with lions, which have reached the pit before them. The fight is always fatal to one or other of the parties, unless the wild beasts take to flight; and even in this case they are followed and tracked to their very dens.

A curious fact, if true,—it is one affirmed by every body—is, that the lions themselves are often caught in the traps, to which they have come in search of prey. It is then easy to kill them, but sometimes their howlings bring their companions to their aid ; and these seizing them by the mane, drag them out of the pit before the huntsman arrives. I suppose it is by carrying away the spoil of the Lighoyas so often that the lions have learned this stratagem, by which they assist each other in times of need. The lioness delivers its little ones, when entrapped, by scratching at the side of the hole like cats, and opening for them a trench or ditch by which they may escape. Should the holes, however, become filled with water, there is no means of escape for the cubs, and they become the prey of the savages.

Leaving Kalasuane, we arrived in about two hours' time at Setlopo, where we encamped. We had then travelled for four hours and thirty-six minutes in a north-easterly direction. We thought, when outspanning there, that we had chosen a very good place in which to spend the night. It was in the midst of immense fallen rocks, which afforded excellent shelter from the winds. Our guides had no sooner given the cattle their forage than some of them took their guns, and scattered themselves over the plain, which was covered with every species of game, such as gazelles, gnus, hares, quails, and partridges, but the evening closing, the huntsmen were soon compelled to return.

The cattle grazed quietly at a little distance from the wagons, in a hollow of the mountain of Setlopo, which unfortunately proved to be the haunt of lions. It must have been owing to the oxen being very much pinched by hunger, that they did not scent the ferocious beasts of the neighbourhood; and I cannot at all understand how the horses remained, even for a short time, in this dangerous spot. There was one of them called Fleur, which upon another occasion had been sorely wounded by lions, and from that time I had a hundred times observed, that he no longer browsed after sunset, but with great caution; for example, he would graze with his nose to the wind, crop a mouthful of grass, listen if there was any noise near to him, then lower his head, raise it, and if there was the least danger threatening, kick up his heels, and scamper away like lightning, to stop no one could tell where.

At Setlopo he must have done the same, for we saw him approaching at dusk, neck extended, mane on end galloping past the wagons. The other horses followed him closely, with all the oxen after them, out of breath and in great trepidation, and three or four lions pursuing them. The foremost of these stopped short at the sight of the wagons, about thirty-two paces distant from us; immediately a discharge of musketry was aimed at him, but without any other effect than causing him to roar most fearfully, as did also the others. The lions then described a semicircle, took a quick turn, and pursued their prey. Our intrepid Bechuanas immediately seized their javelines, and notwithstanding the darkness which had already set in, without thinking of the dangers to which they were exposing themselves, and hungry and fatigued as they were, they followed in the tracks of the lions. It was in vain that we awaited their return; neither they nor the cattle appeared again that night.

As for ourselves and the rest of the party, we surrounded our encampment with fires, and formed a defensive hedge, in the centre of which we kept ourselves close. It was necessary for us to be very vigilant, as we had not a single dog left with the wagons. We, therefore, placed a lighted torch upon one of the wagons, and appointed a sentinel, who had orders to fire his gun from time to time, while another of our people was directed to smack his enormous whip occasionally, to frighten the beasts of prey, and keep them at a distance. In this manner we passed the night, under the protection of the Lord, without any injury befalling us. Early the next day two men were sent out in search of their comrades and the beasts. It was a day of fatigue and of solicitude, but, to our great satisfaction, in the evening the whole of our party rejoined us, with the horses and cattle. They had likewise met some natives who came to demand payment for damages our cattle had done to their fields.

I must also mention, that we had, near the fire, a cannibal traveller, of a savage countenance, and whose whole person was pitted with the small-pox. Happily no one said aught offensive to him. On the contrary, he was supplied with food, and prayers being finished, he quietly encamped with our party. It was amusing to hear the braggings of our people on their return,—this one had never been afraid of lions, the other was not able to count the number he had killed in his lifetime. Each related a thousand acts of valour, and to observe the energy with which they spoke, one might have fancied that they were in the very heat of action. There was nothing going but mountains and vallies, broken lances, unexplored forests, attacks, blood, broken bones, and deaths,—but for all this, there were still some remains of courage in their veins. Thus the tale went round. At length they must know the exact number of the wicked animals that had occasioned to every one a day of so much toil and a night of so little repose. They must find out whether it was three lions or whether it was four; nor must they omit to count also the number of the cubs, for the marks of little feet, mingled with the others, showed that mothers must have been put to flight. And oh,—had it only been daylight, what could have hindered them from catching some of these lion's whelps! Nothing could have been more easy!

CHAPTER XIV.

SETLOPO AND THE MANGOLES.

THE detention to which we were subjected at this place infested with wild beasts, enabled us to procure some interesting specimens of natural productions, amongst which were some of a new species of the silvain, as we were informed by a naturalist of our acquaintance, to whose collection we had the gratification of adding a specimen of these birds. Two specimens were sent also to the museum of the Society for Evangelical Missions at Paris, where they, as well as many other contributions towards the study of natural history, sent by the same opportunity, may be better examined and classified.* In regard to vegetation, Setlopo delighted us. It was indeed a rich botanical garden, requiring only some more skilful

---

* A few setlopo plants, together with their seeds, were sent at the same time to the same place, but in regard to these we have procured no information in addition to our own memoranda made on the spot, which were as follows:

No. 1. Ntsime (name given by the natives.) Fruit like a gherkin in shape. The natives use it as food. It has a nauseous oily taste.

No. 2. Motuku:—Leafy convolvolus, with isolated flower. The ovary encloses three seeds of the form and size of chick pease. The root is cooked with milk, and eaten by the natives.

No. 3. Masibu :—A leguminous plant. The pod about the size of that of the kidney bean. The fruit the same, and of a brown color. Boiled in water it might be used as food.

No. 4. Tula:—A kind of berry of a yellow color, rather larger than an acorn, and used by the Bechuanas as a medicine.

These four plants grow in vallies about three thousand feet above the level

naturalist to explore and describe its treasures. There is there great abundance of shrubs, and of lactiferous plants, such, for example, as the euphorbia. Instead of the bare and rugged rocks, which in other places had fatigued the eye, here numerous saxatile plants covered, as with a carpet, the whole of the mountain, and gave it a most charming aspect. Climbers were to be seen twining themselves around a species of palm common in the Malutis, where it attains a growth of nearly thirty feet in height; and convolvolus, aloes, and geraniums of a deep purple, made the beauty of the place complete. We observed also two species of cotton plants which were new to us. Curiosity prompted us to examine them a little more minutely. Can it be that the Creator has without design furnished them with that little tuft of down in which the seeds are enveloped? Assuredly not. There are moths which clip off the cotton from the seeds, and make of it a covering for themselves, according to an observation as correct as it is interesting, made by the author of *Etudes de la Nature,* to which we may be permitted to refer.

Is it necessary to add, that the more we admired the beauty and fertility of the country, the greater was our grief to see only heaps of human bones in the room of the numerous happy inhabitants whom one might natu-

of the sea. They are very common throughout almost all the country of the Lighoyas. The fruit of the first three serve as food for the baboons, and for a great many birds.

No. 5. Morulane:—A tree bearing a berry, of the form and size of a small apple, but poisonous to man. The Lighoyas dry the pulp of this fruit, burn it in the fire, reduce the ashes to powder, and by means of a small blade of iron they introduce it under the skin as an astringent application.

No. 6. Serue :—An herb which the natives eat entire, root and fruit, without any preparation.

Unless some person in Europe turn to use the seeds of the plants of which I speak, my remarks will be of little use. But any one who may do so can conceive that however uninteresting it may be to others, it must afford a great gratification to those who, like myself, are called to live in the country, and are consequently interested in all that relates to it, to learn the result of his observations.

rally expect to find in such a place? It was, we were
told by the natives accompanying us, formerly the dwelling place of the Mangoles, a celebrated bechuana tribe,
the history of whose destruction presents only a tissue of
distressing details. They were distinguished by their
great veneration for the riet bock, and more especially
by that which they paid to the wild vine, which they
called *morara*. This plant is indigenous in the woods of
the Malutis, and if its stem, on the one hand, does not
exceed a few inches in diameter, its branches, on the other
hand, mount to the very top of the loftiest trees, which it
seems sometimes to stifle in its embraces.

The Mangoles did not refuse its shade, but they never
touched its fruit, and still more unwilling would they
have been to make use of its wood. If any person happened to use it as fuel, they would not take a light from
that fire, and with religious care they would gather up
the ashes, and put them on their forehead, and on their
temples in token of grief. This reverénce, so peculiar,
resembles in some respects the worship rendered by the
Druids to the misseltoe :

> Sur un chêne orgueilleux, des peuples adoré,
> Les Druids sanglants cueillaient le gui sacre ;
> Les autels exposaient au culte du vulgaire
> De la faveur des cieux ce gage imaginaire.

Twenty years ago, this little nation was rich and flourish-
ing; they had seven or eight considerable towns, in the
neighbourhood of Setlopo, which was the capital, and was
governed by a chief named Patsa. Mr. ARCHBELL's
former interpreter, as well as my own, belonged to this
tribe. The late Chaka, say the natives, sent his ruthless
troops against the brave Patsa, who whilst defending
himself fell with many of his people, which was the beginning of the calamities referred to above. Of two sons
who survived him, one was devoured by a lion, and the
other met with a fate still more dreadful.

After the death of his father and brother, he assembled
his subjects, and related to them the immense losses they
had sustained : he then represented to them the imminent

danger they would incur by remaining longer in the neighbourhood of the Matebeles, his sworn enemies, and concluded by declaring, that he was resolved to seek another country, one less exposed, in the north-east. All were of opinion that there they would find safety, and they agreed to the proposal. Then the poor Sebetuane, accompanied by Lekapetse and Ramabusetse, two chiefs who were in alliance with him, descended towards some of the Bays situated between Port Natal and Delagoa. It is scarcely possible to form an idea of the facility with which people emigrate in the continent of Africa! These unfortunate men travelled a whole month in the desert, followed by their wives and children, and drove before them the remainder of their flocks. But day and night they were subject to the greatest anxiety; they equally dreaded the Caffres and the wild beasts; they had neither protectors nor guides. They slept under the rocks, or in the woods; and every warrior, as he laid himself down to rest, fixed his spear in the ground at his head, like Saul when he fled before David.

At length they arrived at the Indian Ocean; but who shall describe their surprise when they saw for the first time that magnificent object, to which at first they could give no name, except that of *great rivers,* or *great waters* * The chiefs immediately began to deliberate on the next step they were to take, and whither they should direct their march. During these discussions some white men arrived, and proved a new subject of wonder. They called them *balupi,* that is to say, *the pretty ones !* These strangers were few in number, and asked them, with much appearance of interest, whence they came. They enquired what they were doing there, and finished by advising that they should follow them the third part of

---

* Great waters,—that is *the sea,*—is an expression similar to what is found in the Old Testament. Thus in the 29th Psalm it is said : " The voice of the Lord is upon the waters ; the God of glory thundereth; the Lord is upon many waters."

a day's journey from that place. They consented ; and then they met with other whites in greater numbers than the first, who descended from two floating houses in the midst of the great waters, and hastened on shore. They also asked Sebetuane and the other two chiefs, many questions similar to those asked by the men who first met them ; and they pretended to feel still greater sympathy for the fate of the unfortunate emigrants. They treated them very amicably, and asked them, if they would not like to be transported beyond the river to the habitations of the Balupis, where they would find better masters than Chaka, a peaceable country, good pasturage, and plenty of excellent ground for gardens. The too credulous Africans, partly intoxicated by an unknown liquor, and weary of wandering in the desert where their lives were continually in danger, hesitated for a little, and then agreed to the proposal.

Immediately, planks fastened together, in shape, said our informants, as if we closed our hands together, and then half opened them (large boats) were brought to the shore. At first the poor creatures were timid, and looked around them, as if they were afraid to enter, but they were officiously assisted ; they stepped in, and their cattle were taken with them.* A cry to which they were un-

---

* This circumstance requires an explanation, which I was unwilling to introduce into the narration of the event. There is nothing, however, to prevent me from giving it in a note. The Bechuanas never move without their cattle, and, as a proof of this fact, I could cite the example of more than a hundred Lighoyas who at present live at Griqua Town. Ten or twelve years ago they were attacked by a party of Griquas, who robbed them of their flocks ; when, rather than see themselves deprived of their cows for ever, these poor people followed on their enemies' track, even to their homes, and consented to live with them and to serve them as herdsmen, &c. The Mangoles had only the remains of their cattle, when they had the misfortune to meet with these slave dealers. If, on the one hand, the slavers are so built that they can receive only a certain number of men, on the other, it may be contended that these pirates would think nothing of receiving on board two or three hundred sheep or goats, and some horned cattle ! Could they not the next night throw them overboard, and is it not very probable that they did so ? But under any cir-

accustomed was heard, and suddenly all were pushed off
from the beach; a river remained before the boats, and a
river behind. Other whites came, and they finished by
carrying off to the ships almost all the negroes, with their
wives and children, their cattle, provisions, and all their
effects. There remained, however, on the shore about
a hundred Mongoles, who exclaimed, with great indignation, No! we will never follow Sebetuane, Lekapetse,
and the son of Mabusetse, to go with strangers, people of whom we know neither the country nor the language, and who will perhaps starve us to death or kill
us; we will rather return to our deserts, when, if we
cannot get beef and millet, we can live on the flesh of
the tiger and jackal, with our brethren:—*re tla ya
linkue le lipokuyue kua ha esu!*

I learnt these particulars amongst the Mangoles, who,
on returning to their own country, related the afflicting
story which I lay before my readers word for word as I
received it, and without comment. They know not what
has become of their countrymen. When they questioned
me on the subject, I replied that I did not know where
they have been taken, and I always added, that those who
refused to accompany them were the more prudent. It
is so painful to me to unveil to these simple people, the
dreadful facts of the slave trade, that I prefer being
silent on this subject when I can. Thus it will be seen
that that diabolical trade has spread even to the foot of
the Maluti mountains; but I do not suppose that it has
reached further on the southern side of this continent.

An english engineer told me that, about fifteen years ago,
two slavers were met by a ship cruising along the eastern
coast of Africa. This ship attacked one of the slavers, the
crew of which, seeing that she was on the point of being

cumstances, nothing could have been more politic than for these robbers to take
on board, with those whom they had inveigled, the only property that was left
to them. If they had refused they must have given up the negroes, for they
had courage to defend themselves, and were far more numerous than the
whites. Oh! if they had but known of the existence of slavery!

taken, had recourse to some large empty casks, into which they put some of the negroes they had on board, and then threw them into the sea, in the hope that they might afterwards be able to retake them. What became of those ill-fated beings is unknown ; might they not be part of the unfortunate refugees whose misfortunes I have described?

CHAPTER XV.

On the 9th April we left Setlopo, and travelled in a north-easterly direction for four hours and twenty minutes, when we reached Motlomo, a village of the Lighoyas, where we unyoked, there to spend the approaching sabbath. The journey presented nothing remarkable. I may simply mention, that we came upon a river, called by the Bechuanas *Tikue*. We crossed it eighteen or twenty miles below its source, about which place there is said to be a very good fountain, a report which may be deserving of the attention of missionaries, in the event of any founding a settlement there, on account of the numerous natives,—Lighoyas, Mantetis, and a remnant of an old cannibal tribe—scattered through the lower vallies, and along the skirts of the Malutis.

The Tikue flows from the south-east toward the north-west. It receives, in its course, the waters of the Keicop, which spring from the neighbourhood of Umpukane, and it then makes straight for the Fal, into which it falls in the 27th degree of south latitude, and about 27 degrees and 30 minutes longitude east of Greenwich. The bed of the river was dry at the place at which we crossed it, but it could not be less than forty feet in breadth, so that the body of water flowing there in the rainy season must be very great. The sand in the bed of the river was so light and so deep, that our wagons and oxen sunk

in it, and it was with great difficulty that we could
get them out. As the Tikue is frequently called in the
country Sand River, I would not be surprised if this
designation should ultimately prevail.

The country continues to decline towards the north,
but it assumes a different aspect from what it presented
up to that point; it is now open and unbroken. The
waters of the Tikue, it is very likely, flow a little below
the surface, though the bed be dry ; and we saw occasionally fresh water lakes, which we had not previously met
with. Towards noon we left one of these on our left,
which was about a mile in circumference. In its vicinity
were herds of antelopes grazing, and on the lake itself we
observed a great number of aquatic birds, amongst which
we recognised wild ducks and teals.

Although the inhabitants of Motlomo had never before
seen white men, from which circumstance they must
have viewed us with a little suspicion, they nevertheless
came freely to our wagons, whither God collected them
to *hear the word*, to employ a bible idiom which is also
used by that people. They had been told of our approach to their kraal by one of our Bechuanas, whose
conversation, and explanations of the design of our visit,
pleased them much, and inspired them with confidence
in us. They, accordingly, all came down to the wagons,
and mingled freely with our own people, to whom they
did not fail to put a thousand questions. At length we
engaged in worship ; our service consisted of three songs
of praise, two short and simple prayers, and an exposition
of that evangelical appeal of the prophet Isaiah, " Ho,
every one that thirsteth, come ye to the waters, and he
that hath no money ; come ye, buy, and eat; yea, come,
buy wine and milk without money and without price."
But how true it is, that spiritual things are little understood by those who are carnal, and by those whose affec-
tions are engaged in the pursuit of earthly good. The
natural man understandeth not the things of God, much
less can he love them. It is necessary that the Holy

Spirit reveal them to us, that he produce a complete change in our tastes and natural inclinations,—that he bring us back to our Creator,—that he explain the doctrines of scripture,—in a word, that he renew the understanding and the heart. Then only will one begin, like Lydia, to listen and to receive the gospel of the grace of God, and be saved. I could not wish a better proof of this important truth than is supplied by one or other of the following facts. During a catechetical conversation which followed the discourse of the morning, one of the natives remarked, We have understood. He was asked, And what? That we must pray to God. And what then? Well, proceeded one of them, you tell us of a rich and benevolent Chief who can increase our flocks, satisfy our mouths with fat things, and fill our dwellings with peace and prosperity ;—these news are delightful : I, for my part, wish to settle near you, that I may hear them again, that I may understand them aright : if I come, will you give me a heifer? A strange conclusion to our worship, said I to myself; does the man really intend to materialise my address ; and yet, ignorant as he was of spiritual things, and altogether carnal, he only reasoned correctly according to bechuana ideas. It was for the very same thing that our Saviour reproached the crowds which followed him from the sea of Tiberias, with seeking him not because they had seen his miracles, but because they had eaten of the bread, and been filled, and therefore was it that he said unto them, " Labor not for the meat which perisheth, but for that meat which endureth unto everlasting life, which the Son of Man shall give unto you."

It will be granted, however, that the mistake of the Lighoya was sufficiently amusing. I mentioned the circumstance one day to a missionary settled amongst the Barolongs, who, not satisfying himself with simply remarking that nothing was more characteristic of the Africans than that trait, related to me a similar incident. One sabbath, said he, I attempted to depict the happiness of the righteous in heaven. The service being finished, one of my hearers came to me, and with great earnestness addressed me thus : " Master, nothing can be finer than the Canaan of the righteous, a country flowing with milk and honey ; the pasturage there must doubtless be rich, and the water plentiful, a country of peace, where there are no enemies, and where a kind and powerful king reigns. His subjects must be happy ! If you go some day to visit that land, master, will you promise to take me with you. I wish to see, with mine own eyes, what it is, and then we will go there,—myself, my wife, my children, and my flocks. I would like much to make it my country."

Although the weather was very bad, we had a short service in our tent in dutch, for the sake of the Bastaards of our party. After which we had conversation with the Lighoyas of Motlomo, on the subject of religion. Monaile also said many good things to them, from which we trust that, through the grace of God, this visit may prove a blessing to them.

It rained at one time, and my colleague and I having shut ourselves up in our wagon, like two hermits, continued almost the whole evening to talk of christians at home. Somehow or other, both of us felt a painful uneasiness, which it would be difficult to describe. It may have been some presentiment of the troubles in which we were about to be involved ; an account of these would almost lead to the conclusion that it was so.

On Monday the 11th of April, Geriet asked for some tobacco to smoke ; we cut off a piece from the roll, which we kept behind the pillow, and gave it him. September came after that to get some tea, and Adam Krotz for coffee. We knew these people enough to gather from their manner that there was some mischief brewing. At length, Adam was sent by Ruiter to get some beef. Some of the *salt beef?* said he. We answered that all the fresh meat must be eaten before the salt, and that for obvious reasons. On this refusal our man began to murmur, *This will not do.* A word which he let drop in speaking to our Bechuanas betrayed his intention. He said to them:—Aye, this is a good distance from our homes. On hearing this, we jumped out of the wagon, to put a stop to the mischief if possible, before it should spread further. " In what direction are we to go to-day?" demanded our driver, in an impertinent tone. We answered, To the North. Upon which he tossed his head and said he would not go. Adam also came to propose that we should go back towards the south-east, in which direction he said there was an excellent fountain, which he wished to show us, but all his entreaties were thrown away, and the rascal tried then to get our Bechuanas to join them. These we had hired as a measure of precaution against any mishap of this kind, as we did not choose to trust ourselves altogether to our bastaard guides; and as we saw that we were now to be left by them, we immediately doubled the wages of the others. One must have heard the thousand-and-one reproaches, excuses, and recriminations which followed, to form any idea of them, "No," said September, " I have found it necessary before now to flee from Mosolekatzi's. I should have taken care not to come near him again. I dread that cruel zulu tiger. He will tear us all in pieces." "And who wishes you to go so far?" we asked.— " We are to turn, when once we have got to the Fal." " To the Fal!" cried Adam ; " that is the place where the horses die of the *pere-sickte*;* I will lose all mine." " Not at this season, Adam ; in the month of February last, you might have lost them ; there is no danger now ; but at all events your horses will be replaced by us, if they die of the *paarde-siekte*." In this way we endeavoured to obviate the different objections as they were raised, but it was lost labour. The Bastaards are a feeble-minded people, of an irresolute, wavering character, from which it might be expected that we should have retained our command of them in a case in which we were so deeply

* *Pere Sickte* for *Paarde Sickte*, or *Horse Sickness.* The Cape Journals say it is a kind of influenza affecting the horses.

interested. But Adam, more decided than others of his tribe, had taken his stand, and was immovable. When we saw this, we said to them plainly, "Go! you may return, both you and yours. Your services are no longer required." "No! no!" replied the rogue, "We must all go together." And he set about attempting to corrupt our Bechuanas. "Nobody knows," said he to them, "where they are going to take you. It may be into the lion's jaws, as they did the day before yesterday; or it may be to the Matabeles, the sworn enemies of your nation, who will kill perhaps every one of you. Return you with us. You are too good. These whites, are they not very much to blame for leading you into a country altogether unknown? Your wives regret your ever leaving them; and, with good reason, they are asking, if you will not come back soon. At what an immense distance from our homes we are already! Come! As for myself, I had resolved like you to go further, but I am afraid. I must return. Come, follow me. There is no want of game betwixt this and home. I will see that you have plenty to eat."

Sekesa and Monaile wavered; they appeared indeed to be very much shaken in their resolution, but happily Raseluyana kept firm. The Bastaards reproached them with being head-strong, and with putting so much confidence in the missionaries. "Can they drive a wagon, asked they. If you go, you will stick in the mud at any piece of bad road you come to." But the Batlapi, with his usual energy and simplicity, rejoined thus, "What I say is this:—these men are the whites, you others, bastaards; you have learned from the whites how to whip a span of oxen. How, then, can you wish me to believe that they cannot do it much better than you can? Go home if you will, but let me alone."

Adam leaped into his wagon with a furious air, took all our goods which he found there, threw them on the ground, yoked, swore, and left us, taking with him the other bastaards. As for us, we made some good cups of coffee, and took them in company with the rest of our people, waiting till the rainy weather should clear up a little, which it did about 10 o'clock in the forenoon. Mr. Daumas then put every thing in order in the wagon, while I arranged the yokes, and calling in the cattle we inspanned. As we were setting off, Raseluyane said to his companions in an encouraging way, "See we have all got a warm belly-full, while the deserters have only had ditch water to drink, and will they pretend that one cannot do without them? Very well, we'll see. Come lay on." It would appear that this young man, at least, was quite satisfied with the result of the morning's adventure. For three quarters of an hour we travelled eastward ; then for an hour N.E., and then for four hours to the N.N.E.

About a quarter past 3 o'clock we passed an old kraal on our right, which had formerly been inhabited by Metsuane, a Lighoya chief destroyed by Mosolekatzi.

It is there that the Enta, one of the most important tributaries of the Fal, takes its rise. Its waters fill a great number of pools, in which the beasts of the field quench their thirst, and, a little further on, it threads its way through some charming hills, which it enlivens with its gentle murmur, the only sound perhaps ever heard there, excepting the howling of the jackal, and the roaring of the panther.

Our camp was pitched on a little flat, rising ground, distinguished only by the number of enclosures of stones, in which the Mantetis formerly shut up their cattle. Thither we conducted ours, to prevent them being dispersed, or devoured during the night by the wild beasts. The evening was cold and dark, we therefore kindled a large fire, around which we gathered close. As in unpleasant dreams, hideous objects seem sometimes to disappear, and again to place themselves before our eyes, so came Adam Krotz and posted himself exactly opposite the wagon about thirty paces from us; it was really he, while we were supposing him far away. At nightfall he came, and seated himself on a rock; there

he sat quietly though it was very cold; he remained
about an hour without speaking a word, and then disappeared as suddenly as he came, and we saw no more of
him. He then sent Ruiter to let us know that he had
killed an elan in the course of the day, and that we
might have a part of it. This we declined, and that without so much as speaking a word to the poor messenger.
For what good could have come of our making fresh
arrangements with such people,* who would not have
allowed a day to pass before beginning again to torment
us? We were too happy in having got rid of them ; and
seeing that we could do without their assistance, we
only wished them safely home. The Bastaards are any
thing but a people on whom you may rely. We had
engaged Krotz and his party as guides; it was not, however,
because we had confidence in them, but because we knew
not where, in that country, better drivers were to be found.
Hereafter I hope the Bechuanas will be able to undertake such work. Many missionaries are endeavoring to
prepare them to do so; but as yet, you will not find one
good *whip* (for that is indeed the only proper designation
for them) excepting amongst the mixed race, unman-
ageable and troublesome as they are. As for Adam, this
was the second time he had left me alone in the fields;
and he had previously left one missionary of my acquaintance, and afterwards another, so that he ought by this
time to be pretty expert at the trick. I knew him,
however, to be a bold and courageous man, and it was
this that recommended him as so suitable for such a
journey as ours.

His departure devolved on us the difficult and fatiguing
duty of driving the wagon ourselves, as our three Bechuana attendants understood nothing about it; and one
of these natives, moreover, had no great inclination to
accompany us. It was Sekesa from Morea. Monaile was

---

* Let it not be supposed that we entertained any rancorous feeling in regard
to them. The principal actor in this rebellion having subsequently made an
apology, we forgave him with all our heart.

rather more disposed to go with us, but his companion discouraged him; as for Raseluyana he never hesitated a moment. "What have you to fear from these deserts in which you yourselves were born?" cried he to his friends in a chiding tone. This Batlapi had left Thaba-Unchu, taking with him his dog, a bundle of assagais, clubs, and other necessaries for the chase, that he might go and seek his fortune. He undertook to keep watch over the cattle, and to supply us with game; he regularly started first in the morning, after having learned from us in which direction we meant to proceed during the day. As for Monaile, he was tolerably well acquainted with the country; one will not meet with many Mantetis more interesting than he. A man of few words, he said to us in a humble manner, "My masters I know to mount a horse, I can accompany you in your excursions round your camp, but we must never go too far from the wagon." And as regards Sekesa, difficult as it was to manage him, he agreed to lead the oxen going before them with a hold of the short thong attached to the fore-most couple of the team. So we could not dispense with his services, except on good roads.

Having made all these arrangements, breakfasted and prayed, we set out on the 12th, agitated and full of anxieties, but commending ourselves to the care of our heavenly Father. I took a strong bamboo about fourteen feet in length, to the end of which I fastened a cord eighteen or twenty feet long; this we call a whip in South Africa, and a tremendous whip it is. Then, seated on a chest placed in front of the wagon, I set my-self to drive our team of ten oxen, fastened in couples to a long rope passing betwixt them, which lengthened the team far beyond the reach of my lash. But never mind; I jumped down, from time to time, to go and whip the leaders, which are always certain to prove the most lazy, whatever care may have been taken beforehand to place in that position the most lively of the team. After having put a little life into them in this way, I jumped up again

to my box seat, ready to jump down again whenever it
came to *This will never do*,—to borrow an expression of
Adam Krotz. My colleague, at the same time, mounted
his horse, and gun in hand accompanied by Monaile, he
rode on before us, pursuing at the same time herds of
elans and of game. In carrying out these arrangements, we acted with some policy ; we were not sure but
our guides wished imperceptibly to turn back towards the
south-east ; he therefore invariable set out toward the
east, and agreeably to arrangements made betwixt us, he
afterward turned toward the north, whither we could not
do otherwise than follow him with the wagon. For a
quarter of an hour, I drove to the North, for an hour and
a quarter to the N.N.E., for half an hour to the East,
for an hour and a quarter N.E., and, then after a halt,
three hours and a half longer to the N.E.

About 2 o'clock in the forenoon, I was obliged to halt for
a considerable time, through the stubbornness of Sekesa,
who absolutely refused to advance further in a northerly
direction. He pretended that Monaile had gone to the
east, and given him directions to follow ; but I stood firm,
and brought into play every possible means to overcome
the obstinacy of the young man ; for example, I asked
him, Where does the sun rise ? Can you tell better than
my compass can ? and this I lent him to examine. I next
put a map of the country before him, and said to him,
See, there, there is such a nation. Is it not so ? Down
there such and such a river flows. Is it not so ? Who
can better direct the journey, you or your master ? But
no, I could not convince him ; and a little after I took to
another plan, and I desired him to tell me, for my information, if he knew to what tribe a hut of reeds which we
found in the midst of the fields could belong ;—when the
roguish fellow answered coolly, "I, how can I tell ?
Does your paper not tell you that ?" I succeeded at length,
however, in carrying the day, and, yoking once more, we
again set out. In the evening, however, this man kept
still murmuring, saying, "These whites, because they fear

God, they have no fear of man." Happily for us he had both of his companions against him. And they replied, "You are not to speak in that way, Sekesa. They like us better than do the Bastaards, whom you wish to go and join, but they are now too far away for you to dream of that. Before us there is nothing to fear, and you know it. There are only some deserted towns, or some small kraals of our countrymen, the Lighoyas, and nothing more. Here you will want nothing, victuals in the wagons, game in the fields ;—And the wild beasts? Oh, you are afraid of them, are you? When did they ever devour you near a wagon, and beside such a fire as we have just made. No brother, it is only the oxen and the horses which are in danger from them ; but we will fasten them to the four wheels of the wagon, and they will be as safe as ourselves." To this sensible lecture we added a little more, mixing with it a little irony, but in no way destroying, by so doing, the adaptation of our address to the circumstances of the case, as nothing else would do.

"Monaile and Rasiluyane" said we, addressing ourselves to them, "Your words are wise, and just, and appropriate ; but do you think that Sekesa will believe you? He has resolved to be obstinate and stubborn. He is no more the humble, laughing companion of other days. He is master now. This wagon is it not his ? To-morrow you will see him sitting in it at his ease, and we shall all have to drive this morema wherever he may command. These oxen, oh yes, they are his! the horses also! Come, we must let him know that each of us will expect a heifer from him when we have conveyed him home ! For you see he is master. He is master in his own opinion. What think you, Monaile and Raseluyane?" Irony, we have generally found effective amongst the Bechuanas, and it was not less so on this occasion. Sekesa hearing us arguing in this way, changed his tone, and began to make excuses. The African tribes may not be distinguished by an excess of courtesy, but they have a little. The lower classes amongst them forget their place much less

frequently than do the same classes amongst Europeans ;
and if it do happen occasionally, it is rectified speedily by
a short representation of the impropriety of their conduct.
Much besides may be told to their praise. They possess, for example, a natural tact, which seldom, if ever,
leaves them, and the reader will find no more details of
unpleasant collisions with our servants in the pages
which follow, as, in this respect, all went well with us
throughout the remainder of the journey. If it happen
that our conduct in this case give offence to any, which
we should regret, let such judge us with that measure of
indulgence which men ought ever to extend to one
another. We did not otherwise towards Sekesa. After
our reprimands, the young man felt prefectly at ease ;
and a little encouragement from us soon led to the recovery
of his usual hilarity. He became very useful to us, as
did also his two companions, and we loved him sincerely
for many reasons. He was naturally of a gentle and
religious disposition. In proof of this let the following
soliloquy suffice ; it will be found interesting, and I insert it here rather than elsewhere, that I may rest and
refresh my thoughts.

    " Your news, oh white man," said he to me one day,
" Your news are just what I wanted and sought for
before I knew you, as you shall judge for yourself. A
dozen years ago, I went in a cloudy season to pasture my
flock along the Tlotse, among the Malutis. Seated on a
rock, in sight of my sheep, I asked myself sad questions,
yes, sad, because I could not answer them. The stars,
who touched them with his hand? on what pillars do they
rest ? The waters are not weary, they know no other
law than that of running without ceasing, at night and
morning alike ; but where do they stop, or who makes
them thus run ? The clouds also go, return and fall in
water on the earth ; whence do they arise? who sends
them ? It surely is not the Barokas who give us the rain,
for how could they make it ? And why do not I see them
when they raise themselves to heaven to search for it ?

The wind,—it is as nothing to my eyes :—but what is it in itself? Who brings it, or removes it, makes it blow, roar, rebound, and frighten us? Do I know how the corn grows? Yesterday not a blade of it was to be seen in my field; to-day I returned to my field and I find something. It is very small,—it is scarcely perceptible; but it will grow, and it will gradually develope itself just as a young man grows. Who can have given the ground wisdom and power to produce it? Then I buried my forehead in my hands.

*   *   *   *
*   *   *   *

" Anew I reflected with myself, saying, We all depart, but this country remains ; it remains alone, for we all quit it to go away ; but whither do we go? My heart answered, Perhaps there exist other men besides us, we shall go to them. A second time it said, Perhaps those men live under the earth, when we depart hence, we may go to join them. The thought returned to me, Perhaps those men live under the earth ; but another rose against it and said, Those men under the earth, whence come they? On this my heart did not know what else to think ; it wandered.

" In its turn my pluera rose and spoke to me, saying, All men do much evil, and thou, thou also, hast done much evil; Woe to thee ! I recalled many wrongs which I had done to others, and because of them my conscience gnawed me in secret, as I sat solitary on the rock. I say I was afraid. I got up and ran after my sheep, endeavouring to enliven myself,—but I trembled much."

CHAPTER XVI.

On the 13th we continued our route, and made at one stretch about 16 miles towards the north-east. It was a long stage, but the griqua travellers would have called it a *schoft*, or an ordinary day's work. We travelled through the ruins of old bechuana villages, as we had also done the day before. Eteletsane, one of these villages, was formerly occupied by the Mantetis, as were seven or eight similar ones situated in the neighbourhood. A group of others were seen a little further to the north. These were not in so good preservation as the first, from which we concluded that they were more ancient. They belonged to a family of Bechuanas, called Barankokoto ; one of their chiefs has bequeathed his name to one of them,—the one which chiefly arrested our attention, from its having been the largest. Two of his descendants live at Moriah, whilst the assagai, as they express themselves, has devoured their brethren and their companions.

There is nothing in this place to enliven the fancy. They are the fields of the dead, and Ezekiel himself would have groaned in spirit had he seen with his own eyes these fields covered with human bones. The huts have been burned, the gardens destroyed ; and nothing remains but the circular walls of stone, standing about four feet in height, in which the natives of that fertile country formerly folded their happy herds.

The Bechuanas are all a pastoral people. When they leave any of their little towns to go and found another in some new situation, better adapted to the support of their cattle, they carry with them the materials of which their cabins are built, their clothes, their utensils, and their weapons. If they be attacked by an enemy more powerful than themselves they flee before him, taking with them what they can of their goods, and the remainder is carried off or destroyed by the invaders. In either of these cases of migration, nothing but the walls for the cattle of the village remain, and for these they have no peculiar designation ; they call them simply *lerako*,—wall. This term is almost always employed in the plural *litaku*. The same name is given to the capital of the Batlapis, probably because they had formerly left that place, and on returning they would say, that they were returning to their *litakung*, the ablative form of the word ; whence has been formed by corruption the Lattakoo of the english. If this observation appear trifling, let its insertion be attributed to the reputation enjoyed by the town of Mahura and of Motibe.

Two or three of the *litakus* which we visited, must have belonged to the Matebeles, as appeared from the subterranean granaries which we met with. there. These granaries are holes, similar to what are made in their cattle folds by all caffer tribes, for storing their millet. All of them have the form of a vault but they vary much in their dimensions. The entrance is just sufficient to enable a man to get in. When the hole is finished, a fire is kindled in it, that the walls may be thoroughly dried ; after which it is swept clean, and when filled with corn, the mouth of it is closed with a flat stone which is plastered over with fresh cow dung ; the cattle may then lie down above these subterranean granaries without doing them any injury. In opening them, the natives are careful to do it in the morning, that the suffocating air generated within, may have time to escape during the day. Towards evening, they may be entered without danger, and the corn is then brought out. If it have fermented, it is only a little at the bottom and the sides, and what is thus injured is not thrown away, but made into beer, of which the Caffers are very fond. Such are the pits which they call *omoleti*, whence comes the sechuana word *moleti*, employed by the Baralongs and the Batlapis as a designation for the infernal regions, by adding to it the word *molelo*, signifying fire: *moleti oa molelo*, the granary of fire,—the pit of fire,—hell,—the fire of Gehenna.

With little more trouble than is bestowed on the making of these moletis, the Bechuanas procure for themselves other and much superior granaries. They store up their corn in *sisius*, without any fear of its mouldering. These sisius are large straw baskets, shaped like the turret of a dome. The Caffers know not how to make them, a circumstance for which we found it at first difficult to account, but we think it may be traced to their not knowing how to plait the rushes of which this kind of basket work is made; the trusses of which the Caffers avail themselves to strengthen the unstable wood work of their huts, and to tie down the thatch with which their huts are covered, is the work of old women alone. With the Bechuanas it is altogether different; and one would almost conclude that the more man is of a warrior, the less does he trouble himself with household matters, and these devolve on the woman as her birth-right,—we may say, her only possession. I do not mean to say that the Caffers might not learn to make trusses and sisius as good and, perhaps, much better than those of the Bechuanas, if they would only apply themselves to the work; for, with this single exception, they have shown themselves much better basket-makers than they. Give to a Matabele, for example, a small sharp piece of iron, flattened and slightly bent, pointed at one end, and pierced with two lengthened slits at the other, that he may get a firmer hold of the blade of grass which he wishes to pass through it in the place of twine,—and, with this kind of needle or bodkin *(letlabo,* piercer,) a little straw and reeds, he will make for you all manner of pretty things,—an *omothlolo,* a sort of basket which serves him for a dish; a *sééki,* a basket of a middling size, and of a very elegant shape. You will see in his *setuto* a neat and well-made round box; his little *omothleloana* will be seen to have been finished off in a tradesman-like way; and when the workman informs you that one of these baskets serves him as a water jug, or beer pot, and the other as a milk pitcher, what will you say? Will you believe his word? Yet examine the workmanship, how close, how fine it is, and you will not doubt it. The Matabele will show you, moreover, simple but pretty mats on which he sleeps at night,—thicker ones on which he rests his feet by day,—and strong hurdles of wicker-work with which he closes the entrance to his hut. If you compare all these little productions of his industry, with similar productions of the Bechuanas, you will not hesitate to give the preference to the work of the Caffer.*

At the distance of twenty or thirty miles to the east, we saw some high hills, which formed the extreme northern prolongation of the Malutis; but from that point the country to the west and to the north is perfectly open. In that range, at the extremity of the horizon, was to be seen Mokoto, the most celebrated mountain in the whole. Like many others in its neighbourhood, it is peopled by Basutos. At the period of our journey, their small towns were under the government of a chief called Tsetlo, a native of that country, and naturally strongly attached to it. There he lived formerly in the midst of his faithful subjects, rich in goods, in valor, and in fame.

War having destroyed his repose, Tsetlo went down to the south, and sojourned for a year or two in the neighbourhood of Thaba Bosio, where Mokachane reigned. He gained the good opinion of that chief, who gave him

* Notwithstanding what I have said in praise of the Caffer, it is but right to add, that their wicker-work will be found very inferior when compared with that of the Indians and the Malagasy; but it is not with these that we are now comparing this people.

his grand-daughter in marriage. Some time after, peace being restored, he was able to return to his country, and he did not hesitate a day as to what he should do. If Tsetlo had had as much prudence as courage on returning to Mokoto, his ancient capital, he would have settled there quietly; but instead of doing so, he entered into a league with the Mantetis against the Chakas; and the Mantetis, a poor people, who had never known any thing but pillage, were not slow to lead him and his people out to war. The expedition proved successful, and it may be that the petty king of Mokoto congratulated himself on having such allies.

Some time after, they sent him word to hold himself in readiness for another attack upon Dingan, which they had projected. Tsetlo at once caused a quantity of millet flour to be roasted, filled some leather bags with it, sharpened his assagais, scraped clean his buckler of buffalo hide, covered his hair and his body with fat, and sent to say that he was ready.

On the appointed day, Sekoniela and his soldiers arrived at the foot of Mokoto; two messengers climbed up to the plateau and went to salute Tsetlo, who made haste to offer them beer, and to slaughter an ox with which to regale them. He then went down with them to the camp. But as soon as he got there, he was seized and bound by order of Sekoniela. They cast him on the ground, where he lay like Chakta, more than surprised, motionless with alarm on seeing these barbarian soldiers, but lately his companions in arms, infuriated against him. When he could open his mouth, it was boldly to demand what wrong he had done to the son of Mokocho to deserve such treatment. His pretended friend replied, " It is because thou hast purchased some horses which were stolen from me." " When, and how many?" " It is now six moons ago, and the horses were four in number." " Very well, then, if thou canst discover them amongst mine, they will be brought to thee at once." Sekoniela rejected this proposal. " What

dost thou want then?" demanded Tsetlo. "Thy flocks."
"Thou shalt not have them." "I will have thy head."
"Take it then, if thou desirest it." The sons of the
captive, however, were not slow to collect the cattle of
their unfortunate father that they might ransom him by
giving up the whole. Tsetlo said to them, " My children,
your filial love is carrying you too far. Keep your
goods. I know how to die. And you, how will you
live if you give up these cattle? Why! Hunger would
devour your families, and my eyes would see it. No;
rather let me die; and you, do you boldly defend your
possessions and your lives after my death." Yet the sons
were determined. They delivered up to the enemy their
horses, their cattle, and their sheep, and this being done,
their father was set at liberty. They conducted him
home with great joy, while the Mantetis took their departure for Merabing, which they entered the next day
in triumph.

Three months later Tsetlo wishing to be avenged for
the affront he had received, and the loss he had sustained,
collected together his impoverished subjects, all cherishing
mortal hatred against the Mantetis. There happened to be
a considerable chief of that tribe, called Ralitaoane, living
in the neighbourhood of Mokoto. Upon him Tsetlo and his
party threw themselves one dark night, and carried off his
cattle. On hearing of this, Sekoniela dispatched a messenger to the chief of Mokoto to say to him what mischief
hath Ralitaoane done to thee? None. Sekoniela, his king,
alone hath done thee harm, and he will do thee more
harm still.

It was a word and a blow. The day after the message
was sent, he threw himself upon Tsetlo, overcame him,
pillaged him a second time, and left him dead on the field
of battle.

One of the subjects of this unfortunate basuto chief,
who had preserved some head of cattle, hastened to go
down towards Bosio, that he might secure them there.
With this design he followed out-of-the-way paths, in-

clining always towards the heights of the Malutis; but
even there he encountered Mantetis, who despoiled him
of all. After that, in pursuing his journey, he arrived one
day at the dwelling of one of the principal warriors of these
cruel hordes, called Masopo. It was a cave in the Blue
Mountains. Masopo pretending to receive the stranger
as a friend, caused some refreshments to be brought to
him,—but while his guest partook of them, he laid him
prostrate with one blow of his club, demanding at the
same time, " Must I put an end to thee ?" " No, I pray
thee," replied the unfortunate traveller, " No, master, for
I have done thee no harm ; thou seest me destitute, I
will serve thee." The ferocious Masapo was inexorable ;
he stabbed the poor Basuto with one thrust of his assagai,
muttering these words, " I must kill thee for all that."
Oh, how unhappy are the Africans, living without God,
without settled laws, and they themselves such enemies
one to another !

In the neighbourhood of Mokoto, where a short time
back there were some thousands of Basutos, there are now
but few to be found, and every day fresh parties are
leaving it, emigrating some to the colony, and others to
the peaceful territory of Moshesh, so that if this go on
much longer, the fine country of Tsetlo will soon be
covered only with Litakus. Such are already almost the
only traces of human habitations, to be seen from the
extremity of the Malutis, to a great distance towards the
east and the north. Our journeys of the 14th and 15th
of April, fully satisfied us in regard to this said fact. We
travelled during these days about eighteen miles towards
the north east, and about fifteen miles towards the north
west, over only the skulls of men, mingled with broken
pots, and the rubbish of the Litakus, which met the eye
in every direction.

There can be no doubt but all the country which lies
between the chain of the Malutis and the French Mountains, was once very populous, and that it would again be
the same in a few years, if the principal chiefs remaining

there would but combine and consider what is their common interest; it is through each thinking only of himself, and considering how he may best secure his own interest, that they cannot afford mutual assistance and protection against even extermination, as in the case of Tsetlo and his people,—a thing of constant occurrence amongst the tribes of South Africa. The details given above, are so analogous to a host of others which I have received, that they force upon my recollection the *ab uno disce omnes* of an ancient poet.

Plenty of water, rich pasturage, and abundance of game, these are the three sources of prosperity offered to new inhabitants by the country of which I speak. The blacks seldom seek for more; one would have been glad, however, if there had been also a little wood and a few mountains, to which they might betake themselves in case of danger; but neither of these are there.

Geographers would give to the whole of the country the designation of a table land. It has an inclination towards the north west, but it is so slight that it is scarcely perceptible, and the rivers which water it are at once deep, and confined by high banks. From Setlopo to the Sekua we were constantly crossing hills, one would imagine there was a continued ridge of them, forming an extension of the Malutis, which are in the very place which these mountains would occupy if they were really prolonged so as to connect themselves with those which we have called the French Mountains, and thence to the mountains of Monomotapa, as almost all the maps of South Africa would make us suppose.

On the evening of the 16th we could not find even three round stones with which, as usual, to construct our fire place; we had to use a couple of clods instead, and in default of rubbish or brushwood we had to use reeds from the marsh and dry herbs to cause our kettle to boil. This was the bed of a little stream which we called the Cocong, the name given by the natives to the blue gnu, a great many antelopes of this species being found in the neighbourhood.—We tried for many hours to get to the top of the banks, but these were so precipitous, and every thing so miry, that we were at last obliged to give up the attempt and to remain in our awkward position, having thoroughly fatigued ourselves and the cattle to no purpose, and broken the handle of the whip into three pieces, an accident which we had no means of repairing but by using the shingles of our wagon. I still recollect that it was not till about one o'clock in the morning that our guides procured for us some refreshments, consisting of a cup of coffee and a kind of porridge made of flour.

Raseluyane remarked that night, " He who is on high still helps us!" We have always indeed found that God was a present help, reviving our strength and restoring our confidence. No one can expect to be without trouble in this life, but the great thing is like the Apostle Paul, to know in whom we have believed. Carrying back my thoughts to the time of which I speak, nothing appeared to me so terrible as the thought of our being then in the middle of the desert, without a bit of wood. We travelled for several successive days through the most lovely herbage and along charming hills, but not a single bush caught the eye ; suppose that an axle-tree or the shaft of the wagon had broken, we would have been obliged there to abandon the wagon and all our effects, and to make our way home as we best could, on foot and empty handed, on account of having no means of repairing the damage. The Lord in kindness spared us such trials, no part of the wagon of any importance broke in the course of the whole journey, which is a very rare occurrence in those districts. In travelling from the Malutis to the French Mountains, we crossed the following streams, the Tikue, the Enta, the Chacal, the Cocong, and the Enketuane, of which the Chacal and the Cocong are sources. The Enketuane flows into the Namagari, about the 27th degree south lat. and the 29th degree east long., after having watered that district from one side to another. At their junction the one of these two rivers may have a breadth of about sixty feet, the other of about thirty. There the Namagari, which is the larger of the two, exchanges the brown color assumed by its waters in the Blue Mountains, for a yellow hue imparted to it by the chalk and the sand over which it rolls. In some places also its bed is paved with black and glistering rocks of granite and feltspar. I was almost drowned under one of these blocks, my strong and vigorous Ruiter, on which I was mounted, was thrown flat amongst the rocks, and his rider left at the mercy of the stream. We both found it a difficult matter to extricate ourselves. The poor horse, moreover, had been suffering severely for two days from violent cholics, brought on by eating too freely of green rushes. In the evening he laid himself down on the grass and was unable to rise again, so that we believed we should have to abandon him, amidst the wild beasts of the field. Sick as he was, however, he afterwards bore me on a long journey up the river towards Intsuana-tsatsi, one of the three little mountains whence flows from the east to the west, and into the Namagari, a little stream called by the natives Noka, or Little Elephant River, because formerly many Elephants were caught there, and also Hippopotami. This spot is very celebrated amongst the Basutos and the Lighoyas, not only because the *litakus* of the tribes are there, but because of a certain mythos, in which they are told that their ancestors came originally from that place. There is there a cavern surrounded with marsh reeds and mud, whence they believe that they have all proceeded ; and yet, man does not in their language, as in many others, bear a name recalling his origin. *Motu* in Sechuana, the same word as *montu* in Caffer, means *the speaker*, and this is the generic name of the race, so that in that country, as well as in the schools, man sees himself described as the *speaking animal.* He is also spoken of as the man in contradistinction to *mosari* the woman. *Monna,* the term there used, being formed from *mo,* a prefix, and *nna me* signifying *I who am.* Mosari, is a name more humble, but very beautiful, being the derivative of Mosagari, *the graceful.* As for the long word Intsuana-tsatsi, it signifies the

east, a name applied to this spot, apparently simply in consequence of that mythos. The word *machaba nations* has no
other etymology than the Sechuana and Caffer verb *chaba*
to pierce,* used in reference to the sun. In their ablutions
these tribes turn themselves towards the east, in which
direction also they turn the face of the corpse when buried.
Every thing, in short, intimates that they have preserved
a vague recollection of the east having been the cradle of
the human family.

* *Chaba*, to pierce, to point, comes from *cha* to burn, and from *ba* to be.
Bochabela, the burning side, the east.

CHAPTER XVII.

From the Noka-Tlou, stretching away towards the east and the south, on to the Indian Ocean, there lies, as we have been assured by the natives, a country rich in pasturage and in wood, healthy, well watered and abounding in game of all sorts,—as the elephant, the unicorn, the rhinoceros, the hippopotamus, the buffalo, the giraffe, the elan, the gnu, the quagga, and a great variety of gazelles, as well as lions, hyœnas, leopards, jackals, wild dogs, and wild cats. The climate there appears to be, generally speaking, temperate ; but in the lower districts many kinds of fevers prevail, and the *paarde ziekte* is there very severe after the rainy season, which lasts almost from the month of November till that of April. That fine, wide country, in fine, is studded thick with lesser mountain chains, and is peopled almost exclusively by the Zulas.

I have collected a good many notices of that people, which I would fain insert here in preference to bringing them in at the end of my narration, which would require a tour into the country ; and, perhaps, the reader will pardon me if I do so, even though the digression should threaten to be somewhat lengthened.

These Zulas are a fine race of blacks, superior in stature, in elegance of shape, and in muscular strength to the Bechuanas.—These, as mild and gentle as the others are ferocious, have invariably suffered much from their aggressions when they have come into collision with them. A Basuto speaking on this subject, said to me, " On seeing these men, so strong and well made, entirely naked, of a cruel and ferocious countenance, armed with short handled but larged headed assagais, the *mokondo,* and with a shield of buffalo or bullock hide twice as large as ours, we were all seized with fear, and called them *Matebeles,** but amongst themselves they are called *Amazulus.*" †

The Matebeles have driven from their immediate neighbourhood all the powerful bechuana tribes, which they found in that place. They fell upon them like lions, to borrow the energetic expression of the natives. The dread which they inspired is astonishing. There is not a more powerful caffer nation known. We calculate that they must be about one hundred thousand in number; but others reckon that there must be at least fifty thousand more capable of bearing arms; and, if so, the number of the tribe must be much greater than even we have supposed. Be it as it may, it is a difficult problem to solve. The matebele chiefs are full of cunning; when an intelligent traveller wishes to ascertain their strength, they cause some thousands of the troops to pass in review before him, and then they take him four or five miles away to show him others, and he is not unfrequently met there by the same forces. An order has been given, and individuals already

* *Matebele,* those *who disappear,* or are scarcely to be seen behind their immense bucklers.

† *Amazulu,* the Zulas, that is to say *the Celestials.* This proud title reminds one of the Celestial Empire, and the Celestial Court of the Chinese. In general the African tribes name themselves after their chieftain; but I am not acquainted with any case of a chief bearing the name of heaven or earth, or any similar designation, so that *Amazulu* can only mean *the Celestials.* The *a* at the beginning of the word is an adjunct, which serves to determine the word to which it is joined after the manner of the Greek article, or more correctly speaking, like the letters called *prefixes* in the semitic languages. The prefix *ma* combined with Zulu, which signifies *heaven* or *celestial,* shows that this word is in the plural. The Zulas are also called *Amazaze, those from down there,* the lowlanders, because they lived for a long time on the sea coast. The Bechuanas more generally call them *Bakoni,* and sometimes they give them the nickname of *Lifakani,* that is to say, *those who hew down,* or cut their enemies in pieces with the *chake,* their formidable battle axe.

numbered in the note book of the traveller, are at the appointed place, and mixed up with some hundreds of other soldiers, so that it becomes impossible to make a correct estimate of their numbers; such is the singular policy they adopt to conceal their real strength. They thus blinded the eyes of their enemies, and led them to consider the Zulas as at once invincible and innumerable; and in more engagements than one have other tribes fled at once on their approach, without striking a blow. It is no bad thing for a people to be able to render themselves formidable to feeble ones arround them, simply by their renown, as the Midianites and the Philistines of old did to the children of Israel.

Amongst the Matebeles the youths tend the flocks, the men go to battle. On leaving the service, at about the age of forty, they set themselves to make weapons, pickaxes, or clothes, and they constitute a kind of veteran corps, never going to battle but in cases of great necessity. The women make the pottery; and the cares of house keeping and husbandry, moreover, devolve almost exclusively upon them. The troops are all divided into distinct regiments, dispersed through the country, and kept apart from the rest of the people, and even from their wives and children. These regiments, it would appear, are composed of from six to eight hundred men each. A certain number of cattle is alloted to them by the chief of the nation, but these they dare not touch without his orders. A few years ago, he sent and massacred a whole regiment, because a few members of the corps had killed an ox without having first obtained his permission. When the despot orders it, the regiments go to the attack of different villages according as he may appoint,—this to this village, that to another.

Their war cry is, " *To conquer or to die.*" The sovereign does with them whatever he pleases. When they are absent, and even when they are present, he sacrifices to his ambition whom he will. His soldiers on returning from an expedition victorious are rewarded, as the soldiers of

Mahomet were; the chief divides amongst them the captives, and a part of all the booty. If the expedition has proved unsuccessful,—if, for example, they have fled before their enemies,—they must lay their account with certain death on their return. On this account, numbers never do return to their homes, but, to save their lives, take refuge in the countries around.

I have known a great many of these refugees. They have,—as is common, both with men and women amongst the Matebeles,—a long slit in the curvature of the ear. The rich wear copper earrings, about one inch and a half long, and collars and bracelets of the same metal, or of ivory, or of different kinds of beads, and in some cases of iron. The common people introduce into large holes in the lobe of the ear bits of reed, or they suspend from it plates of iron, of copper, or of leather, as ornaments. The children, both boys and girls, go naked; but the latter, on growing up, put on an apron of cords or of skin, and throw over their shoulders the softened skin of an ox or antelope. The sovereign levies a sad tribute on them; every year he causes to be brought to him all the virgins to whom he may have taken a fancy, and he only permits them to return to their parents for the time which they may require to suckle their children, which is about three years; at the end of which period they must again appear before him, as if they were so many concubines, and continue with him till he gets tired of them, and sends them away.

Like all the Caffers, the Zulas are very superstitious; they have magicians, both men and women, who are in great repute for the power to curse or to bless, which they are supposed to possess. They are most commonly a kind of soi-disant physicians, but at the same time wicked denouncers of suspected or imaginary crimes. The people have recourse to them in general when they wish to make away with some relative or friend. In this way they often subserve the ambitious designs of the chiefs. For example, a young man has taken umbrage at his elder brother, but as he does not like to sacrifice him without some plausible pretext, he gets him denounced as a traitor, or as ambitious, and immediately a sharp spear is buried in his heart, or more frequently stones are heated to redness, and, by a concentration of cruelty, the accused is forced to sit upon them, and they are renewed from time to time till the wretched victim is burned to a cinder; sometimes, however, his sufferings are cut short by a *coup de grace*. Shall we not extol the Holy Scriptures for having made it a law of the Hebrews, to extirpate from the land the unprincipled people who gave themselves out as sorcerers, necromancers, and wizards!

The other crimes punished with death amongst the Zulas, are adultery, murder, and speaking against the chief. This last crime, however, is of rare occurrence, as the chief has spies every where, who report the most trifling remarks of his soldiery and of his subjects, and this being known, every body is guarded in his expressions. The supreme judges of the country are Omthlola and Tapuza. Criminals are generally executed at Mokokutlufe, the capital; and although executions there are almost of daily occurrence, and the people are butchered like cattle, to use one of their own expressions, the executions always take place in the face of day.* The condemned have their necks twisted, or they are strangled, or impaled, or stabbed to the heart with an assagay, as is generally done when the royal guards receive orders to go and slaughter a chief, together with his wives, his

---

* Amongst the laws of Moses, there is one bearing some resemblance to this custom, which may possibly throw a little light on the design of the practice,— "If a man have committed a sin worthy of death," it is said in the book of Deuteronomy, chapter xxi, 22, 23, " and he be put to death, and thou hang him on a tree, his body shall not remain all night upon the tree, but thou shalt in any wise bury him that day; (as he, that is hanged, is accursed of God;) that thy land be not defiled, which the Lord thy God giveth thee for an inheritance." Such an one is accursed of God, for he hath forfeited his life in the eye of the law, and "cursed is every one that continueth not in all things which are written in the book of the law to do them."

But even supposing that the Zulas may have retained something of this tradition, it is painful to think again, that the great majority of the people condemned to death amongst them are the innocent victims of suspicion or of envy, and often, also, of the mere caprice of their judges, as is but too notorious.

children, and his subjects, and to burn his villages to the ground. Then, nothing belonging to the condemned man survives the execution but his herds.

The Matebeles bury their dead with great care; they purify themselves for the departed, and offer sacrifices to them, in itself a proof that they have some idea of the superiority of the soul and of its immortality, as they have also of the erroneous doctrine of the transmigration of the soul. Every Caffer pays the greatest reverence to a serpent if he meets one, because he believes that he sees in it one of his ancestors, who has appeared to him in that form. If it be in the hut that he has found it, he endeavors to drive it out with the greatest gentleness; or more frequently he presents food to it as an oblation, and goes out himself, shutting the door behind him, and waiting outside till the god (*Setunta*) has eaten, which may be not till the following morning. Some Zulas burn the corpse in the midst of fields of millet. Those of the Mosiniate, beyond Intsuana Tsatsi, expose the dead bodies of their chiefs upon the branches of trees, leaving them there for a certain time, then burning them, and throwing the ashes into the river. With these exceptions, the common practice is to bury the dead in round strait holes, the body being wrapped up in a skin cloak, but with no ornaments, the hands laid on the breast, the face turned towards the east, and the knees bent up towards the chin, which is the attitude of suppliants in that country. The widow is transferred to the brother of her deceased husband on his death. The orphans are brought up by tutors or *malumes*, who are held in as great respect as the parents themselves. There is not, perhaps, a single case known of a child being so entirely abandoned as not to have some relative, near or more remote, who would take him under his care. In this respect the laws of the people are most admirable; yet, I have, and that but lately, seen a boer, displaying ostentatiously two young Matebeles, whom he had just captured, and when I reproached him with what he had done, he replied that it was an act of humanity on his part, as the two little slaves were orphans. Poor little things, they would not let us see their youthful faces, so conscious were they of the degradation which had befallen them.

All the youths amongst the Zulas were formerly circumcised; but the predecessor of the present king, with a view to the improvement of his army, restricted that rite to his soldiers on their leaving the service. They are circumcised in the month of February by an *enianka* or magician, at sunrise and near a running stream, into which the foreskin is thrown. Not a word is spoken, no one is allowed to be present excepting the fathers and the intimate friends of the circumcised. The strictest secresy is observed in regard to every thing done at the place, but there are war-dances and libations of beer at the town, and there both the priests and the people make themselves beastly drunk. The neophites are the only persons who do not take part in these orgies.

To the last king of the Zulas we must also attribute the abolition of marriage amongst the soldiery, for neither he nor his successors, in taking wives, have followed the custom of the nation. Both of them have condemned family ties as prejudicial in every respect to the profession of arms, and it is only those troops which have borne the brunt of war who are allowed to marry, the other soldiers are punished with death whenever they violate the law of celibacy. When the soldiers leave for the war, young girls run before them naked, and they are promised that one of these will be given to them in marriage when they return from the expedition, if they acquit themselves valiantly. Every thing,—rest, agriculture, commerce, and domestic happiness,—every thing is sacrificed amongst this people to the demon of war, and this because the chief of the nation wishes to be a god, and to make his subjects slaves. He takes the title of *inkosi*, a designation which will be best explained, perhaps, by first explaining the word *mokosi*, the one being a derivation from the other. Mokosi is applied alike to an *alarm* and to a *national assembly*, and the right of giving the alarm and of sum-

moning the troops to deliberate on important state questions belongs exclusively to the *inkosi*, who is a true
sultan in absolute power, in tyranny, and in supercilious
contempt for all beneath him.

He shares his power with two soldiers of his choice;
Omthlela and Tapuza, already referred to,—the one cunning, the other cruel. Together they form a triumvirate
of the most convenient sort. When it is something bad
that is to be done, it never fails to secure their unanimous
approval, and so to acquire the force of law. But when
it is something good which is to be done, some one of the
three votes is always wanting to give the proposal effect,
and, as may be readily imagined in such a case, the good is
left undone. The court of the Zulas sometimes, however,
sacrifices some little personal interests to public opinion.*
These two ministers of the chief are considered, according
to the phraseology of the country, the two eyes, the two
ears, the two arms, nay forsooth, the two nostrils of the
monarch. They are distinguished moreover with the title
of *great indunas*, a word which literally signifies *males*, but
figuratively *powerful nobles*. Omthlela and Tapuza are
accordingly the two first dignitaries of the nation of the
Matebeles.

The military force of the nation is composed in all of
twenty-six regiments, at the head of each of which is an
induna or commander, a lieutenant, and two sub-lieutenants. These regiments live in garrison towns, which are
surrounded by pallisadoes in lack of better fortifications.
They are not subjected to frequent change of residence.
By a very prudent arrangement their inkosi passes a month
with each of the corps in succession, and sometimes he
leads them to war himself. An armour-bearer marches
before them. The armour-bearer of the present ruler is
called Mokafane. This distinguished officer keeps always
two paces in advance of his master, to shade and protect

* As for example, when Dingan filled the hands of Cumete with w' alth, to
which an allusion will be found in the praises of Dingan with which this chapter
concludes.

him with an immense ægis of bullock hide, around which one might fancy that they saw grouped, Terror, Discord, Might, and War. Be it in token of respect, or be it from fear, Mokofane never looks his Jupiter in the face, and excepting through him, no one, not even the two grand viziers, Omothlela and Tapuza, can have any communication with their sovereign. Well may we say with a judicious writer, " When we see some chief of a negro tribe, crushed by his own haughtiness, and his subjects rendered nearly as wretched as himself, those in civilized nations who are in rank elevated above their fellow-men may easily perceive that pride is not the measure of true greatness." The Bakories find their prince so difficult of access, and when approached so formidable, that they have adopted, as their national mode of swearing, this short sentence, 'nkene 'nkosene, that is to say, I cannot better attest the truth of my affirmation than by promising that if it be found incorrect *I will go in to the inkosi*.

The chief of the Zulas has also a lance bearer, and two great chamberlains, who are pretty well named the *two wolves of the king*. These two officers never move in the seraglio, but upon their knees, and with their eyes to the ground ; incredible this may be, but it is nevertheless true. In conclusion, it is but proper that I should name the two principal cooks of the prince, Omolete and Mokobulane. Their situation must be no sinecure, for their master has such a repute for voracity that his subjects say of him he swallows up fountains, like as Job says of Behemeth, *Ecce absorbebit fluvium, et non mirabitur !*

Sa gueule du jourdain engloutirait les flots.

The allusion to scripture may require apology, but it shows that hyperbole has always been indulged in by man. The following is a synoptical list of the existing regiments of the Zulas *

* I have got my information in regard to these, as well as a good deal of what I have obtained in regard to this people, from Rasekuai, an inhabitant of Moriah, who spent four years in the service of Dingan, and in the seraglio of that chief.

ARMY OF THE ZULAS.

Nos.	Names of the Regiments or Lebantla	Commanders or N'duna-e-nkholu	Lieutenants or 'Ngenana	Sub-Lieutenants or 'Ngenadzana. (Plus, Omzepa et Omozezoa.)
1	Omobapankue	Omthlela	Ototala	Taoane, Onomapeta.
2	Nkompa	Po°kane	Koboka	Nomotane, Makakabula
3	Setlepe	Omaniune	Omozezo	Makutumane, Kopueana
4	Mokokonthlofu	Omozempa	Eentoa	Oniepeze, Nobanta
5	Bommelebele	'Nkobonka	Onuntabula	Oputele, Kakane
6	Bosuku	Omofungusi	Sepenia	Mothlathlo, Nokonkela
7	Ontubu	Okhaoe	Masetela	Ofoluze, Molota
8	Ofasepe	Omozezoa	Opankubane	Opetene
9	Amakethla	Mokhèkhèkeke	Nonkokela	Chunku, Mochochi
10	Eboea	'Ntaoane	Kochuo	Mongaiela
11	Omokaze	Onutsikeluane	Mokubulane	Mopeezoa, Kueabuntala
12	Zeetane	Cheba	Fefe	Obote, Sepezi
13	Sepeze	Ezoakana	'Ntaba	Osama, Funtuene
14	Obolaoanko	Ontene	Onthluane	Thlakathla
15	Otuguza	Opakazeta	Okoza	'Mpetene
16	Mokamule	Omafungusi	Mosesane	Balela
17	Enkuebane	Omofane	Mokhose	'Nkantane, Omocheloa
18	Eziniosi	Omaziezulu	Omoketeza	Ofusi, Osengata
19	Mokolujane	Osekhèkete	Otlapo	Motetoa, Maueue
20	Otibitlaku	Bolota	Mothlathlo	Okaza
21	Onkankèzüe	Nobanta	Okuathlampa	Makuatza, Opotu
22	Onthlankeze	Ofèfè	Kochoa	Oselelcane
23	Onkome	Okopulane	'Ntanio	Othleka, Maiekeza
24	Ofoloze-e-Moniama	Omaniinu	Esepaze	Opetana
25	Ontena	Ontubula	Pankobane	Othlaza, Othlothlo
26	Empotlo	Tapuza	Okuai	'Mpatlane

Besides all this force, very considerable certainly for such lands as these, the Zulas reckon in addition five tributary nations, of which the following are the names, capitals, and chiefs.

Nos.	Name.	Capital.	Principal Chief.
1	Atoantoas;	Thlasaioé;	Mauéué;
2	Amazouazés;	Pongolé;	Séopazé;
3	Amankoloupézas;	Omokankala;	Onjobé;
4	Maguégués;	'Mpentabantou;	Mo'koiéloa;
5	Machanganes;	Masanzéné;	Mankonouto;

These nations which are altogether unknown, are all Matebeles in their manners and language, except the Atoantoas, who speak the sesuatse, a dialect related to the zula, but so despised at Mokokutlufe that the subjects of Maueue are there usually nick-named the *maguelegas*, or the *stutterers*. It is said that the population of these five nations amounts to upwards of twenty thousand souls, and that they live along the sea-coast on the Lepokole, to the south of Saint Laurent Marques. The servitude to which they are subjected, in common with the other nations tributary to the Zulas, is very great; but these details being, in some measure, foreign to the subject which at present engages our attention, we must leave them to give some information respecting the regiments we have already mentioned. The first thirteen consist exclusively of tried soldiers, and they are distinguished with the designation of *Emetlopes*, the *whites*, while the others are called *Emeniamas*, the *blacks*. The former have only white or variegated shields; while it is not permitted to the latter to bear any but those of a black or olive colour, according to the color of the ox hides which they receive from their master to cover them. Nor to any but the whites is it permitted to shave the head and chin, which they do with pride, notwithstanding the danger of adopting such a fashion under the burning sun. They leave a small crown of hair growing on the very top of the head, and on the forehead they gird pads formed from the skin of the otter. Into these is stuck a crane feather, which floats gracefully backward from the brow. The *black* warriors do not wear this feather, but they load their heads with dense plumes of others, by which they add not a little to the confused entanglements of their crisp-matted locks, which, instead of cutting, they carefully cherish, and mat compactly together, as if an african head of hair were not nearly thick enough for them, or sufficiently inconvenient. But no, we must give blame where the blame is due. It is the folly of the zula chiefs which is alone responsible for all these ridiculous customs. They wish their soldiers to have as much the appearance of wild beasts as possible, and it must be acknowledged that they have not succeeded amiss in their endeavors to make them seem such. The matebele soldiers, when they go on a campaign, take off their ornaments of beads, their collars of iron and of copper, and their copper bracelets, and they cover their bodies with ornaments borrowed from the beasts of the field. Round the ancles, the knees, the elbow, and the wrists, and on the breast, they put ornaments made of flattened ox tails so as to resemble a hairy covering like a beard on these places. While round the loins they fasten a girdle, suspending some hundred straps of the skins of wild beasts, so twisted as to bear a striking resemblance to tails, so much so indeed that strangers almost invariably mistake them for such, which mistake never fails to afford great amusement to the natives.

We have never seen any thing of a more savage appearance than these matebele soldiers, of an athletic frame and savage mien, and quarrelling with every body. The neighbouring tribes say of them proverbially, that *they are not men, but eaters of men*, so formidable have they become. In the morning they drink a kind of beer, made from millet and said to be strenghthening, which intoxicates them; and in the evening they make a repast on beef, but without vegetables of any sort, or with these very rarely. This regimen renders them robust, enduring, ferocious, and capable, we have been told, of going

without food as long as the vultures. The war-dance
constitutes the most important part of their training, and
they engage in these frequently. The white warriors
excel in these, and the appearance of their shaven heads,
with the sun's rays falling directly upon them, is very imposing. All the Zulas use, in this kind of exercise, a short
hilted staff, which they handle with great dexterity. In
war they use a longer one, which aids them in climbing,
and in descending mountains. Their master allows only
one assagai to be given to each soldier, that they may be
under no temptation to throw the lance in the fight, the
law being that they must battle foot to foot with their
foes. If they once allow themselves to be disarmed by
the enemy, they must perish, and this circumstance con-
tributes not a little to make them careful in this respect.
In the attacks, moreover, the blacks, who are the youngest
soldiers and the least accustomed to war, are always in
the front, having chiefs selected from amongst the whites
following near them, and these are authorised to slay all
fugitives without exception.

In their military expeditions every one sleeps naked.
They live on pillage, and on oxen taken from home as
provisions for the way. There are other oxen which they
are not allowed to touch, because they are destined to
serve as guides to the captured cattle, and, if need be,
to the troops themselves on their return. So instinctively
do they return to their accustomed pastures.

All the whites are married, and never do their wives
look with a dry eye on their husbands going out to war.
After their separation they all hang up, upon the walls
of their huts, the nuptial couch, a simple mat of rushes
which they have themselves plaited. As long as that
casts a little shade upon the wall, the credulous woman
believes that her husband is safe ; but when it ceases to
do so the sight of it is productive only of grief.* The

---

* Along with the mat she suspends also the billet of wood, which has been
her husband's pillow, and the iron spoon used by him when at home. It is
when she gets up in the morning that the zula woman looks at these objects;

black soldiers never marry but in virtue of an imperial
order, which is always long in coming, but which, when
it does come, is often found to be a general order for
a whole regiment, and sometimes for two of them to
marry. Neither can they, like the others, employ servants and armour-bearers. Their mothers and sisters
can alone prepare food for them, and add to their
provisions, if the rations served out to them be found
insufficient for their support.

In regard to the names of the regiments, the whole
have got significations more or less curious. Thus, for
example, that of *Omobapankue* (the 1st) means *panther
catcher*. They say, that about twenty years ago a panther
having devoured a young shepherd of the king's, de-
tachments of this regiment were sent against her; she
was taken by them, and brought alive before the late
Chaka, who, addressing himself to her, asked, amongst
other things,—" Where is thy retreat, and what is going
on there? Why hast thou killed a man?—If thou wert
a man thyself we would put thee to death: say, then,
what is to be done with thee?—I order that she be
thrust through with a dart!" It was done at once, and
the regiment that had captured her was called Panther
Catcher. They affect the howling, and the extreme
ferocity, of the animal whose name they consider it an
honour to bear. The officers wear only cloaks of panther
or leopard skins.

As to the fourth, the word *mohokonthlafu*, (mokokonthlufe) signifies *elephant's hide*. About the year 1823, the
present king of the Zulas left Nobampa, his native town,
to found another some miles distant to the west: there, in
the course of one year, he killed no less than twenty-eight
elephants, and of the tusks he had a number of ivory
bracelets made for his mistresses. The animals were
taken by a singular stratagem. As the elephants gene-

and they are placed in such a way, that the light coming through the door of
the hut, which is not quite on the ground, falls upon them from above, and
occasions a shade more or less perceptible at the bottom.

VI. MARIMO or Bechuana Cannibal

Lith Paul Petit

On the head three *likharés* or tufts of porcupine bristles, skilfully crooked to spirals; three bladders or amulets, two crane wings and a jackal tail — on the neck a *gaup* or copper plate and a necklace of sacred wood — a panther skin over the shoulders — a *lebeko* hanging round the neck — a cuirass of hide — in the right hand a buckler or *tébé* of ox-skin, surmounted by a *mokhélé* or plume of ostrich feathers, and a *molamo* or club — on the legs *likhotlos* or calf-skin buskins.

N.B. This costume does not belong to the cannibal only, it is also the complete costume of a Basuto or Mantetis warrior. With the exception of the costume this cannibal resembles very much the Kafir cannibal. If a portrait of this latter has not been given it is because his disgusting nudity would have offended the eye.

rally lean against a tree when sleeping, the savages made deep cuts in the largest trees of the country, and the elephants, coming to seek support there, fell with the trees, and were immediately covered with a shower of spears.* The capital of Dingan, and the regiments stationed there, have received the one common name of *Mokokonthlufe.*

The Zulas take many young prisoners of war, who afterwards become soldiers; they also stop a great many native travellers, whom they reduce to servitude, and in these ways have been formed the numerous and dreaded corps of the *Litane* (No. 12) or *Travellers.*

The *Eziniosi* (No. 18), or *Bees,* are said to be as numerous as a hive of bees; the buzzing of these they imitate in battle, and like them they sting, and from this they obtain their distinctive designation.

The 25th regiment is called *Ontena,* or the *Victorious,* from having destroyed a powerful chief of a tribe called Sekognane.

The 26th is the only regiment of body guard;—summer and winter they sleep around the harem without a shred of covering. The soldiers of that corps are the favourites of the prince, and he employs them as his executioners. A few years ago he ordered them to destroy some myriads of locusts infecting the fields; the next day it was found that there were still some in the fields, and the barbarian took his revenge by putting the lieutenant to death. On another occasion he took into his head to order them to bring a lion to him alive. Away go the *Empotlos* seeking after lions: they find one; they attack him; four men are devoured by him; Umpatlana at last seizes him by the tail, Tapuza jumps to one of the jaws, another soldier to the other, and the

---

* The hunters were, of course, on the watch not far from the trees most frequented by the elephants. The savages made also other traps for these animals. Thus, they dug on their tracks large pits; these pits were carefully covered with branches and rubbish; and in the bottom they fixed strong upright posts well sharpened, that the elephants falling upon these might be so injured that escape would be impossible.

king of the forest is brought alive before the king of the Matebeles.

So also the *Otibitlaku* (No. 20) caught a hyæna one night, and kept her carefully till the morning, that they might present her alive to their master on his getting up. And the celebrated Mokofane, of whom mention has already been made, went one day and thrust his spear into the toothy gullet of a crocodile, which had taken away a heifer. The dangerous reptile was killed at the river Folutzi, dragged to Mokokutlufe, and laid at the feet of Dingan, who would probably repay the hero for all the trouble and danger he had encountered with a simple—*Go gentle; it is well.*

It is indeed the case that the zula emperors make no account of men. There the subject cries to his master in the most respectful manner :—Zii : *our father ;* and he coldly replies—*I have seen thee, as thou has said.* There is no to-morrow for the unhappy Zula, and therefore does he reply to every promise with the proverb—" Give it to-day ;—before to-morrow I may be killed." For the same reason he never stores up wealth ; he knows too well that *the mouth that does not eat puts apart for the mouth that does ;* a maxim having a particular reference to the danger in which he is kept of having his life taken by his chief. That people know only fear : they have scarcely one social or domestic tie. They trust in no one, and the few thousand Matebeles which we have at and around our basuto stations absolutely refuse to listen to the good tidings of the Gospel. Young and old are exceedingly obstinate, which we can only attribute to the vicious education of the nation ; for naturally they are intelligent and brave.

In vain would we seek for interesting facts or pleasing incidents in the history of the kings of that unhappy people; it contains only horrible details of cruelty. Chaka, to speak only of him and of his successor, was an awful tyrant ;—absolute, stern, and cruel beyond expression. It is said that at a general review of his troops he wept from joy and vanity, saying—See the extent of my power! I alone hold the life and death of these men in my hand! But there was not one of them that loved him; on the contrary, his own soldiery attempted many times to put an end to his days. On one occasion he was stabbed under the arm with a spear of a peculiar shape, so that it could not be found out who had made it.

According to Caffer law, marriage is legalised by the bridegroom giving a certain number of cattle to the relations of the bride as a dowry; the son of Seatsakakona* was the first to deviate from the custom.

Another law requires that the successor to the king should be chosen from amongst some of the younger princes, the two eldest sons being deprived of the right of reigning after the father,—*because,* say the Zulas in a vague way, *they are the sons of the womb,* or the *firstborn.*

The deceitful Chaka pretended that he had no successor, and by this reason, that his wives were nothing but courtesans; and this sophism, originating in an excessive fear on the part of the despot lest some one should arise to supplant him on his throne, led him to commit the most cruel deeds. Thus, for example, Botekatze, his favourite concubine, finding herself with child, left the seraglio of Bolaoako under pretence of being ill. She would have wished to have returned to her parents, but Nate, who loved her much, took her home to her house, and promised to keep her safe. Nate was the king's mother, and whenever her son came to see her, she entertained him with long stories about Botekatze's pretended ailments; and Botekatze never spoke to the king but with sighs. Meantime she was delivered of a son, whom Nate got suckled by Nobaguebo, her faithful handmaid. This second Joash was concealed for five or six months in an earthenware pot, and when he could be concealed no longer, his foster-mother took him away amongst the Mathlekas, beyond the boundary of the zula territory.

* This was the name of the father of Chaka.

But Popa, the cousin of Chaka, was informed of the circumstance, and he told his master, who gave him orders to go to the hut of Nate, in the middle of the night, and stab her to the heart, taking care, at the same time, to stanch the wound with a piece of skin, to conceal the fact that her death was the work of an assassin.

The next day, at an early hour, it was told to the king, that Nate had either *been cut down by her ancestors*, or that she had died by sorcery. He immediately went to inquire into the matter, taking Popa with him ; finding her really dead, he made haste to get her buried ; and he abandoned himself to the most extravagant lamentations, which, of course, were only feigned. He went so far as to kill, with his own hand, some unaffected spectator of his extraordinary grief ; and he blotted out for ever from the language of his brethren the word *nate*, which means good, and ordered the word *motunti* to be substituted in its place. His emissaries then spread themselves over the town, and cruelly put to death all who were not mourning the death of the old queen, alleging that they must be suspicious persons, and perhaps sorcerers. Those whom they found at their meals they asked,—How do you find it ? And all who happened to answer *nate*—good, were massacred at once. Who could question, then, that he who ordered so many executions was deeply affected that his mother was no more ?

But God, who seeth the heart, will not hold the guilty innocent, and does not allow himself to be deceived in this way by the workers of iniquity, to whom, as to the sea, he hath said,—Hitherto shalt thou come, but no further ! Behold, then, the end of Chaka !

It seems as if the parricide could not be allowed to perish otherwise than by the hand of his relations. It was but a short time after the horrible crime which I have just related was committed, when the relatives of Nate determined to revenge her death. It may have been from perfidy, or it may have been from a desire to secure his own safety, but be this as it may, Popa himself entered into the conspiracy along with Mokofane, who was at that time first officer of the bed-chamber to Chaka. All that was wanting then was a favourable opportunity to execute their design, and this soon presented itself,—the king having sent a great army against Lepalule, and by that means considerably diminished the force at the capital. Two sisters of the deceased queen, Makhabai and Mama, went to Dingan's, where were also Mothlankane and Mokubane, their brothers. They said to them—" The blood of your mother cries for vengeance! The tiger who hath drank it is thirsting for your own: go then and kill him, before he can throw himself upon you; the troops will be thankful to you if you do! On their return from Lepalule, you may be certain that they will look to you to become their leaders." To that address the caffer princes simply answered—*You have spoken ;* but that short sentence implied much.

The next day Chaka went out, as usual, with Mokofane, at sunrise, and seated himself on his royal chair in a retired spot behind the cattle fold. While his servant was washing him, who should appear but Dingan, Popa, Mothlankane, and Mokubane, all four armed with assagais. While they were yet at a considerable distance, the king cried to them, in great trepidation, —Where are you going?—To the hunt, they replied. But why do you come so near to me, and all armed? Have I done you any harm?—He speaks, and tries to escape, but Popa, Mothlankane, and Mokubane thrust him through with their spears; he falls under their blows, weltering in blood. Why do you kill me, my brothers? he asks, groaning.—Dingan answered,—It is because thou hast murdered thy mother! Quick! speak in your own defence. Thou art a treacherous sorcerer!— " I repent for ever—you have corrected me—let me alone now!"—" Barbarian, leave thee !—Thou wouldst slay us all !—implacable Chaka—thou skilful impostor— thou stern inkhosi!—Thou preventest the marriage of everybody but of thyself—thou dost not allow us a moment of rest.—Dost thou not cause thy soldiers to be put to death if they but spend a few days in fine weather at home, instead of engaging incessantly in war? Dost thou not send even the sick soldier to battle, saying, in mockery, that the road will do him good?"

" But I have repented."—" Blood-thirsty tiger! thou wishest to devour us all. Thou hast killed Botekaze, Nobaguebo, Tsetlatla, Baehenka, Chochokile, Umpato, Kopoi, and Nomao, thy sister, and thy mother, and—"
At the words *thy mother*, Popa threw himself the first upon Chaka; and Mokofane got from the hand of Popa a spear, with which he also stabbed his master; all except Dingan covered him with darts, and, seizing him still quivering, they threw him into a hole. Filling it up, they cast the imperial throne into the dung pits. The garrison had remained quiet; the people also had maintained a perfect neutrality, and did not dare even to go to the fold on hearing the noise there. But when all was done Dingan and his brothers heard nothing but acclamations throughout the whole of Bolaoako.

But, such is human misery, the very next day after the death of Chaka, his brothers, spear in hand, contended for the throne; on the one hand Dingan, on the other Mothlankane and Mokubane. These, proving the weaker party, they had to leave Bolaoako along with their adherents, and to go elsewhere.

Some time after, the troops arrived from their expedition against Lepalule. They returned weakened and decimated by the war, hunger, and fatigue of a two months' unsuccessful campaign. In the capital the people were singing a new song, of which this was the burden—
" We have thrown away the yoke of Ramotetoa (Chaka)!"
On reflecting on what had occurred, Mothlege, the first captain of the host, cried—" Why, my lords, do they murder one another?" and, making an attack upon the town, he captured some thousand head of cattle, with which he and his army made off to the east of the Malutis, where he settled, and still remains.

These commotions once settled, Dingan remained master of the kingdom, which he governs as badly as did his predecessor, instead of profiting by his fate, and trying to improve. From the descriptions given of him by the natives, he appears to be a man in middle life, of ordinary stature, and very stout; he is, moreover, very black; he has bushy hair and many wrinkles. He is rather ill-favoured, but he is apparently unwilling to admit it, for he takes the greatest possible care to conceal that he has three decayed teeth in the front part of his mouth. This accounts for his speaking always in a half whisper, and most frequently with his mouth covered with his hand. Rasekuai, who knows him well, says that he affects " a jovial outside, *but without being for all that happy behind.*"* He suffers from vertigo, and from strange fears, and a thousand apprehensions of death, and other misfortunes. In the dark he always imagines that he has before his eyes the shade of Chaka. To which we must add, that in damp weather he suffers severely from four wounds which he has on his person. The atrocities which he has already committed would fill a volume. From all that we have heard of him, it would appear that nowhere in the world will one find pride more manifestly enthroned, or tyranny more openly displayed, than at Mokokutlufe. At the very mention of the name of the tyrant who reigns there you ask yourself, with trembling, if it be indeed a man, and not the devil, who in human shape sways his iron sceptre over a herd of hardened and degraded slaves, reduced to the last degree of wretchedness, not to say almost to the state of the black spirits of the bottomless pit!

The arch tyrant of the Malutis caused himself to be designated alternately by the sad title of the Ravisher,† because he has ruined many nations, and the presumptuous title of the Saviour of his subjects, because he has slain their former king, his own brother, though only to usurp

* Could Montesquieu have expressed himself better ?

† *Otengane* (Dingan) Go tenga ; to rob, to ravish.

his place. He suffers them also to call him the Peace-maker, and the Vulture, the devourer of other birds. He allows them also to make the most prodigal use of the epithets the Noble Elephant, the Black, *par excellence*, and the Generator of Men.

Thou who art high as the mountains; Thou who art exalted as the heavens; Thou who livest for ever!.... Such are the blasphemies addressed to him daily by those who approach him. If in the evening he goes out with his harem, his sultanas cry to him—" O hard-hearted lion!" and it is anything but offensive to him. His soldiery do not simply request him to send them to lay waste some province, but they say to him—Thou human hyæna, give us nations to devour. They have no idol but he; it is before him, literally, that they prostrate themselves. He grants them permission to live, or he slaughters them according to his caprice. Can the devil really have whispered to the Zula (the celestial) that he is a god? Be this as it may, many of the Matebeles, of the same people, believe, on the word of their princes, that the ancestors of these have sprung from the reeds of a fountain, instead of being born of a woman, as other men are. Add to this black catalogue of repulsive traits, that the fear of being supplanted makes Dingan worse than even the she-wolf refusing to acknowledge her young. One of his wives, too confident in this respect, on one occasion unhappily presented to him one of his sons, doubtless in the transport of her joy. The monster took the sucking child by the feet, and, with one toss of his hand, dashed him to death on the ground; the mother, at the same moment, was thrust through with a spear, and died looking on her new-born babe expiring. It is a well-informed native to whom we are indebted for these details, which are, unhappily, but too true,—and yet, can we believe them?

The Zulas celebrate annually, in the month of January, the great national feast of first fruits. On that occasion they congregate in the capital from all parts of the

kingdom. The crowd, with barbarous pomp, gather around
the seraglio. The god comes out at the very moment of
sunrise; the people cry out *Ga-ba-a-ente!*—*let him be
magnified!* and at the same time they prostrate themselves before him. The idol of the blind multitude then
magnifies himself above the star of day, and spits at it
three or four times, by way of insult, and goes in again.
It reminds one of the celebrated verses which follow, but
which one would rather have read as the dream of the
poet than as the record of history.

> Le *Nil* a vu, sur ses rivages,
> Les noirs habitants des déserts
> Insulter, par leurs cris sauvages,
> L'astre brillant de l'univers.
> Cris impuissants, fureurs bizarres!
> Tandis que ces monstres barbares
> Poussent d'insolentes clameurs,
> Le dieu, poursuivant sa carrière,
> Verse des torrents de lumière
> Sur ses obscurs blasphémateurs.

To conclude, and at the same time to verify the picture,
gloomy but faithful, which we have given of the matebele
nation,* we shall now insert an ode in metrical verse, in
which Okopulana and Omokotunguana have preserved
the exploits of Dingan, which to them, as to many others
of the Zulas, appear most sublime, though these exploits
are by no means uniformly deserving of applause. With
less pain we admit that the piece is not altogether devoid
of true poetry; and we have seen, with no little satisfaction, that the zula idiom is not very different from the
sesuto: it scarcely differs more than the dutch from the
german.

The first lines of this remarkable panegyric,—almost
all in apostrophes,—are as follows in the zula language:—

EMPONKO ZA OTENGANE.

1. Egnoné éa suléla,
2. Ea suléla qua Bolaoako.

* Since these lines were written the social position of the Matebeles and their
chiefs has been completely changed. Attacked by the emigrant dutch farmers,
Moselekatzi and Dingan have been beaten and put to flight, and the greater
part of their troops have been destroyed.

3. Egnone éa thla régné zégnoné ;
4. Ea thla O'khèlè la qua Bolaoako.
5. Makhubalo a thléoa ca capate ;
6. A thléoa ko Mama no Makhabaï.

7. Egnoné é thlètzé qu'o sanguéné, qu'o Nobampa.

8. Ea thla Opucaché, oa Botélézé.
9. Ea thla Omocoquané, o' Poko.
10. Ea thla Séthlépuna, sa Babananko.
11. Ea thla go ba qua Masumpa.
12. Ea thla go Matuané.
13. Makhubalo a thléoa ko Nomapéla.

14. U Fézé! ua zéféza bantu éné ;
15. U lamuléla éntumpé,
16. Na manéna, na matota, na macacassana.
17. U Mocabateri! u cabatella makhosé amagné.
18. U nomaquélo, ka u quéla énthaba.
19. U fégnané léyé lé sé na énthléla.
20. Ua lé banta, ua lé éza énthléla thléla.
21. Ua thla énkhomo za qua Ontungéla ;
22. Ua thla énkhomo za malala a Babananko.
23. U m'oézé omotala !

24. U Nquézé oa léoanthlé,
25. Oa Motéto, qua Ntéméntoa ;
26. U Nténquézé zé machumé.
27. U fulatéla Moghoma lé Quathlampéné,

THE PRAISES OF DINGAN.

1. There is a bird hovering .
2. It hovers above Bolaoako.

3. This bird devours the other birds ;
4. It has devoured the sagacious one of Bolaoako.(1)

5. The lustral waters have been drank in silence ;(2)
6. They have been drank by Mama and Makhabaï.

[1] *The sagacious one* is a periphrasis for the elephant, and the elephant a metaphor for Chaka. This is a double figure, common with the Zulas when speaking of their kings; the power and cunning of whom naturally recall to the minds of these savages the greatest and most sagacious of quadrupeds.

(2) *The lustral waters, makubalo*, are composed of milk and water, and the juices of certain bitter herbs, which the relatives of the deceased, according to the religious rites of the Caffers and Bechuanas, drink in the retirement of their dwellings for ceremonial purification. It is a practice very similar to that according to which persons who were defiled amongst the Jews were sprinkled; they sprinkled their furniture and their apartments with water, mixed with the ashes of a red heifer, sacrificed by the high priest on the day of solemn expiation. The Zulas purify themselves also with water from running streams, and by sacrificing an ox or a calf, according to the age of the deceased, were he a man or a child. They cast away, as altogether defiled, a part of the clothes of the

7. The bird has perched at Nobampa,(3) in the cattle fold.
8. He has eaten up Opucache, the son of Boteleze.
9. He has eaten up Omocoquane, the son of Poko.
10. He has eaten Sethlepuna, the son of Babananko.
11. He has torn in pieces the Masumpas.
12. He has devoured Matuane.
13. The waters of purification have been drank by Nomapela.(4)

14. Liberator! thou has shown thyself to this people;
15. Thou hast delivered from oppression the virgins,
16. The women, the men, and the children.
17. Thou art a king, who crushest the heads of the other kings.
18. Thou passest over mountains inaccessible to thy predecessors.
19. Thou findest a defile from which there is no egress.(5)
20. There thou makest roads; yes, roads.(6)
21. Thou takest away the herds from the banks of the Letuele,
22. And the herds of the Babanankos, a people skilled in the forging of iron.
23. Thou art indeed a green adventurer!(7)

24. Thou art victorious over the nations of the sea,
25. Over Moteto, king of Ntementoa.
26. Thou art a conqueror, chosen amongst ten tens of others.(8)
27. Thou hast passed over Mount Moghoma and the Quathlampenes.

Thou art the pillar which supports the house of Nate.
Thou art the ally of Cele, king of the Taquenes.
That is something different from being the ally of the Basutos.(9)

dead man, his buckler, the shaft of his assagai, and the bed on which he died.—Every one knows that the nations of antiquity all attached an idea of great defilement to death : thus the fleet of Æneas, after the death of his friend, is represented as entirely defiled.

> *Præterea jacet exanimum tibi corpus amici,*
> *Heu nescis! totamque incessat funere classem.*

(3) *Nobampa*, the capital of Seatsakona, situated in the neighbourhood of Bolaoako and of Mokokutlufe. It appears that the best pasturage is to be found at Nobampa, and thither they accordingly lead the flocks. Dingan is represented as going, after the death of Chaka, to place himself at the entrance to the folds, and saying,—Now, this prey is mine!

(4) *Nomapela*, the uncle of Matuane, and one of the lieutenants of Dingan.

(5) *Thou findest a defile, &c.*—The original is *lege, a stone*, and by metaphor *a mountain*. It is in the same sense that the Borolongs and the Batlapes call the mountains *maye, stones*. The bushmen say only *Komao*, a stone; *Ikomao*, stones, mountains.

(6) *Thou makest roads; yes, roads!*—Literally, *thou makest it* (the mountain) *road, road*. It is a caffer idiom.

(7) The expression *a green* man, is employed to designate a vigorous and healthy man; it is an expression not less common in caffer and in bechuana than in french.

(8) A phrase somewhat similar may be found in Scripture.

(9) The Basutos are very much despised by Dingan, their greatest enemy. It is worthy of remark, that under this designation the Zulas comprise all the Bechuanas in their neighbourhood, the subjects of Moshesh, the Mantetis, the Lighoyas, &c.

Before thee the true men of the nations(1) faint in their heart.
The true men of the nations faint away,
Even those of the Boko 'khu 'khus.

Thou sayest to the Motetos and the 'Kuabes,
What ill have I done you,
In snatching you from the flames
In my mercy ?(2)

King! deliver us, oh saviour!
Thou, who subjectest to thy sorcery the greatest of kings,
Throw a spell over Bosaze and Mozeugnane;
And the Mokhatanes, and the Mokheme ;
For the food upon which thou feedest
Is mighty kings.

Bird of the morning! give in secret thy commands
To thy soldiers ; to the veteran and to the more youthful.
They will go, before the dawn of day,
To ravage every place whithersoever thou may'st command them
To carry desolation.
Of night we know nothing!

Formerly we used to say of him,—He is a man of no importance.
We did not know thee!   ,
But now we know thee :
For thou hast cast a death spell on the Chakas.

Author of our tranquillity !
Thou givest us flesh and marrow;
We are no longer lank and lean.
Of old the hostile nations disturbed our repose ;
They did it as do the *mazeze*.(3)
To-day they trouble us not,
For thou hast caught and crushed them.
Thou makest all the world to keep silence :
Thou hast silenced even the troops ;
Yes, the troops of Moyokuane,
Of Enteba, of Mageala(4)......
Thy troops always obey thee :
Thou sayest, and they go;
Thou sayest, and they go again ;

(1) *Montu oa sonto*, a *true* man. This caffer idiom is equivalent to the french word *preux*.

(2) That is, because after having surprised them in the night, he was satisfied with carrying away their herds without burning their towns, as was his usual practice.

(3) That is to say the *fleas*. Thus they describe in derision the enemies of Dingan.

(4) Three ancient kings of the Zulas. The following is a more complete list of them : Chaka, Seatsakakona, Yama, Punka, Makheba, Mayokuane, Entaba, Mageala, Mageala Kuycloa, Mageala Kugnegnezela, Sekofa, Sesanguene. The greater part of these kings lie buried at Nobampa, or as it is also called Macasana.

Thou sayest yet again, and they go to fall upon Sekognana.
Thou art master of the great garrison towns
Of Mocamula, Moculuyane, Nquebane,
Of Kaquezoa, of Enthaba-Eukholu........

All have respect for a king whom no one can approach unto.
When the king eats there remains with him no one but Ceyelele ;
For Ceyelele has his confidence.
The king speaks not to Pante,
Nor to his other brothers.

Thou art he who hath filled with goods
The hands of Cumete, father of the Quezazes ;
Thou art he who preservest their heads
To the troops decimated by Chaka.

Ravisher, thou art held in repute amongst the Basutos,
At Khobas,(5) and amongst the Balunques.(6)
Thou hast plundered the cattle of the Amakozas,
Of the Suqentos, of Cutene, and of Maculoge.

Thou art the purple dawn of the morning.
Thou art beautiful as an isle in the Mosiniati.
Thou art the salvation of the towns of Kankela, of Mabelese....
Thou sittest on the throne of Kankela.(7)

Thou puttest to death the Basuto—to death the old men.(8)
Thou hast despoiled the troops of Makheta.(9)
The smiths themselves are torn in pieces by thee,
Without their hearing a breath of thy approach.

Thou puttest nations to silence,
As thou wouldst silence thy cooks.(10)
Thou art the salvation of thy subjects.

(5) The present chief of the Tambukes, or Amatembus, which is their real name.

(6) The *Balunques*, that is to say *the pretty ones*. These are the Portuguese of Saint-Laurent Marques. It is said that on one occasion Dingan took from them a wagon, and forty-two horses, &c. The horses were all thrown to the vultures, after having been brought and speared at Mokukutlufe. " What good will these animals do us," said Dingan, " when they could not save their former masters?"

(7) It would appear, that Kankela is the ancient name of Mokokutlufe; as for the word throne, *mo' kupe* is the name appropriated to the chair of Dingan, made simply of the trunk of a tree.

(8) That is to say, Thy rage respects neither the quality of strangers nor of old age ; O terrible is it when enkindled.

(9) *Makheta*, a basuto prince, who lived, not long ago, in the vicinity of Moriah, on the summit of a high hill, which has retained his name.

(10) Amongst a thousand droll accounts given of Dingan, it is told, that his barber, when on duty, dares not look upon his master's face but so as to see his profile. He breathes upon his *quecu* (a wretched little knife), to warm it a little, shaves away a hair or two, and breathes on it afresh. If, by mishap, the despot turns around, or

Thou art not the man to rest at ease in thy palace !
Thou delightest in the military expedition !
Out then ; flocks have been seen
Going up from the sea-shore,
And proceeding towards the Mathlekas.
Pursue these herds and seize them.
The ox of the Zula is his assagai.(1)

The government of thy forefathers thou hast surpassed,
Leaving it at Macasana.
Thou art the master of Mayokuane,
Of Entaba, of Mageala, of Kuyeloa,
Of Kugnegnezela, of Yama, of Nomakueba,
Of the great and wonderful court of Kankela.

Enter thou into the magnificent house.
As for me I dare not enter it
Unless thou shouldst grant to me the favour ;
And even then I must be introduced by a servant, the old Ngeto.

Father of praise, give an ox,
The ox of thy troops.
New troops have arrived,
Who stand before their king,
To receive from him their food.
They are the Omokaze,
The Eziniosi, the Onkankezue.
Thou art indebted to no one for what thy belly devours,(2)
But thou fillest all bellies,
O conqueror of kings !

Thou, the only one issuing commands,
Issueth orders even to thy seniors.
Thou art not young, for thou art powerful.
Thou hast the god of the Mozeakazes for a familiar.(3)
If some head of cattle have gone astray,
The herdsmen fear to come and inform thee.
Macheche, that chief of the herdsmen, trembled

makes some other movement, the terrified barber runs away to conceal himself in some corner of the hut. After a time he re-appears, and recommences the dance of his wretched razor over the face of his sable majesty.

Ici c'est un metier que je n'entends pas bien.

(1) *Enkhomo, qua Amazulu, ki mokondo.* This line has the force of a proverb, and perhaps it is one. It tells in a few words what the Zulas are.

(2) Dingan is extremely scrupulous with regard to captured herds, and never touches them himself. He lives on the cattle of his fathers, which are called *oxen for the mouth.*

(3) *Ubapanyene Setunta sa Bomozeakatze.* Is it not a curious fact that Dingan should be reputed to have communication with the dead ? still, be it remarked, it is with the most ancient representative of a most noble zula family,—that of Mosolekatze, or more correctly, as one may see, Mozeakaze.

.When the black heifer disappeared.
He pulled up the supports of his cabin,
And went to plant them far from thy wrath
At ¸Mokoagnane's.

Noble sovereign, reign over the subjects of Nate,
Of the land of Buza.
Thou art a vulture, thou hast pounced upon Busako.(1)

And thou sayest, Soldiers, it is not you who are avenged, it is the court.
Moko'khu(2) is known here, he is known at Mokokutlufe.
Ga-ba-a-ente! Ga-ba-a-ente! our king, our father!
Moko'khu is known here.
Thou art he who abaseth all other men ;
Thou art Chaka, thou returnest from Tebethlango ;(3)
Thou hast taken away both the calves and the mothers from Tebethlango,
All the oxen of Mega(4)
With the heifers of two years old, they and their mothers.

In the race, by thy agility, thou causest to pant
The lungs of the Basutos.(5)
Dost thou not say to them : Ha ! ha !
When they speak they tell lies.
They are beasts of the fields from all lands.
If they slaughter an ox, the cutting up
Begins with the shoulder;
They cut first the shoulder, then the leg,(6)
And the other flesh remains there ;

(1) *Busako*, town of Motlanckane, where Dingan caused his brother to be massacred some years since with all his people. According to a horrible law of the zula despots, when a chief is put to death they exterminate also his subjects. " Your father is dead, who will be able to support you?" is all that is said; and it is the only trial they have. Tyrants are everywhere the same. The first who appeared amongst the Greeks had he not a sycophant who wrote to him : " I have concealed nothing from the man whom you sent to me : I have led him into a corn-field; I have cut off before him all the ears which rose above the others. Follow my example if you would wish to secure your domination ; cause all the principal men of the city, to perish, be they friends or foes ; for a usurper ought to be distrustful even of those who appear to be his greatest friends."

(2) Moko'khu, chief of the Boko'khu'khus [*page* 158]. He was a powerful king, from whom Dingan took everything, even his name, which he sometimes in pride assumed himself.

(3) Name of the grazing ground of Chaka,

(4) One of the chiefs ruined by him.

(5) The tactics of the matebele soldiers is to pursue an enemy at the utmost speed for one, two, and even three days, in succession, a feat in which they greatly excel all the other tribes; carrying their large buckler greatly incommodes them. It sometimes happens that they throw it away when sore pressed by the enemy, which is considered a great defeat, as may be supposed.

(6) The Zulas, on the contrary, at one blow cut off from the carcase the two legs ; there remain then the shoulders, the breast, and the head, which together present a appearance less disgusting according to their taste.

A pretty spectacle it is !
These gross Basutos are numerous ;
Multitudes of petty tribes,
Which know not whence they have come,
A host of beasts of the field from all countries.

Thou hast the whole nation under thee.
Thou causest to groan the subjects of Zeku.(1)
Thou art Chaka ; thou causest to tremble all people.
Thou thunderest like the musket.
At the fearful noise which thou makest
The inhabitants of the towns take to flight.
Thou art the great shade of the Zula,
And thence thou expandest and reachest to all countries.
Thou puttest out of breath thy soldiers.
Thou art like the door of a house :
If it close itself upon an adversary
He must perish.
So it happeneth to those whom thou shuttest up,
Even amongst thine own people.

Thy granaries are larger than those of Kokobane.
Thou art sagacious as the elephant,
Thou stabbest the other elephants :
Thou hast stabbed the elephant of Tebethlango.

Thou slaughterest the nations as thou slaughterest a lamb.
Thou hast slain a great number of them,
Who no more dared to make a noise
Than the dumb sheep.

Hast not thou devoured Chaka ?
Hast not thou devoured Mothlankane ?
The bitter herbs of expiation,
It is thyself who hast eaten them.

Boko'khu'khus keep quiet.
You are, indeed, men of courage ;
But we know one
More courageous still :
It is your conqueror.
Submit your soul, obey him.
Sleep a tranquil slumber.
All the horses of the nations are his.
All leaders belong to him.
Silence ! silence ! obey him without a murmur ;
Or else, murderer of men, do thou arouse thyself and slay.
Cause the blood of thy foes to stream at the dung-pits,
Amongst the rocks of Quelile, and of Baghagha.

(1) His uncle.

VII. MARIMO OF LERIBE

Lith. Paul Petit.

He who scattered the Mathluibis on the Mosiniate(1)
Is no youthful warrior.
Do not fear
That he will ever want fat oxen
Wherewith to feast his concubines.
Do not fear
That he will ever permit any to take away his flocks.
King of kings,
Put to flight the army of Contuane.
Powerful conqueror,
Triumph over all the powers of the east.
Thou art violent ; thou art cold
Like the wind which comes from the sea,
Thou causest to perish all the nations.
It is said that thou hast wrenched from the Tseles their herds,
From the Thlankanthlas, their herds,
And that thou hast delivered to the flames their habitations,
Forcing them to go and construct new ones elsewhere.
Thou art Mayoye, thou hast wrenched from Mayoye
All, even his name.
Thou hast subjected the tribes on the Folose,
And on the Folosane.(2)
Conqueror of the Manquanes,
Ravager of provinces,
Deep abyss, which engulphest all :
Thou covetest all the riches of the tribes,
And thou hast gathered them together as into a pit.
Go, thou sagacious one, take away the cattle of the cunning.
Take away, as if in play, the oxen of Sepampo ;
From their race, take away those of Mozeakaze.
Bird, king of the other birds, scream,
Since thou hast been placed at the head of the troops.
Call Petlelele, thy faithful herald,
Give to him thy commands, and our chiefs, with speed,
Will run from all corners of the realm
To appear before thee at the appointed day.
Thou reignest here, thou reignest there ;
Thou reignest in all directions.
Send for thy favorites Otengua and Mocubula.
Go in pursuit of Sango, aud of Empeane,
Surprise these two kings, and slaughter them
In the cavern of Kome.

(1) A considerable tributary of the Letuele. The natives say that it takes its rise at Thaba-Enkolu [Great Mountain], beyond Instuana-tsatsi, and that it flows nearly from the north to the south. We believe that the Mosiniate is the same name as the Nlaniatu.
(2) Two other tributaries of the Letuele, but much less than the Mosiniate.

CHAPTER XVIII.

THE country of the Zulas is bordered on the north by numerous unknown Caffer tribes. One of these bears amongst the Basutos the name of Maghobas. Their last chief was called Mate. He appointed for his successor his son Mantlakapeze, who governs only some ten or twelve towns, and who appears disposed to submit to the king of Mokokotlufe, of whose cruel power he stands in dread. The Maghobas speak the setebele. Their country, rather small but pretty, is fertilised by a river of considerable size, called Pongolo, which flows into the Osuto.

A little further towards the north live the Baraputsas; a tribe so powerful and warlike as to render themselves formidable even to the Chakas, who have succeeded, indeed, in depriving them of their herds, but have never been able to subjugate them. These Caffers are recognised amongst themselves by a slit along the external ridge of both ears. They carry the short assagai of the Zulas, whom they resemble in manners and language; but they are less ferocious than they, neither are they, perhaps, so much addicted to wars of extermination. They and the Zulas, having vowed perpetual hatred against each other, have no intercourse whatever.

A young inkhosi, called Motsueze, governs the Baraputsas. He resided at Elange, a considerable town, built of a round shape, according to the fashion of caffer towns. In its vicinity flows the Inkonto, a tributary stream of the Osuto, which is said to traverse the states of the oldest son of Putsa (Motsuase,) before losing itself in the Indian Ocean.

This tribe, however, does not extend to the sea. Between it and the coast there is another caffer tribe, called Makasana, from the name of the reigning chief. Although the Zulas have greatly enfeebled this tribe, the natives assure us that it is still somewhere about ten thousand strong. The Makasanas, it would appear, work in iron and in copper. From the first of these metals they forge hoes of an inferior quality ; and from the second they make earrings, collars, and bracelets, which they exchange with their neighbours for skins and cattle.

Such details derived from native travellers, and often vague and general, we cannot multiply without a risk of their being some day found incorrect; but the following may be relied on as more authentic, and they may be introduced, we consider, with all propriety at the close of what has been said in regard to the Baraputsas. They relate to a certain german naturalist of the name of Seidenstecher, and an Irvingite called Martins.

The first of these gentlemen was well known at the Cape; he was also seen by the missionary at Philippolis, where he arrived about the beginning of December 1832. The missionary, who had received him into his house, found him absent in his manner, and sometimes singular in his behaviour. As they sat down to table, he invited him politely to take his place; but the traveller made no reply, while a few minutes after he drew near of his own accord, and dined with an appetite. It was the sabbath. Seidenstecher nevertheless saddled his horses, and civilly taking leave of his hosts, set off in an easterly direction, accompanied by a young Hottentot, called Jacob, who was engaged as his guide, to the capital of the Basutos. The two unknown travellers arrived there in the last quarter of the December moon, with six horses, medicines, and

other baggage. Seidenstecher wore a simple straw hat,
but his valet wore a very fine one of white felt. When
they asked the Hottentot the name of his master, he
replied, *mynheer*, (sir,) and that is the only name the
german traveller ever had amongst the inhabitants of
Thaba Bosio. In the meantime, Moshesh, the chief of
the town, received him well, and offered to him a kind of
yard, constructed of reeds, in which to put his goods; at
the same time he caused two kinds of milk to be brought
to him, the one sour, the other sweet, which the traveller
drank with pleasure; after which he fell asleep and rested
there all that night, his head supported on his saddle.
The next day he carefully took his baggage to the rocks
of the mountain, and there changed his linen. Moshesh,
in accordance with the custom of the petty kings of the
country when they wish to honor any one, caused an ox
to be led before the stranger, and presented to him for
food; but Mynheer declined it. They then brought to
him cooked meat, and that he took. Every body looked
on with wonder, mixed with terror. The natives asked
one another, on account of his color, quite new to them,
"Is it a *man*, or a *god*, or a *beast?*" Be that as it might,
they feared to approach him, and above all to eat any
thing which his hands had touched. And poor Jacob,
who did not know one word of sesuto, could do nothing
to deliver them from their fear. Towards noon, his
master rose, and went to examine the mountain, running after butterflies by the way. Then he showed his
gun to the chief, and fired at a mark, that he might see
the force and precision of that beautiful weapon.

The next day, there was a *battue*, in which the stranger
took part; but he had the precaution to cause his horses
and all his baggage to follow him to the field. The
savages killed many elans, a portion of which they presented to the white huntsman; but he would not touch
the meat, because he feared, as they supposed, that the
darts with which it had been killed might be *unclean*.
Moshesh then kindly sent to the village of Mocheri for

milk for him to drink. He sent by Leoatla, to whom I am indebted for these particulars, and who is one of the most interesting of my catechumens. As it was getting late, they bivouacked that night in the fields. The following day swift runners drove some elans before Seiden-stecher, who, firing at one with his gun, killed it and cut off some pieces, which he caused them to cook on the embers, and which he ate. The chief of the Basutos having also killed two elans, they put all the flesh of these, and of those killed the evening before, on the pack oxen, and went to regale the town of Bosio with it.

There they found an Englishman of the name of Martins, who had just arrived. The preceding night he had passed on the other side of Jammerberg, under a bush which I have often seen. There the only horse which he possessed was devoured by a lion. His few effects and his purse remained, no one knows how, in the hands of some natives settled in the neighbourhood. Martins went on foot to the chief Machosa, who gave him a man, called Molefi, as a guide to Bosio. The poor traveller had nothing with him but an umbrella, which he presented to Moshesh, and a pocket bible from which he was often reading ; then raising his hand to heaven, he would say to the natives, *Koto-gorimo-leserimolelo o chessang !* that is to say, *God—heaven—light—burning fire !* * Moshesh offered to him a hut in which to lodge, which was accepted with thankfulness.

It was now getting near the end of December, and Jacob, Seidenstecher's young Hottentot, had been missing since the beginning of the hunt. He had run after the cannas, mounted on a vicious grey horse called Vrolk, which had thrown him near Umpukani, and came at full speed to join the others. Some Makantas found the unfortunate little cavalier in the fields, and brought him back to Bosio. Seidenstecher on seeing him again, gave him two buffets, saying to him, " Where did you go to hunt alone ? you are always losing yourself; get away ;

* The savages imagined that Mr. Martins, in speaking to them of a *burning fire*, was foretelling to them a year of great drought.

I do not love you any more." The "father of Jacob" then requested Moshesh to take care of the child, and to give him better guides, who would conduct him further towards the north east. But to this the chief at first made objection, declaring that it was dangerous to travel in that quarter, and that the state of the country in general was far from tranquil. The German, however, insisted on proceeding, and therefore two men were furnished to him ; they were Leonatla and Turu.

Of five pistols which he had with him, Seidenstecher presented one to his benefactor. He had still four left, and a gun of large calibre. He gave him moreover two worn-out horses : Vrolk, which is still alive, and as wicked and vicious as ever, and Fekis, which Moshesh lost in a military expedition against the Tambukis, and also a mare, with a colt which she was suckling. In return for all these presents, the chief of Bosio presented to his guest three pack oxen, and a cow, with her calf, to furnish him with milk. He was thus enabled to continue his journey, the principal object of which was, it is said, to find out and examine the mines whence the Caffers obtain their iron and copper. Desirous of following Seidenstecher, Martins intreated him to lend him one of his horses ; but to this he replied that he could not lend him one, as he had only his pony for himself, and Schoenberg as a spare beast of burden.

On the day after that on which they returned from the battue already mentioned, Seidenstecher left Bosio with his two guides, Leoatla and Turu. In the evening they encamped in the fields. Leoatla went to seek milk for the traveller in a neighbouring village. On his return he found that Turu had run away. The next day Seidenstecher and Leoatla came in sight of Merabing, when Leoatla said to the former, but without being understood, "There is the capital of the Mantetis. These are the sworn enemies of my tribe; they will kill us; I leave you ;" and there he left him as he had said. Seidenstecher, however, reached Merabing, where he spent two days; after which he departed for the Namagari. But his pack oxen escaped from him in the fields, and returned straight to Bosio. After that, he was seen amongst the Baraputsas, by whom in all probability he was murdered. The persons who saw him there in 1833 are two native traders, called the one Sebatane and the other Pole.

As for the disciple of Irving, he remained upwards of a month at Thaba Bosio, and preached in his own way throughout the neighbourhood; after that he set off on foot for Merabing, and thence for the country of the Baraputsas, visiting, in the way, a tribe of Caffers called Mathluibis, from whom he sustained no injury. But going further up among the Baraputsas, he was murdered by them, if the unanimous report of the natives is to be believed. Martins and Seidenstecher were fanatics, the one in religion, the other after the fashion of the disciples of Rousseau; can it be cause of astonishment that they both fell victims to their stubbornness?

To the north east of the Baraputsas, between Delagoa Bay and the country of Mosolekatsi, there is a numerous and very interesting tribe of Bechuanas, called Baperis or Malekutus. Amongst the Basutos there are many individuals, who trace their descent from this tribe, which makes us more or less acquainted with it. Nevertheless, if we may be permitted to insert here a notice of it, we shall introduce nothing but what we have learned from the Baperis themselves. During the past year and the present, we have had a small company of them at Moriah, where they remained, reckoning the time of both visits, about two months. The chief, who was called Matimulane, had been deputed by his tribe to arrange certain matters regarding peace and commerce with the subjects of Moshesh.

These Baperis bore a close resemblance, both in colour and figure, to the Basutos. They found the country of the latter, however, cold in comparison with their own, where the heat of the sun is so great in summer that sunstroke is of frequent occurrence, and ophthalmia also is very common. The women clothe themselves pretty decently, but the men simply tie a piece of sheep or gazelle skin round their loins. It is the *popotane*, a narrow girdle, common to the Barolongs and to the Batlapis. It constitutes, along with a short cloak, the only dress of the Malekutus, who are distinguished, moreover, from the other bechuana tribes by an oval tuft of hair, which they allow to grow on the front of the head, while the hair around it is shaved off very close in men, women, and children. Their ornaments consist of two bits of reed, which they pass through a large hole, made a little above the lobe of the ear, and collars and bracelets of blue, red, and yellow beads of Portuguese manufacture, proving that they have communication with the traders at Delagoa; but this only by means of natives belonging to other tribes, as they have assured us. Matimulane wore sandals also, and he had suspended at his neck a tooth of the porcupine as an amulet, and a whistle with which he used to collect his travelling companions, his sheep, and his dogs. It was made of two blades of hollowed wood, so closely applied to one another that they seemed more like one stick than two distinct pieces; they were inserted in the last bone of the tail of the blue gnu, as a sheath, and at the end there was a beautiful tress of the mane of a giraffe, and a little brass wire. It was open only at one end; at my request Matimulane applied his lips to it, and drew from it some notes which were very shrill and piercing, but which seemed not to be the less pleasing to him on that account. The Baperi on his journeys had often used his whistle, sometimes to drive away ennui, at other times wild beasts, and a new Tityrus, he had also sometimes in his own way charmed the woods and echos with its notes. Now, however, thanks to his obliging disposition, his precious whistle, or *pala*, has passed into other hands. The huts of the Baperis, so far as we can learn, are low and circular in shape, and in structure similar to those of the Basutos; but the kind of screen, called *lelapa*, placed at the entrance, instead of being

made of marsh reeds, as with these, is made of the
stalks of the large african millet, the millococo, and
sometimes, like those of the Barolongs, of branches
of trees and stakes, which make a stronger enclosure than the first. Their caverns are made of a kind
of bamboo carpentry, or of laths covered with dry grass.
They resemble in form a baker's oven, but they have an
oblong, and very low entrance, so that they cannot be
entered but by crawling on the belly, and a man can
scarcely stand upright when once he is in.

The Malekutus speak sesuto, retaining the sing-song
accent of the Batlapis, with whom they must have frequent communications; they have many words considered
peculiar to these, and also their hard *g*; whilst among the
Basutos, and some other tribes, that letter is comparatively
soft; thus the expression *ma a ge* his mother, which is
pronounced *ma'ghe* in the north, becomes simply *ma'e*
amongst the southern tribes. The *h* of the Batlapis is
changed into *f* amongst the Basutos. They consequently
say *mafura* instead of *mahura*, fat; *fela* instead of *hela*,
only; *ka-go-fela* instead of *ka-go-hela*, all,—literally, *to
end it*.

These are the permutations of letters which constitute
one of the greatest differences bitwixt the caffer and the
sechuana dialects. But for that, the dialects of the
Baperis and the Basutos would have been the same; but
the former have *ch* for *s* and for *ts*. For example, *ba echu*;
in sesuto, *ba esu*, ours; *chepe* instead of *tsepe*, iron. *Dj*
is used by the Baperis, moreover, for *y*; thus they say, *dja*
instead of *ya*, to eat. The *s* of the southern tribes is
changed into *sh* in the words *bosigo*, night; *mosima*,
terrier; *mosimo*, a field of millet, &c., which are in the
north pronounced *boshigo*, *moshima*, *moshimo*. On the
contrary, the *sh* of the Basutos becomes simple *s* among
the Baperis; thus they would say *sua*, to die, instead of
shua. With the former, *sua* signifies to soften a skin.
The twelve months of the year have not all the same
names in seperi, as in sesuto; and in the two idioms they

reckon also a little differently. In the south the Bechuanas all say *batu ba bangata*, many people ; in the north
they say *batu ba bantsi*. Those draw their comparison
from a sheaf, *ngata*, the latter from the word fly, *ntsi*, an
abbreviation of *ntsintsi*. With these and a few similar
exceptions, the language of the Baperis, as has been
already remarked, is the same as that spoken amongst the
Basutos. Matimulane narrated to me a tale, occupying
three pages of manuscript, in which it would not be necessary to alter above a dozen words, to render it entirely
sesuto. In speaking of stealing, the Baperi told me that
a maxim of his tribe is that a *robber* is *a dog which pays
with its pate*,—LEGORU *ki mpcha, e lefa ka tloga ea e
ona*. The Basutos would say, LESHULU *ki mpch'a e
lefa ka tlogo ea e ona*.

The tribe of which we are now speaking have nothing
but sheep and goats, the cattle have been carried away
by their enemies. They live chiefly by the chase, on millet,
and on beans. Maize is not cultivated amongst them, an
evident proof that it is an exotic, though it is now generally
diffused over southern Africa. In 1838 Matimulane planted
half of a bushel of it, which he had obtained from Moriah ;
his chief allowed him to attend to it, to reap it, and even
to eat it, but he would not allow him to sow it again,
alleging that the plant was unknown to their fathers. So
powerful and injurious is the force of prejudice in every
country.

Amongst the beans cultivated by the Baperis, there is a
new species of very small gray beans called *litlori*, which
we are endeavoring now to naturalise amongst the Basutos.
About thirty grains of them were furnished to us by a
chief in our neighbourhood, who went two years ago with
his toops to attack a feeble tribe in the north. This seed
happened to be found at the bottom of a sack in which the
soldiers of Pushuli had taken black beans as provision for
the journey on their return from their unsuccessful expedition. In the account given of their food, the Baperis
described also a pistatio nut, very common along the coast,

and a common root called *chuge*, in form and taste very like to the potatoe. In regard to fruits or berries, they eat that of a large tree, called *mofuru*. From a tree which they call *morula*, they extract an inebriating drink. The *motlatsoa* grows, it would appear, to a great height, but the natives cut it down by means of little hatchets of their own manufacture, and suck the reddish bark of it, which they find at once refreshing and nourishing. Under the name of *morokuri*, I believe that they describe the cedar ; they obtain from it a fine aromatic wood, the smoke of which is considered a specific for the cure of headache· The acacia, also, and the wild olive are very common amongst the Baperis, and many other trees of great height, unknown amongst the Basutos. In the more wooded parts of the country, it would scarcely be possible, it would seem, to open up a bridle path. There elephants, buffalos, and giraffes disport themselves, and also two distinct species of the two-horned rhinoceros ; the one of a reddish brown, large and comparatively gentle, called *mogufu*, the other smaller, of a darker colour, and surnamed the wicked or *magale*, on account of his extreme ferocity.

Amongst the numerous antelopes which cover their country, the Baperis have described to me several unknown in the south. I shall mention only the *pallah* (*A. melampus*, Lichtenstein,) which they call *pale*, and the *blauwbok* (*A. leucophea*, Pallas,) of which I have seen a magnificent skin, and also the horns which fall back like two arms.

But there is an antelope altogether unknown to me, which the Baperi travellers called *kharapa*, of a red colour, and of the size of the ritbok (perhaps the *antilope fulvo-rufula* described by Afzelius and H. Smith;) another, the *khorumo*, of which these strangers spoke to me, and which is also of a reddish color as they affirmed ; also their *tolo*, fawn coloured, of the size of the canna, having two very pretty long slender horns ; and in fine their *tiagnane*, a kind of gazelle, the peculiar movement of which the natives playfully endeavored to imitate to me while going on softening skins. In telling me of lions and hyenas, Matemulane assured me that with them these formidable animals go *in herds*, that is to say, they are very numerous, which shows also the abundance of game, which is to be found there. The Baperis have four different spears, used in war and in the chase, the *chuane* or common assegai; the *patsoane*, armed with a serrated blade, like the zagai of the west coast; the *pataka* and the *chulu*. They also take game in deep and narrow pits, which they dig in the paths followed by the animals in going to the water. These they cover carefully with brush wood, which has secured for this kind of game trap the name of *marema* or *branches*, from the verb *rema*, to cut wood. The young elephants sometimes fall into these, but it happens not unfrequently that the mother comes, and with her trunk pulls out the captive.

The Baperis call their country *Mogaritse*, and describe it as hilly. It is bounded on the west by a chain of mountains which separates it from that of Mosolekatsi. It is the same range, it would appear, as that of the Fransche bergen. The highest point is called Morimotle. Two principal rivers water the Mogaritse; these are the Lepelule and the Mogala-Kuena (Crocodile's bank,) which flow towards the east into the Indian Ocean; while two smaller streams, the Maope and the Utsane, follow the opposite direction, as the natives assure us. The Malabela* or *boilings*, is a lake of fresh water, above a mile in circumference in the country of the Baperis. These say that there is smoke arising from it morning and evening, that it is shaded by trees, destitute of fish, and avoided by the natives, and that it is also called *Bela-bela-a-maluti*, strictly speaking, *the Boiling boilings of the mountains*. These waters give indication of the existence of subterranean fires, of which the Malekutus have not the least idea. Nevertheless, at the base of a small mountain which they call *Mole*, is a deep cavern called *Marimatle*, *fine bloods* or *pretty races*, because they maintain that men and the other animals came out of it; and not only so, but that the souls return thither after death ; an opinion which reminds one of the old pagan doctrine of the infernal regions. * But we shall let Matemulane himself speak. " When we take a resolution," said he to me, "to go and visit this long, damp, dark, very frightful subterranean place, it is not without laying in a good stock of courage. We lower the head, for the entrance is low, taking hold of each other's hands; we cry all at once, *Barimo boelang teng, kunupa! Infernal Gods, return into the interior, we throw stones!* We find a path, we follow it, it leads us to a cattle kraal, where there is to be seen only cow dung, some milk pitchers, some beautiful skins hanging on the walls of the cavern, and a stag or canna stretched lifeless on the ground, but without any wound. This no one is permitted to touch, nor may we touch any thing there. There the stream Tlatlana, which traverses the cavern, murmurs fear in our ears. Without daring to taste its waters we flee ; no one looks behind him. Once out, if you follow the course of Tlatlana, it will lead you to the lake of Tlatle, which it feeds with its waters, before pouring them into the river Gori. The lake is surrounded with reeds, and infested with crocodiles and caymans. The hypopotamus is the only animal which goes near it."

The Mogaritse is divided into fifteen cantons, which take the name of the clans or families which inhabit them. These are as follows,—Sekuati, Mangana, Matulo, Mat-lankana, Masuene, Magasa, Matamoga, Marema, Lipitsi, Pognane, Mashikare, Matlari, Marima, Mapetluane, Manaile. Sekuati is the name of the reigning king of the Baperis. He resides at Makhoarane (the vallies) where are found a variety of minerals, such as peridot, talc, mica, &c. At Masuene, at Lipitsi, and at Matulo, they are also found. Iron abounds in the country. The natives forge out of it pickaxes, twice as heavy as those of the other bechuana and the caffer tribes we have known, and

* Marimatle signifies *happy* in ordinary language. Applied to the cavern whence the Baperis allege that the human race have come, and whither it must yet return, this name appears to be employed as synonymous with *place of happiness*, or elysium.

twice as good. Like all the other natives of these countries, the Malekutus venerate their ancestors almost to
adoration. They believe in diviners, sorcerers, and rainmakers, and they are extremely superstitious. Their great
oath is that of *ka noku, by the porcupine*, because the
majority of them *sing*, to use the consecrated phrase,
intimating that they feast, worship, or revere that animal.
From this comes the common designation *Ba noku*, those
of the porcupine, applied to the Baperis. When they see any
one maltreat that animal, they afflict themselves, grieve,
collect with religious care the quills, if it has been killed,
spit upon them, and rub their eye-brows with them,
saying, "They have slain our brother, our master, one of
ours, him whom we sing." They fear that they will die
if they eat the flesh of one. Nevertheless, they believe it
to be beneficial for a nursling to introduce into the joints,
of its body, certain parts of the belly of the porcupine,
mixed with the juice of plants of a virtue equally occult.
The mother gives also to her new-born child the remainder of this *setlari*, or medicament, to drink.

The other Baperis, on the contrary, worship the *khabo*,
a species of monkey unknown here. Others swear by the
baboon. At the new moon they stop at home and do not go
out to the fields, acting in this respect like those who *sing*
the sun. They fear that if they should set about their labor
at that time, that the millet would remain in the ground
without sprouting, or that it would fail to fill, or that it
would be destroyed by the rust. *Those of the sun*, or the
Baletsatsi, when the brilliant star of day rises in a cloudy
heaven, do no work, saying that *it afflicts their heart*. The
food prepared the night before is all given to the matrons or
aged women, who alone may touch it, and who give part to
the children under their care. The people go down in a
crowd to the river, there to wash their whole body. Every
one casts to the bottom of the water a stone from their
hut, and replaces it with another taken from the bed of
the river. On their return to the town after their ablution,
the chief kindles a fire at his house, and all his subjects

go to get fire from it. Then begins a general dance in the public place. He who has lost his father raises his left hand towards heaven; on the contrary, he who has lost his mother raises his right; the orphan who has lost both father and mother raises neither, but crosses both of his on his breast. This dance is accompanied by a monotonous song, or every one says :

> Pina ea Morimo, u ee gae!
> Ki lema ka lefe?
> U ee gae, u ee gae !
>
> OR,
>
> Song of the Morimo, go home !
> Which is it that I raise ? (which hand)
> Go home, go home !

The word *gae* which we have translated *home,* is strictly speaking *there where one has built,* or where one dwells, corresponding exactly to the english word employed. The Baperis assign a *home* to the *dead,* or the morimo, or household god. They do not believe that every thing dies with the body. Their religious ideas are very vague, but they have some.

As it is very dry in their country, they know no greater blessing than a little rain or a good fountain of spring water ; and to this they attach the greatest importance in the choice of a place in which to reside. The favorite song of the tribe is that of *the rain,* the first part of which is as follows :

> *The two choirs.*
> Build, build,....
> The rain comes to us.
>
> *The men.*
> Build, build,....
> The rain is coming.
>
> *The women.*
> Build, build,.....
> The rain, where is it ?
> Build, build,....
> The rain where is it ?
>
> *The men.*
> Drizzle.....

The women.

Drizzle, rain!

The men.

Drizzle. ...

The women say at the same time.

The striped one (the quagga) brays for thirst.

The men.

Drizzle.....

The women.

We invoke the rain.

ORIGINAL.

U age, age, ...ge....ge....

Pula e ka ana.

U age, u age....

Pula e ka ana.

U age, u age

Pula e kai?....

U age, u age.

Pula e kai ?....

U niere....

U niere pula!

U niere....

Moguari oa lela.

U niere ...

Rea rapela pula!

But for the fear of being too prolix, we would give more lengthened details respecting the Baperis. We may, perhaps, be allowed to mention here the names of some of the predecessors of Sekuati, their present king. *Sekuati,* Malekutu, Tulari, Makao, Mosheleri, Mosepe, Mpche, Tlopane, Morikue.....

All that is known of this last chief is, that he dwelt on the Mogala-kuena. It may be presumed that the river Morikue, beyond Mosiga, derived its name from him. As for Tlopane and Mpche, their history is equally unknown. Mosepe and Mosheleri both perished in a military expedition against the Bapenas. Tulari, when old and blind, died at Bogalaka of a quinsy, which prevented him from swallowing any thing but water. Malekutu, his successor, was slain by Moselekatsi on the expedition of that caffer prince to the north in 1822. It is from Tulari, otherwise called Moperi, that the tribe has received the name of Baperis, the import of which is simply *those of Moperi.*

This king is still highly esteemed amongst his people.
Daily they celebrate his praises. Of these the following
fragment may serve as a specimen :

"Tulari, son of Makao.

"Tulari paints himself above the eyes with yellow ochre.*
In spring his feet are as light as those of a party colored
heifer.

" He begets daughters who do him no honor. Tulari!
Their eyes are large behind, but very small in front.

" Earthen pots for household use !†

" The uncle of Lekoti is gone to Magakala to seek jackal
tails along with Pitsi. He is a zebra courser of the
plains !....

" The father of Malekutu pastures (pillages) only at
night like the hypopotamus. This worthy chief of mount
Masueme, There, says he to his subjects, By day raise
the fruits which support you, the fruits of a cherished soil.
At night rush to the cattle fold along with him who never
fights but in the dark. Am I Setlatlare or Setamanga ?
(*his youngest children*) I am the aged Lerima. I was
circumcised by Tseke, son of Masimola."

With the exception of these little heroic poems, and
similar traditions, savages are without a past, neither do
they give themselves like us, to speculations concerning the
future ; nay, even that which is going on amongst their
neighbours gives them little concern, provided only that it
be not a question of war. So the baperi travellers
who were able to give me a great deal of interesting information in regard to their own tribe, could scarcely give me
the names of those around them. They only told me that
to the east of the Mogaritse, there are two considerable
tribes of Bechuanas, called Batlapatlapus and Bamulechis,
who are always at war with each other ; and a third called

---

* The mark of great military exploits.

† The natives burst into loud laughter while reciting this ridiculous passage,
which it would seem is by no means flattering to the king and the princesses,
his daughters. As for them their little eyes suggest the appearance of cooking
pots, large in the middle, but small at the top. The idea of beauty is almost
the same every where.

Makopas, the reigning chief of which is called Sengalela, and the capital Matselana. It is in this direction also that the Matlekas live. These are a caffer tribe, having an incision in the nose similar to the cuts with which the Portuguese mark their slaves, and they have also the singular custom of filing off the teeth,* so as to leave only the stumps, from which they have got the nick-name of *stutterers* given to them by the neighbouring tribes, who do not follow this custom. They procure copper, beads, and stuffs at Laurent Marques, and go to exchange these for ivory, horns, cattle, and furs in the interior. It is from them, for example, that Sekuate has purchased the red scarf, with which he is said to deck himself on féte days.

It is difficult to believe, yet Matimulane has twice sworn to it, that according to the custom of these Mathlekas, a man when he is married eats the elder brother of his bride! He leads into the cattle fold of his wife's father the cattle which he gives to him as a dowry for his daughter. He, on the other hand, calls his eldest son, and commands him to feast his sister. He binds back his two arms, as if they were the two horns of a blue antelope, runs to the fold, and there he is thrust through with a spear, and eaten by the bridegroom and his friends. The pretended sorcerers, moreover, when they wish to injure any one cast lots upon him, declare him mad, and then slaughter and eat him. I repeat, that all this appears to me incredible. Perhaps, it is the caricature of some atrocious deed, although the natives generally testify to the truth of a similar report in regard to such a custom.

To the north of the Baperis are the Batlous or Batlu, *those of the elephant.* They are a new nation of Bechuanas, more powerful as it appears than that of the Mantetis. They live at the foot of high mountains of a most sombre rocky aspect, similar to that of the mountains of Mogaritse, but less wooded. Tobacco, on the other hand, grows there much better, and there is a great deal of business

* A custom prevailing on both coasts of Africa, says Capt. W. Owen in his narrative of voyages, &c.

done in it amongst the natives. In this district should be found the sources of the Muri, a river on the east coast, which is larger than even the Orange, according to the report of the natives, who say, moreover, that the bed of it is very broad, but that it is not so deep.

The Batlous possess a race of oxen of very fine shape, with horns of almost incredible length, namely, from four to five feet, so that from tip to tip they cannot be less than seven or eight feet.

The capital of this people is called Mamakao. It is governed by Mokopane, son of Kekane. This Mokopane is so valorous that they have surnamed him *sechuamara* or the *bloody*. It is not very long since he went and besieged Nguanalelle, the town of Seamoga, younger brother of Sekuati ; he there killed every inhabitant of the place, and carried off the whole of the herds. On the northern frontier of his country there is a salt pit called Matlatla, from the name of a little village of Bechuanas, who have settled there under a chief called Sebula. This natural salt pit or *lechuaing* has been described to us as measuring nearly three miles in circumference, so that it must present the appearance of a true *salt marsh*. The inhabitants procure there without trouble as much salt as they wish.

The only white man, I believe, who has penetrated so far north is a certain dutch boer from the Cape, who arrived there with his family in the month of April or May 1836, with a Basuto from the neighbourhood of Moriah for his guide. After having filled his wagon with salt, the stranger wished to return ; but his oxen, too feeble to drag the load, left it there, and perished one after another. They had been bitten by an insect, very numerous there, called *fly-flea* in Sechuana (ntsintsi-a-tsetse) on account of its bite. The natives give to this insect the size and greenish color of the flies which ordinarily live on meat. They say also that it is armed with a long red trunk, which they compare to the beak of a bird. It appears in February with the great heats, and does not disappear till towards the end of summer. Its bite blisters the skin, and causes

a very acute pain, but this does not last above a day,
which may possibly arise from the flow of blood generally following the bite, at least in man, whom it
attacks as well as the beasts. The oxen, in particular,
are so tormented by them that the natives always take
care to keep them far from the reeds where this dangerous insect abounds, and to lead them to pasture in
the high grounds, and even into the country of their neighbours. As for the travelling boer, we understand that
after the loss of his team, he procured another by his
musket at the village of Ramapulane. Some inhabitants
of the place were killed, the others, all affrighted on seeing
these bit and killed from such a distance, took to flight,
leaving in the power of the formidable white man their
oxen and some cows, which he also led away with him.
He arrived safely with his prey amongst the Baperis, and
from them he went down to Delagoa Bay, but I do not
know exactly what has since become of him. I have been
assured that he has perished along with his children and
his slaves.

It is very painful to witness the infamous manner
in which certain whites behave in these countries. Not
to multiply examples, let it suffice for me to state that
I knew an individual of this kind, who had taken no
less than thirty caffer women with whom he lived in true
morena style. I also received into my house one day two
english traders, whom I had afterwards to show to the
door, having received a letter which unveiled but too truly
their sad character, leaving my house loaded with provisions for the journey, and furnished with a french New
Testament, that they might learn to do well; they stopped
at Thaba Bosio, where they lived nearly a month *as
shameless Adamites.* Thence they went down to Port
Natal; the more intelligent of the two became chief of the
other whites whom he found settled there. And some time
after he fell in an expedition against the natives.

Every one knows that such crimes, unhappily too common, exasperate the Africans, and cause them to judge

erroneously of the moral character of the Europeans, so
that in their justifiable mistrust, which is naturally great,
the savages often repay on peaceful travellers the crimes of
those who have gone before them. One man, thinking
thereby to praise the cape farmers to me, told me that they
do this good wherever they pass,—they make the name of
the whites most formidable to the natives. The remark is
correct, excepting in the use made of the single word *good*;
it would be more befitting to replace it by the word *evil*,
or even *great evil*. The boer, for example, of whom I have
already spoken, has excited a very stong feeling against
us amongst all the natives acquainted with his conduct.
The Baperis, in telling me of his behaviour, told me that
that which saved his life was his strange white colour;
and still more his arms not less frightful than his face.
If they had only been a little more accustomed to these
things, he might have laid his account with being torn
in pieces at Ramapulana.

About fifteen degrees of latitude may separate the
country of the Baperis from the Lake of Maravi, of
which I have not been able to procure any positive
information, although it is not entirely unknown to
them. They call it Marabai, and believe it to be fresh
water ; assuring me that it is fed by a river called
Tubatse, of which the Mogomatse, referred to in certain maps under the name of Mofumatsi, is one of the
principal branches. These two rivers are inhabited by
crocodiles, which are also said to live in the lake in
question. It is also surrounded with deep bogs, which
render the approach to it very difficult for the natives.
These particulars, vague and imperfect as they are,
are, I repeat, all that the Baperis could give me on this
important point.

In speaking to me of the country situated to the west
of their district, they informed me also that they are
bounded on that side by a very strong tribe of Bechuanas,
called Bakuenas, from whom a good proportion of the

Basutos seem to have derived their origin. These Bakuenas are governed by a king called Sebetuane, who lives on the shores of the Ueri, one of the most considerable rivers in these distant regions.

In conclusion, to the south west of them these Bakuenas have as neighbours the Baharutsanas, and the Bamanguatos, two other bechuana tribes, already known to us under the names of the Baharutsis and the Bamanguetos.

CHAPTER XIX.

IT is among the Bamanguetos and the subjects of Sekuati that we should find the Zulas, who are subjects to Mosolekatsi, the formidable inkhosi, who causes both his own people and the numerous tribes of Bechuanas which we have noticed to groan under his despotic power. What is known with the greatest certainty in regard to him, is, that some twenty years ago he was living about three days' journey to the north of Mokokutlufe, in the town of Umtulu. His father bore the name of Maehobane, and was descended from a very noble zula family called Suanazene.

In 1822 an independent matebele chief, called Sekognane, declared war against Mosolekatsi, overcame him, and carried off a part of his herds. He then went up with his people towards the north west, plundering and killing on his journey the Makoros, (a feeble tribe of Zulas,) and the Makhatlas, a tribe of the Bechuanas, who appear to have been so reduced that they have never recovered their strength, and have, in some measure, become cannibals.

After this success, Mosolekatsi went to attack the Bauanketsis or Wankits, and lastly the Baperis, who fought and defeated him, however, at Matamoga and at Marema. Four years passed on without these people hearing any thing more of the aggressor. In their

national songs they were celebrating their victories over
him, and laughing at their terrible enemy,—" She is
asleep, she is worn out, the wicked brute, her bellowings
do not trouble us more." But the chief of the Zulas was
not asleep. In the fifth year, in 1827, he presented
himself before Makhoarane, took, plundered, and sacked
the town, and carried off all the cattle.

Six months later he sent one of his officers, called
Kutsane, at the head of a battalion of soldiers, who captured the inhabitants of Matamoga, and led them away
to Motlatlantsela, the residence of Mosolekatsi, who employed them in constructing a pallisade around his harem,
which consisted in all of forty-four huts. This enclosure,
made almost entirely of mimosa stakes, has been described to us as upwards of half a mile in circumference,
about six feet thick, and the same in height. The king
of the Zulas used to take a singular delight in walking
on the top of this terrace, whence he could command the
whole town. As for the poor workmen, they did the
work,—" by day their eyes in tears, at night sleeping
with hunger," to use their own expressions. When they
were completely exhausted with fatigue, they were sent
home, and their brethren from Marema came to replace
them. Scarcely had the latter labored five days, when
Omthlela arrived at Motlatlantsela with an army of Zulas,
sent by Dingan. The town of Mosolekatsi was invaded
and plundered. Part of the inhabitants fell under the
steel of the enemy, the others fled from the field of battle
in confusion, and their chief, being in the midst of the
fugitives, escaped without being recognised.

As for the Baperi woodmen, they received no injury.
The conqueror sent them back to their land, and returned
himself to his own, taking with him great booty. In the
meantime Mosolekatsi, who had gone down to Kafela on
the Morikue, sent orders to the Baperis to bring him
millet and other provisions, which they did through fear
of that formidable *lion*. As he had previously taken from
them all their oxen, the transport of provisions was

effected with very great sufferings by the women, who crossed the deserts in small parties, each with a sack of corn on her head, and a suckling on her back.

A thousand facts prove that Mosolekatsi has been as cruel and absolute as the Chakas. He follows out their political and military system. The countries to the north of these do not know a greater scourge than he. He reduces to subjection all the bechuana tribes in his immediate neighbourhood. His principle is to exterminate the men and women, and to bring up their children in the ranks of his soldiers. By a ridiculous presumption he adopted, it is said, as his maxim, Two chiefs may suffice, one in heaven, and the other on the earth,—nor has he deigned any further explanation on the subject.

A mission to his people would be of immense importance, and in all probability it would rectify that state of things; but it is not probable that it would succeed during the life-time of such a despot. Nothing, indeed, could be in greater opposition than the gentle law of the gospel and the brutal conduct of a mad zula emperor. It is indeed true, as we are told, that religion surmounts all obstacles; but she does not always attack them in the front. Her march moreover, to be sure, should be progressive. Follow the steps of the gospel from Table Bay to Lattakoo, and consider well all the blessings which it has procured for the lands over which it has passed, and the people which one by one it has subdued. This is evidently the river of Ezekiel, the waters of which increased without ceasing as they went; or rather, if you will, the net of which our Saviour speaks, which must cover, one after another, all the nations of the earth. If, then, securing that which they have already conquered, the missionaries labor still to bring under the influence of the Cross the pagan hordes of Bechuanas to be found betwixt Moteto and the Morikue, who can doubt that their efforts, humble as they may seem, will be crowned with success, and that, sooner or later, we may see the

Zulas also embrace the christian faith, as their neighbours have already done?

With this view, a mission to the Baperis would be
most important, and, perhaps, indeed it would succeed
better than all those which have already been tried to
the west of the country of Mosolekatsi. This we know
for certain, that Sekuati and Seamoga are well disposed
towards the reception of the messengers of salvation,
for they have earnestly entreated us for them, and it was
not without deep regret that we found ourselves unable
to give other answer than this, "There is a lack of
laborers."

During their sojourn at Moriah, Matimulanc and his
travelling companions regularly attended the religious
services. At the first in which they took part, one of
them was seized with a panic of fear on hearing the
singing of the psalms ; he went out from the assembly,
trembling all over, his body covered with perspiration ;
and he appeared again amongst the audience after having
breathed the open air for a moment. "His heart was
desiring two opposite things," said he to me afterwards,
"to fly from our worship, and to remain there."

These people when they returned to their country,
took with them the sesuto alphabets, of which they had
learned to form some words. They knew, in general, the
fundamental doctrines of the bible, and one of them could
repeat correctly the Lord's prayer. Besides the presents
made to them by our chiefs, they received from the
members of the mission a sowing of wheat, of maize, of
potatoes, of white beans, called in this country french
beans, together with some of the most useful tools, such
as an adze, a file, some domestic animals, a couple of
grey hounds, two goats of a species new to them, a cock
and a hen, &c., all being things unknown at Makhoarane.

The subjects of Mosolekatsi extend to the south as far
as the 26th degree of south latitude, and the 30th degree
longitude east of Greenwich. Some years ago they robbed

some griqua hunters in a valley, upon which I came
unexpectedly with Monaile on the 16th of April. We
had gone on horseback to examine the confluence of the
Namagari and the Lekua, two rivers of about the same
magnitude, and whose united waters form the Yellow
river, otherwise called the Fal (*from the Dutch Vaal.*)
The Lekua comes from the east, and throws itself into
the Namagari, at the base of a ridge of mountains previously unknown, which we called *Fransche Bergen* or
French Mountains, for lack of a better name. They form
a regular chain, which runs at first from the south west
to the north east, and stretches very far into the interior,
according to the uniform testimony of the natives, who
have observed them, as has been already seen amongst the
Baperis, and further. These mountains, at the spot where
they commence, may be upwards of two thousand feet
above the surrounding soil, and about five thousand feet
above the level of the sea. The natives assure us, moreover, that they increase greatly in magnitude, as they
advance to the north. They are covered with snow in the
month of August, and three months later there falls at that
place abundance of rain. Every thing then assumes a
lovely appearance of verdure, and antelopes swarm there,
as do also lions and hyenas. At all times there is found
there great numbers of baboons, of coneys, called by
others rock badgers, of panthers, of jackals, of wild dogs,
and of wild cats. Olive trees and acacias are also very
common there, with many other trees of a great height.

Along the banks of the Fal I saw a new species of Ibis,
which I first observed on the Enta. I have examined
one that was full grown, and from it I have made the
following notes:—Neck completely devoid of feathers; skin
of a reddish grey colour (*glaucus,*) like the nose of a
horse; claws of a deep red, naked under the wings,
color scarlet; plumage white; end of the pinions of a
light green; the cubital feathers white, with a gray lustre
towards the extremity; length of beak 7 inches; length
of the bird itself 2 feet 4 inches; it is a little larger than

the sacred Ibis of the Egyptians. The designation *ibis nudi colis* would suit it well.

There is also in these countries a large ibis, of a brown lustre, commonly called by onomatopy *addadu*; and another deep blue ibis with red head, called from this peculiarity, though improperly, by the English at the Cape, *wild turkey*, and by the dutch farmers *wilde kalkoen*, which means the same thing.

I might have remarked, in speaking of the Fal, that its banks are very bare where I have seen them, only a few small willows show themselves here and there, while after its junction with the Lekua it is covered with firewood and even with timber.

Along the river in the driest spots there grows a prickly bush, scarcely a foot in height, which bears a fruit pretty like the jujube in form, and having a juice which is rather sweet. Monaile and I supported ourselves on these almost the whole day of the 16th of April. We had left the wagon at an early hour without any other provision than a large piece of the flesh of the gnu, which was as tough as leather, and which hunger alone could lead us to consider eatable. It was in the midst of the fields, on the banks of a small lake, where we lapped a little water to complete our repast. Then, remounting our horses, we held on towards Mauliri, a small stream running into the Namagari. Its bed is almost even with the ground, and its water as clear as crystal. After having crossed this brook, we expected soon to find our wagon, or at least its traces, as it had been agreed in the morning that the rendezvous should be about that place; but nothing was to be seen. Leaving the encampment, situated about ten miles on this side of the embouchure of the Enke-chuane, it had moved away west-south-west instead of due west, and made five-and-twenty long miles that day.

As for us, with the design of seeking the track of the wagon, we rode in a direction to cross it, and thus we succeeded in finding it before night fall. At first we followed it courageously and at a good pace, until our beasts were knocked up. Then, Monaile dismounting from his, and giving me his gun to carry, walked behind with a switch of buffalo hide, and thus urged the animals on a little further. But at length my poor eyes could no longer perceive the traces of the wheels; I then put forward my young man, who understood better than I how to follow them. Our progress was thus retarded greatly. The horses appeared to be sorry for the change, but with myself it was a little different. The sun had just set, leaving behind him darkness and gloomy thoughts. I was conscious of nothing but fear; the desert, hunger, and dangers of every kind presented themselves before me to frighten me; silence surrounded us on every side. From time to time, however, this was disturbed by some ferocious cry, by the yelping of the jackals, or by the hollow flapping of the wings of some bird, which crossed our path, as if to multiply our fears. On the other hand also, there was the alarmed voice of my guide, repeating without ceasing, "They have made us lose ourselves, where are they leading us? Are we still in the track at least?" And this young man had to stop continually, groping for the rut with his hand. How little does one appear in his own eyes at such a time? Oh, how blessed then is the thought that there is a God in heaven who sees us, who knows us by name! Lord, said I to him in my heart, (with too little confidence I must allow):

Seigneur, tu grâce infinie,
Au fidèle qui te prie
Fait ressentir tous les jours
Les effets de ton secours.
Puisqu' à toi seul je m'arrête,
Seigneur, entends ma requête,
Qui, comme j'espère en toi,
Daigne prendre soin de moi.

When there was nothing more visible on earth, we raised our eyes on high to look at the stars. Orion for nearly an hour directed our uncertain journey; but he too must in turn be hid from our view. There sprang up a west wind which gathered a thick cloud over our heads; large drops of water fell every moment upon us, and at last all nature was enveloped in darkness. I dismounted to fire a gun, hoping that perhaps they would answer with a similar discharge from the camp, which we supposed could not be very far distant; but it was of no use. In my confusion I lost the ramrod, which could not be found again to enable us to re-load. What was then to be done? There was nothing for it but to lie there, each in his little cloak, crouching close together, and that immediately under the nose of the horses, which we held by the bridle all night for security, in case the lions should have attacked us; a few grains of gunpowder and a small bit of paper put into the touch-pan procured us a light; but unhappily we could procure no firing but rubbish, and even this the wind and the rain speedily extinguished. But further than this, no other evil befell us, for which we desired to be thankful. The night passed quietly. The next day at dawn we resumed our journey, but on foot; partly because we were stiff with cold, and desirous of warming ourselves by walking, partly from pity for our beasts, which had the day before been fourteen hours under the saddle,—and then again it was the sabbath. To be short, we had not much more than half a mile to go to the wagon. M. Daumas was still in bed. He had the kindness to get up, to let me lie down; and he immediately prepared for us two cups of *eau sucrée* a little warm, which did us unspeakable good.

This was a dull day, monotonous as solitude always is. We were encamped on the ruins of old dwellings; the ground was every where covered with human skulls; we placed one in the wagon as a *souvenir;* so easily does the soul associate with itself, and bind to itself, any thing which bears the impress of misfortune. This sympathetic law of our being, so common and always speaking, dates from the fall of which it is doubtless one effect. At the close of the day a Lighoya from Malibaning came out of his town, situated in the neighbourhood, to see us. He told us that Lumisi, his chief, having learned from some native travellers that we were *whites*, and white bearers of good news, wished to hear us, which did not fail to give us joy.

The next day we went to his place where we delivered two addresses. The inhabitants of the place were exceedingly obliging as they brought even the old handles of their hoes to feed our fire of reeds.

Before leaving these good people, we made them a present of some potatoes for seed. Do people eat these things? they asked. Yes, all who have them. And whence do they come? From under the pickaxe. But how, and when do they plant them? We caused them to bring us a common hoe, and showed them how it should be done. Excellent,—said one, holding his two hands full of them,—excellent! This, indeed, is very little; but I go next September to put this in the ground where it will grow; I shall then make my harvest; I will take it; I will go somewhere and purchase a she-goat. This she-goat will give me a kid, &c. &c. Let us hope that the good man will succeed better in his projects of aggrandisement than poor Perrette, whose language did not differ so much from this, but that the one recalls the other.

On the 19th, after having bidden adieu to the inhabitants of Malibaning, we directed our course towards the west, and encamped that day in the fields, in the midst of the wild beasts, which scattered all our cattle to a distance. In the vicinity there was found a kraal of Lighoyas, but so small that a native told us, showing five of his fingers, " *There are there just so many women, neither more nor less.*" The next day we reached one somewhat larger. It was built in a hollow, on the banks of the Kokuatsi, a tributary of the Yellow River. The inhabitants of this place on perceiving us hid themselves in their millet fields, others took to flight, trailing after them all that they could of their possessions. Upon this our young men were sent to them to reassure them. They brought back Sebuku, the chief, and, by the way, an old cannibal. This petty morena held in his hands some heads of maize and a pumpkin, which he presented to us in token of friendship. After having returned his salutations, we explained to him the object of our visit, which he seemed to understand, but he was doubtful of us, as was very obvious through his constrained demeanour, contrasting, as it did, with the lively movements of his head, and the sharp glances of his eye. Notwithstanding that, he collected his people, and we offered a prayer, after which every one fled on all fours, except Sebuku and his chief man, whom we succeeded in retaining near the wagon. Never shall I forget the original way in which one of our Bechuanas spoke to them of our character of messengers of God, and of God himself. His short address, if it may be permitted to me to introduce it here, was nearly in these words :

" These whites," said he, pointing to us with his finger, " These whites have a father, and a mother, brothers, and friends. They have left all these. They have come from beyond a country of water (the sea) ; they love people; their parents have sent them to us. You see well that they are young men ; they cannot have come of their own accord ; no, their fathers also love us.

" Look into their wagon, there is nothing awanting ; it is full of meat and of corn. Besides, do you not see that it is a small one ? Can you believe that they would wish to take away your crops ? These are not birds of prey. For all that they receive from others they pay.

" Of cattle you have none. They covet neither your millet, nor your maize, nor your pumpkins. Do not fear either that they want to carry off your children as the Bakotus did (the Korannas.)

" If you find them lean, it is because they are travellers.* At Kokuatse, when a traveller arrives what is done ? I suppose that they gather around him ; every one wishes to see him, to hear him ; every one is desirous to be seated on the flaps of his mantle to enquire of him

---

* Amongst the savages poor fare is inseparable from journeys.

whether he brings any news. Thou, Sebuku, you, his
principal men, what are you about to day? I assure you,
I your own brother, that these whites are indeed the
bearers of good news; but you have lost your usual
eagerness! They have come to make you acquainted
with their God. Do you know who he is? *Yes*, answered
a voice eagerly, *It is the sun;* but many voices replied
with one accord, *No, it is the Creator of the sun.*

" Their God hath made the sun, continued the Orator,
he hath created the high heavens, and the earth, and the
waters great and small. He hath also given his only
Son. He hath given him for us. It is chiefly about him
that these people speak to us, and what is his name?
His name is Jesus the Saviour.

" Does it not often happen to shepherds that their
sheep wander? Yes. And what do the shepherds do
then? They put aside their kaross, run to seek them,
go in spite of hunger and fatigue, and make themselves
anxious about them. If they find the sheep they bring
them back with joy. Jesus is the shepherd of men,
their good shepherd. His sheep have all gone to feed on
cursed pasture lands, the grass and the waters of which
cause death. He has seen it; He has come to seek
them; He leads them back to blessed pasturage.

" The whites say that these are good things, to love
one another,—to assist one another,—to live in peace,—all
that is well. To kill one another,—to seize the flocks of
one another,—to quarrel with one another,—to lie to
another,—all that is bad. The conscience of the blacks
says to them the same thing.

" Sebuku, chief of Kokuatsi, now what wilt thou reply?
Why dost thou dread my masters? When one does evil,
they are grieved, their heart weeps. How could they
possibly do it to you? Their God, Jehovah, punishes with
a chastisement which never changes (*eternal*) whoever
commits that which is displeasing to him, such as robbing,
adultery, drunkenness; and to wash us from all such pollu-
tion, this Jehovah gave up his Son to death.—That is all."

CHAPTER XX.

FROM Kokuatsi we came to Sisiyue, passing through Tsikaniane, where we preached the gospel to the inhabitants. They pointed out to us at a little distance from the road Moghotli, Monchunyane, and Chupane, three villages of Lighoyas, who but a short time ago were cannibals, as were also the inhabitants of Sisyue. The extreme wretchedness and frightful manners of the inhabitants of the place, forced themselves on our attention, but notwithstanding their ferocity, they fled at our approach. Almost all left their cabins, though it was nightfall and the weather very bad. It was not till the next day that they permitted us to get near them to give them some tokens of our good will, and to tell them what we had to say to them about the Saviour.

A man, with numerous gashes in his face, sang, danced, and pirouetted near the wagon, assuming a thousand low comic attitudes. "Wonders!" cried he, "Wonders! what have we here? Yesterday, on perceiving this *house* in the plain (the wagon covered with a large linen sail) I swore that it must be *a walking rock.* To-day I see heads with crops of *horse hair* (our locks, every where wondered at, sometimes envied, sometimes ridiculed, happening not to be crisp,) I see white faces, white hands, oh! oh! my white men, oh! oh!" This old cannibal ridiculed many other things about us; but when we put a mirror before his eyes, in order to procure for him once in his life the pleasure of beholding his hideous figure, he made some amusing somersets, and fell on his back, on which he lay for several minutes laughing at himself like a great fool.

From that place we went to Machogane, where we found a people who were true materialists. An old man asked of us with naiveté, whether the God of whom we spake to them, would give him sleep, provided he prayed for it. Another requested us to give him a heifer, although he saw that we had none with us. Millet constituted the principal riches of this village, as it did of the two last named. Their inhabitants possessed, moreover, a small flock of goats, and there was no want of game in the fields. The natives take the game in round pits, dug on the banks of standing waters, or in the paths of the antelopes, which renders this country rather dangerous to travellers. In prosecuting our journey from Machogane to Matlaking, we had to travel with very great care, to prevent our falling into some one of the innumerable traps which beset our path.

Our way led across low marshy ground, out of which we got with great difficulty and fatigue; one of our oxen sunk under the exertion; that with which we replaced him, proved exceedingly restive and untractable; a third, in trying to escape, broke a necessary part of his yoke. The handle of our enormous whip next broke, this was mended, and it broke again. The wagon had to cross three difficult streams, one after another (the sources of the Enta.) My colleague marched on foot at one side of our team, armed with a double strap; I walked at the other side with a good stick; one of our Bechuanas occupied the seat; thus we went on flogging the poor bleeding oxen, hollowing with all our might, while the lions at a distance were, by their horrid growlings, predicting for us a troubled night. At last towards nightfall we arrived at Matlaking. There we unyoked in the river, after having done all we could to get out. One of our oxen entangled himself in the traces, and had very nearly broken it all in pieces, and then almost strangled himself. Without wood, without fire, the rain pouring, what could we do? We put ourselves immediately under our cloaks, and our people under their karosses. As soon as the shower was over, however, hunger led them to the kraal, where they made us a cup of tea and some porridge, which was not eaten without a relish. It was then eleven o'clock at night.

The next day it continued to rain, so we slept till late in the morning, and we read in bed portions of the *Archives du Christianisme* of *Le Semeur*, and of Buffon, to pass the time. Then the Morena of Matlaking having come to pay us a visit, we showed to him a number of little things, about which our young men had told him. He found us *so* rich, *so* happy, in having been born in a country in which so many things *grew*,—for the good man imagined that with us every thing comes of itself, at least he pretended to believe it, that he might get the more presents from us. To undeceive him, we told him to look at our hands, saying, " It is with these that the white men procure all their good things ; God has only given us two, as he has to the black. What do you do with yours ?" The chief laughed, and then he ingenuously pleaded guilty too little idleness, as well as to a little leaning towards plunder, which he called *the law of the country*.......
Amongst the negroes the assegai spoils every thing. The blacks are not fools, neither, strictly speaking, are they idle; the great defect in their character is their inclination to pillage. This is daily involving families and tribes in ruin. Once impoverished the work is complete, and therefore it is all gain for them to go to their neighbours to try to make depredations upon them. The losses sustained justify the attack. Besides, hunger is there a cruel counsellor ! They say on this subject *that hunger is also chief of the town.* That is to say, as is well understood, that there she also prescribes laws.

In the evening a group of people gathered around the

tent, and we had prayer together, which prepared us for the engagements of the following day, which was the sabbath. The weather was clear and serene. "An african sky!" we cried full of joy in getting out of bed. The air was full of perfume To enjoy the morning more, my travelling companion and I took a long walk. The one said, "The sabbath is always delightful to the christian." The other replied, "Especially under a serene sky." Under our feet we trode a thousand odoriferous plants, such as lavender, sage, mint, white gilly flower, variegated carnations; and by the side of the common dandelion, and other humble herbs, rose geraniums of a bright scarlet, as if they would arrogate royalty to themselves amongst the flowers of the desert. To this one must add the lovely appearance of the seventy huts of Matlaking, which we had before us, the one half on a little table land, shaded by a quantity of brush wood and thick bouquets of furze, and the other on the stopping brow of a hill, at the foot of which flowed with a gentle murmur the brook Sisiyue; when we looked at this little hamlet through our pocket glass, we regretted much that we were not draftsmen. But we were going to seek retirement for communion with our Saviour. We meditated on his word, and presented before him our prayer, under a wild olive tree, which we had approached, humming these two verses of a hymn :—

> Jour du Seigneur,
> J'ouvre men cœur
> A ta douce lumière.
> Jour solennel,
> A l' Eternel,
> Consacre ma priére.

> Dieu Tout-puissant,
> Dieu bienfaisant,
> J'ai besoin de ta gràce.
> Eclaire-moi !
> Soutiens ma foi !
> Je viens chercher ta face.

After that, we returned to the wagon. The natives

assembled there, and there they heard an exposition of
these words of the gospel, " God so loved the world that
he gave his only begotten Son, that whosoever believeth
in him should not perish but have everlasting life." They
paid a commendable attention, but apparently without
being able to understand much of what was said. The
discourse, however, being ended, there was soon heard
amongst them a confused murmur of people, who wished
all at a time to tell what they had retained, or to put
questions to one another. Our Beehuanas, in particular,
were diligent in explaining to them our songs, our prayer,
our addresses. Following us as they did wherever we
went, it was no small service which they thus rendered
to us.

In the afternoon we went to the village to see a poor
blind woman, whom we found in a sad condition, and
banished to the inmost recess of her hut; for in this
country the unfortunate dare scarcely show face amongst
the living. At our invitation, however, she came out
from her dark corner, and also from her continual sullen
silence, and entered into conversation with us, in the presence of a considerable group of her townsmen.

"Who are these men?" she first asked. "Whites,"
we answered. " But do the whites also speak our language?" "Yes, we have learned it, and like it much ;
we are *barutis* (teachers) who go about the country,
preaching good news to the unhappy. Do you know
that you have a Saviour in heaven?" "No, what saviour?"
" Jesus, the master of things." Thus we were able to
give her some instruction, and to encourage her as much
as we could to trust in the new God, whom we preached
as the Lord of her household gods, whom she accused of
having taken away her sight from her. " I was one day
in the fields," said she, poor woman, of her own accord,
" The heavens became darkened, I hastened to take my
child on my back, and to regain my cabin; a common
pot was on my head, and my hoe in my hand; I ran with
all my might; but the storm broke, vomiting forth rain

in floods; the lightning fell before my feet and took away my eyes; from that time I have lived alone and desolate." "But was that in this village?" we asked her. "Oh no," replied she, "it was far from this, far, very far!" "And how comes it that you are now at Matlaking?" "My husband led me by the hand across the great deserts, when we were all obliged to flee before the wicked Mosolekatsi, twelve summers ago." "And where is this good husband? We should like to make his acquaintance too." She informed us that he had gone out in the morning to the chase. We read the word of God, sung a hymn beside the poor blind woman, offered prayer on her behalf, and recommended her neighbours to take care of her; we gave her also some little assistance, and we took occasion from that to speak to those around of the invaluable blessing of sight.

I could not forget at such a moment that one of my best friends had been blind for nearly half a century; and affectionate was the prayer which I then breathed in spirit for him. This good old man has never lost, during all his blindness, the sight given by the *eyes of the heart*, to borrow a beautiful expression of the people amongst whom I labor; and it is to him, moreover, next to God, that I owe the little faith I have. My prayer for him was indeed earnest!

To conclude, the blind Lighoya had by her side a *tumo*, or kind of simple balafo furnished with one calebash. I had a great desire to procure it, but God forbid that I should have taken it away from such an unfortunate creature. It was that little instrument, combined with pity felt for its owner, which suggested the following verses, which I may surely be permitted to insert in this journal :—

Qui me rendra la lumière des cieux ?
Un long ennui m'accable en ces bas lieux.

Jadis j'aimais les aubes matinales ;
J'aimais l'ardeur des plus brûlants soleils.
Qu'elles étaient pures et virginales

Les cent couleurs de nos couchers vermeils !
On me dit bien qu'elles sont toujours belles
Pour qui les peut encor voir de ses yeux ;
Mais les deux miens y sont fermés, grands dieux !
Pour moi les jours, ce sont des nuits nouvelles.
Qui me rendra la lumière des cieux ?
Un long ennui m'accable en ces bas lieux.

Rien ne me plaît dans le bruit des tempêtes ;
C'est tout horreur que leurs mugissements ;
Quand les autans les versent sur nos têtes,
Je suis en proie á d'affreux tremblements.
Viennent les eaux, nobles après l'orage,
Belles à voir rouler en tourbillons.
Belles à voir inonder les sillons,
Couvrir les camps de fleurs et de ravage.
Qui me rendra la lumière des cieux ?
Un long ennui m'accable en ces bas lieux.

Ne suis-je pas cette plante inclinée,
Qui tristement languit dans le vallon,
Qui, faute d'eau, sera déracinée
Par le fougueux et cruel aquilon ?
J'ai des ennuis que nul ne peut comprendre.
Hélas ! je vis sans présent, sans futur,
A charge aux miens, dans uu état si dur,
Formant des vœux que nul ne peut entendre.
Qui me rendra la lumière des cieux ?
Un long ennui m'accable en ces bas lieux.

Cruels aïeux, ô mes dieux tutélaires,
Quoi ! me priver de la clarté du jour !
Quoi ! vous montrer mes plus grands adversaires !
Dites : ma foi, mes dons et mon amour
Seraient-ils vains ? .... Ainsi que la colombe
Je dois gémir, végéter, puis mourir,
Sans qu'un ami daigne me secourir,
Même au dela de mon avide tombe !
Oh ! rendez-moi la lumière des cieux ;
Mon long ennui m'accable en ces bas lieux.

On Monday, the 25th of April, we had another meeting
for worship with the inhabitants of Matlaking ; after
which we bade adieu to them and to their pretty village,
to resume our journey. We travelled four hours towards
the south, and came upon the Enta, in the water course
of which we had to pass the night.

The banks were so steep and so sandy that it took

us the whole of the next day to scale them. To effect this, it was necessary to cut down the bushes by which the passage was obstructed, to smooth the bank, to unload the wagon, then by dint of shouts and blows to rouse our good but stupid beasts ; and thus we got out of that horrible place. A team of horses does well in making a desperate effort to get out of a difficulty, but it is very different with oxen. These dull animals, if they feel that the load remains behind, draw-back and get cooled, and then the more you beat them the more stubborn they become ; it frequently happens, moreover, that they get entangled in the traces, breaking the yokes and the thongs, bellowing, kicking, and putting with their horns like wild bulls. Let the traveller of an impatient disposition, who is obliged to be drawn by them across the vast solitudes of this continent, restrain himself, and borrow from the cape boer a little of his phlegm ; there is nothing hasty about the temper of the oxen.

Their power of resistance is very great in miry places ; on the other hand they always pull well when the stones rattle under the wheels,—that is to say, on dry and rugged rocks ; even in going up a hill they go well, provided that they are allowed a moment's rest every five minutes or so.

Never had we felt so much the inconvenience arising from the total want of roads in this portion of Africa as at the passage of the Enta ; but it must be admitted that we Europeans have the misfortune to take things often too warmly. We are easily excited, and we are hasty in casting the coat, when there is no real necessity for our doing so.

The natives who take every thing easy, do not find things the worse on that account. Had any one seen my colleague and myself on the 25th of April, both of us in our shirt sleeves, laboring away, covered with perspiration, and had he seen, at the same time, our three Bechuanas going on quietly at their usual pace, running from the oxen to the coffee pot, which, thanks to their care, never got off the boil throughout the whole of that day, and from the coffee pot returning quietly to readjust the team,—yes, doubtless had any one seen the whole five,—he must have been struck with the strange contrast. In the evening things were reversed, but it was the same story at bottom. Seated around a large log of the prickly mimosa, by the blaze of which they were cooking their pot of meat and millet, our good people laughed away at the expense of their oxen, all the adventures of which they went over again in. detail, with all their good and bad qualities, without forgetting one. These three men were happy as happy could be; their very discourse breathed delight. At last they supped; then each being well wrapped up in his kaross, they lay down in the same place where they had laughed so heartily, and with their feet in the ashes like salamanders, they slept as soundly as possible till the morning. But my travelling companion and I were laid down in the wagon, both of us worn out with fatigue, and our blood too much agitated to permit us to repose, and our arms in fine so sore with wielding our enormous whip, that we seriously believed that we had been seized with rheumatism. Our anxieties occasioned our troubles, the thoughtlessness of the savages, their happiness. One is always seeking for differences betwixt them and us, I find this one as marked as any other, and I insert it here *en passant*.

As for the Enta, the upper sources of which we had crossed beyond Motlomo, it is at this place about twenty feet wide, and flows gently towards the west, away to the Yellow River, of which it is one of the most lovely tributaries. Thick mimosas shade its banks, along with willows of considerable height, and wild olive trees, &c. Many hyppopotami frequent its waters, which are generally deep, and consequently preferred by the amphibia.

On the 27th, following still a southerly direction, we arrived at Matloang, a charming little Lighoya village, built on a stream whose name it has appropriated (a source of the Tikue.) Mapika, the chief of this place, a civil young man, pleased us much. We preached to him the truths of the gospel in regard to which he said to us after prayer, *Thanks! thanks!* and his subjects after him, with one accord, called out, Thanks!

It was there that we set at liberty a little prisoner that he might have a chance of saving his life. For three days he had been suffering at the bottom of a lanthorn from cold, from hunger, and from thirst, resisting all our endeavors to make him take food, so that it had become necessary at last to give him his liberty. This prisoner was a young hedgehog. Every one knows that this animal is naturally timid. It is no sooner touched than it cries out, contracts itself, rolls itself up in the form of a ball, and presents nothing but spine. From this comes the name it has received from the natives,—*Tlong,*—a word, the plural form of which is employed to express a very abstract thought,—that of shame, *litlong.**

The Bechuanas, to amuse themselves with a bashful man, tell him to comb himself with a hedgehog, in order that his natural shame may pass over to that, which is the type of the feeling; the huntsmen also, when they can lay their hands on one of these harmless little creatures, scratch with his prickles the muzzle of their dogs, that they may become more hardy in catching game and attacking wild beasts.

In regard to the formation of the abstract term which I have just mentioned, I may observe that it is not the only one of this kind known in Sechuana. The word *piri,* for instance, which means hyena, has given rise to that of *sepiri,* secret place, and to the expression *ka sepiri,* in secret. In itself the word *piri* is only an onomatopee of the roaring of the hyena; but this animal lives in the most obscure and deep recesses, and the term has been transferred from the animal to his cave, and from this to whatever is done in private without being seen.

Is another example of the formation of these abstract terms desired? In Sesuto, *tlumula* signifies *to unsheath,* then *to pierce,* used figuratively; and by a double meta-

---

* The word shame in English has no plural, that of *litlong* in Sechuana has strictly speaking no singular.

phore, *to be afflicted, to suffer,* in the passive sense.—
Matlumula-a-pelu, sorrows.   If instead of this last word
one were to use the phrase *poignards of the soul,* he would
not be far from the original.*

---

* It is scarcely necessary to remark that this kind of analogy betwixt words
and their meaning is very common in all languages.   To give only one example *crux* with the Latins signified a *cross,* a *gibbet;* *cruciare,* to suffer punishment, pains of body, and of spirit.   Amongst christians *to have many crosses*
is to pass through many trials and afflictions, which brings us pretty near to
the sense of *matlumula-a-pelu,* as explained above.

CHAPTER XXI.

FROM Motloang we had only to travel about eight miles to reach the capital of the Lighoyas, which is called Entikoa. We entered it on the evening of the 27th, amidst the acclamations of the people. A line of men, armed with short but strong javelins, was formed to mark our way, who cried on seeing us : *Lumelang, Makhoa lumelang!* That is to say, Hail, oh Whites, Hail! For some days they had been expecting our visit without knowing us. So that little reasonable as was their joy, it was neither defective in order nor in affection. They helped us to unyoke, and they made for us a fire of brushwood, around which they seated themselves to look at us. Makuana, their chief, soon appeared, and he grasped our hands. He sat down on the ground like his people, by the side of us, and we heard him say to our mantetis guide, probably without supposing that we understood what was said, " Brother, tell us, are these men men of peace ?" " Thou hast said it, my master," answered Monaile, " They are men of peace." " What is your name friend ?" " I am Monaile." " Monaile ! What has brought your masters to our place ?" " They are barutis, who go from place to place publishing good news. As I have told them that you govern this people, they have come to see you in order that they may teach you also some of the truths which they know." " You say that

they do not rob others of their goods. Do they not?" "No,
Makuana, they do not rob others of their goods." "Good,"
replied the chief, " Good, it is very good." And on
that he turned to us to ask a small present of tobacco,
which was given to him.

He wished then to learn from our own mouth, what was
the design of our visit, on which point we fully satisfied
him. The negro petty king had heard tell that there were
missionaries in the country, but *missionary* was to him
a man, and nothing more. It was of importance to enlighten him on this subject, and to make him understand
every thing aright ; for otherwise the savages would not
have believed that strangers had come amongst them
without some bad design. If they had more confidence
on this point, they would seldom lay murderous hands
on travellers whom they and all fear and respect at
first, though they become free and importunate* with them
afterwards, without making use, however, of violence.
The Lighoyas, at least, throughout looked upon us with
a respectful fear, which would almost have sufficed to
have kept from all wicked attempts, a people naturally
timid, who scarcely know the whites, and *their iron
pots*, but by what they had learned from old legends.†
The word morimo, which we frequently employed, produced moreover a magical effect on the minds of the natives; many of whom took us for tutelary gods (merimo.) I have not a doubt that others, on the contrary,
took us for some new kind of *beast*. No one, however,
did us any harm, nor probably did they dream of doing
so, for which we desire to bless the Lord.

---

* This remark recalls one with which we were struck, in some book of
travels, in which it was said, that the savage scarcely knows more than two
feelings in regard to strangers, an extreme mistrust or an unlimited confidence.
It is all the one or all the other, he does not admit of any intermediate degrees
of these in his intercourse with others.

† They have a story of a race of men who use *iron pots* for the cooking of
their food, and who live in the upper parts of the house, while their wives
keep below, being busily occupied with cooking their meat. They use
earthenware pots, and their huts have no upper story.

His name was proclaimed and invoked at Entikoa, on the very evening of our arrival in that town. It was a fine sight to see the natives collected together for the first time for such a purpose, listening with profound attention to the word of life, uniting their hoarse voices with ours to sing christian hymns, and bending their knees with missionaries before their Creator. The vault of heaven, which served for our canopy, appeared to me more splendid and magnificent than ever. It was studded with an infinite number of stars, in the midst of which the queen of night gently glided through the azure, presenting to my ravished sight her noble silver front, a fit emblem for modesty. *The sight of that star of night is at once affecting and sublime!* There, in so retired a corner of the world as that in which we then were, I felt as if enchanted on hearing an assembly of rude Africans repeat, word for word, the vows and supplications which were ascending from my heart on their behalf to the Giver of every good and perfect gift. The following day my colleague preached in his turn to the inhabitants of Entikoa the doctrines of salvation, and made them acquainted at great length with the object of our journey. At the same time he demanded of Makuana, if he wished to be made acquainted with the truths of the gospel. To this question, the prince answered joyously in two words, *Yes, I and my people!*

We went then to examine the valley at the top of which stood the town. One might have imagined that he saw a group of sixty or eighty soldiers' barracks, built in a circle, on an artificial terrace. We found also an extensive piece of excellent land, black and sandy, where a number of plantations of millet and of maize, as also of sweet reeds, rose to the height of upwards of seven feet. It is watered by a considerable stream of good water, called also Entikoa; on its banks the foundations of a missionary station might be dug if necessary, although the Enta or Matlaking, and above all the Kei-cop, appeared to us preferable for this purpose, were it only for the abundance of

wood found there, while Makuana's place is rather far
from wood. The chief himself seemed inclined to go
down a little further to the south, in the direction of the
Kei-cop, and he assured us positively that he would do so
" if we could procure a missionary specially destined for
him."

I cannot tell what it was that pleased me so much with
this man ; perhaps it was his affable and smiling air, the
sweetness of his eyes and his voice, his open forehead, his
mien, ordinary it is true, but for all that pleasing ; also a
tendency to corpulency, with a handsome person, and at
an age when a man is most agreeable,—namely, about
forty-five.

As our young men found Makuana so good natured,
they made him eat potatoes, on which they had spared
neither salt nor pepper, for they had laid on both most
plentifully ; but one thing not less amusing than that was
that the chief so far from being put about, returned without ceasing to the dish, saying, that our spices were *the
little things which make one eat the rest.*

A recital of his misfortunes, and of those of his tribe,
will enable others to understand what idea we had formed
to ourselves of the petty king of the Lighoyas. This good
man is rich in land, but is poor both in goods and in
talents, and consequently he is but ill obeyed, being
indeed known, as they say, by his misfortunes alone. He
related to us himself, that his father Mopete was slain by
the father of Moroco, the reigning chief of some thousands
of Barolongs, who reside at Thaba-Unchu ; his other
forefathers, Motete and Moisetse, lived on the Noka-
Tlou, where there are still a good number of old towns of
theirs, but quite abandoned. From that quarter the seat
of the small lighoya empire has been transferred more to
the south-west, to Entikoa. This removal took place in
consequence of the continual provocations to which they
were subjected by the Zulas of Mosolekatsi and the
Mantetis. But here Makuana found in the Korannas
enemies quite as much set on his destruction as were they.

VIII. CROSSING THE ORANGE RIVER

Indeed, these brigands have never ceased to plunder the tribe from the first day that they knew it. They possess no advantage over it, either in numbers or in courage, but that which fire arms gives over an insignificant assegai, and horses, over a people who go only on foot. More particularly Piet Witvoet has constantly made war against Makuana and his subjects, from whom he hath taken away in succession their herds of oxen, of sheep, and of goats, their millet, their maize, and even their children, to procure in exchange for these little slaves, powder, and brandy from the cape farmers, or from the *smousen,* or travelling dealers, who engage in such traffic.* Oh the deadly inequality of arms! Nothing has done so much harm as this to South Africa. A kraal of Lighoyas is always certain to take to flight before seven or eight Korannas or Griquas on horseback, and who come each armed with his gun. Then all is taken away, and the huts are often burned.

After so easy a victory, these heroes return to their mole hills, where they tell, like arrant scoundrels, of booty, of carnage, of exploits, and of plunder, and say, full of pride, of the poor Lighoyas, " that they are the cows, and themselves the calves," or again, " that the Lighoyas sow but that they reap." Still the ten or twelve thousand subjects which Makuana may have would give much less advantage to their enemies than they do if they were less widely scattered than they are, and less under the control of subaltern chiefs, who unfortunately heed little their petty king, and if he in form would adopt some system of general policy, instead of leaving every thing to be rectified as it may. Even his own brothers, Maleke, Raleketuane, Engatu, and Molitsane, contravene his orders, which tends not a little to the dismemberment of the tribe. The last, in particular, is remarkable for his spirit of independence,

---

* The dutch word *smous* means German Jew. This name is given at the Cape to those shopkeepers and retailers who go to barter, in the country, clothes and divers other articles for cattle and ivory, at the usual profit of *cent per cent.* They call them *smousen,* or usurers.

and I suspect that he has retained much more of the Lighoya than the name. This Molitsane, in 1823, when he was, it is said, very powerful, and also very absolute, destroyed the settlement of Makuasi, compelling the Wesleyan missionaries, whom he found established there, to abandon it. Then he moved into the district of Philippolis, where his people lived in a great measure on depredations which they committed on the colony of the Cape. It is now some years since Molitsane passed from the neighbourhood of Philippolis to Beersheba, and then he came to live in the missionary district of Mekuatling, with a retinue of six or seven hundred men. This vagabond chief, for the designation is only too appropriate, adroitly assumes the dress, speech, tone, and manners of the tribes around him, as the camelion is supposed to take the colour of the objects which are near it. Does he go to see the Burolongs, he puts on, like them, a long and well fitted cloak of jackal skins, gaily anoints his body with yellow clay, and speaks serolong with a tone rather loud, it is true, but liked by those who know that dialect. With the Basutos, on the contrary, Molitsane appears in a costume more modest than the first, and not so well fitted, and he speaks sesuto. He visits the Griquas in leathern or moleskin trowsers, a vest of the same, a striped shirt, and with wretched shoes of the country on his feet, his head covered with a stuff hat, very much slouched ; he arrives amongst them on horseback, a gun on his shoulder, and followed by a young *agter ruiter*, their kind of groom, nay, (can one say more ?) he tries their dutch brogue, of which the following may be taken as an example : *Ih is hier maar gekome.. om een spraak met u alles te heb..en zeg..dat ons moet niet altoos so baia steel..en malkanderen plaag.* That is to say, for this will require a good translation, " I have only come to speak to you all, and to say that we must not be always robbing one another, nor molesting one another so much."

For all this there is nothing to hinder Molitsane going to Entekoa (if he ever go there) accoutred in true lighoya fashion, that is to say, his loins covered with a jackal skin, a gnu skin thrown over his shoulders, sandals on his feet, carrying in his left hand, besides his little square shield, a javelin or two, and to complete the whole a good club in his right hand. Arrived there, perhaps it might happen that he would meet with people who would refuse to give him the title of *Motaung* (*the lion* man,) but he would claim it as his right; and probably he might set about, swearing by the lion in every respect as much as they do.

I must explain this expression. All the Bechuanas and the Caffers have *national names*, which are very variable, and they have names *of tribes*, which they do not change. Under the first of these designations I would class the natives of the country subject to a petty king, and under the second, all those who have sprung from a common parent, like the different tribes of Israel amongst the Jews. When they speak of themselves as the people of a nation, the natives employ the term *Sechaba*, which corresponds exactly to our word nation, as I have just explained. They say in that sense, the nation of Moshesh, of Sekoniela, of Makuana. If on the contrary they speak of the ancient families to which they respectively belong, they use the word *seboko*, which signifies literally *glory*, and in such a case the *cast, tribe, or family* of a people. In this way it would be most incorrect to say, the cast of Moshesh; it would be necessary to say, the *glory of the crocodile* (kuena;) for such, in fact, is the reptile which the tribe of Moshesh *reveres*, which *they sing*, from which *they designate themselves*, and by which *they swear* (all expressions consecrated by use;) they say also, without being able to tell why, that it is *one of them*, their *master*, their *father*; in fine, they represent the elongated form of its mouth in marking the ears of their cattle, not only as a distinctive mark for the cattle, but in some measure as a kind of family coat of arms.

In the same way the Mantetis are generally called *Bakuabi,*—*those of the wild cat*; and they are distinguished by their reverence for that animal. It is not with them any more than with the others a *national* name, but the name of the family or of the tribe.

As for the ancestors of Makuana, they revered the lion, which is still done by their descendants; whence comes the ancient and celebrated designation (as ancient as it is celebrated in the country) of *Bataung,* or *those of the lion,* but commonly called the Lighoyas. Not that there are not to be found amongst this people, as well as amongst others, many people who revere instead of it some other animals, according to their respective casts; but the majority of that nation are *Bataung,* and, of course, do not recognise as sacred to them any but the king of the forest. They never kill one but with deep regret ; with the false fear of losing their sight, they look towards him when dead, but if the thing must be done they carefully rub their eyes with a piece of his skin, in order thereby to avert the imaginary danger, as well as to perpetuate a superstitious reverence. They carefully abstain from touching his flesh as other people do ; for how could one think of eating his ancestor (mogolu) ? Whilst the powerful chiefs of these lands are proud to clothe themselves with his skin, which they ostentatiously throw over their shoulders by way of royal mantle,—at Entikoa, and throughout the territory of Makana, no one dare use it as fur.

The denomination Lighoyas comes from a powerful chief, whose subjects did him the honor to assume his name, a custom which thereabouts is very common; and in the same way they are now sometimes called the Bamakuana. It remains to be seen which of these names will prevail some time hence. But that of Bataung cannot be changed in that way, which is a happy circumstance for those interested in statistics. The evil attaching to the ancient but permanent designations of the *tribes* assumed from the animal held sacred amongst them, and sometimes

from a vegetable similarly regarded * is that they all, to
say the least, foster superstition, besides having all the appearance of bordering on the doctrine of metempsychosis,
and even to a certain extent on idolatry.

The Lighoya nation is, as has been already seen, pretty
numerous for these countries, but too much scattered, and
held slightly together, except in the indissoluble bonds of
the tribe which have just been discussed. It is necessary
to add that since it has been itself almost entirely deprived
of its cattle by its neighbours, it has given itself, in a very
great degree, to agriculture and the chase. If the tribes
which have done it so much injury, would only apply themselves as much as they to the labors of the field, there can
be no doubt but they would soon become more honest and
more wealthy than they now are. The Korannas in particular would suffer a little less from hunger, and would
give himself less to plunder.

The cultivation of the millet, to which the Bechuanas especially give themselves, requires incomparably more care
than wheat; it occupies them eight months in the year.
At first sight this might appear an evil; one pities them,
and yet it is that, in a great measure, which renders them
so gentle and so quiet, compared with the tribes which are
less laborious than they.

The millet seed has scarcely been put into the ground,
when they have to fear the worm and the caterpillars, especially if the ants fail to destroy these animals. The natives
ingeniously endeavour to call these to their assistance, by
means of bones which they bruise and bury in their plantations. Then come all the little insects, commonly called
wheat lice, which get into the stalk. Often also a great
frost comes which blasts it in a morning; then after that
there are myriads of locusts. Against all these evils,

---

* I know also a tribe of Caffers, tall, strong, and most symmetrical, called
Amalaka, or *those of the sun*. Their natural designation is *Balegao*, from the
name of one of their chiefs. They came, some time since, from the neighbourhood of the country of Dingan, and settled in the country of the Basutos ;
many of them in Moriah itself. These blacks reverence the sun.

except that from frost which is irreparable, the natives make fires of brushwood, the smoke of which in some measure destroys or drives the enemy away ; especially, as these credulous agriculturists imagine, if these fires have been lit by the hands of an avaricious and cheating sorcerer, who may, with a mysterious air have cast therein certain plants known only to himself, with a little sheep or cow dung, and some of the hair of a klipspringer, or of the pluck of an elan. Who can tell all the ingredients which may enter into the product of a pyrosophy so new ?

I may mention, moreover, that it is necessary to repeat and pay again for these *purifications* of corn (*meseletso,*) when the birds in their turn attack it. So the poor content themselves with raising in the midst of their field a mound of clods ; mounted thereon, they fight from morning till night against all kinds of winged robbers, such, for example, as the sparrows, the finches, the rooks, which cut off the stalks most neatly, and carry them away. I have heard many Lighoyas say to the wild pigeons, " Begone, ringdoves, pass on to my neighbour !" And I have also seen them, at once shout with all their might, clap their hands, cry, wave clothes in the air, strike their shields, and throw stones at the enemy. They would then add, " Away, go, I chase, I must also eat !" Such a racket reminded me of the precept in the Georgics : *Et sonitu terrebis aves,* which Delille, I may remark in passing, seems to me to have mutilated in neglecting to render the word *sonitu,* which there is no reason to suppose a parasite in Virgil.*

But since it is with him rather than his translator that I have to do, I may observe in regard to what he says of the goddess of the harvests,

> *Prima ceres ferro mortales vertere terram*
> *Instituit....*

that he is not the only one who, together with antiquity, has attributed the invention of agriculture to a female.

* He translates it simply : *Chasse l'avide oiseau.*

In a country like Africa, where the woman at once sows, weeds, watches the corn, reaps it, grinds it, and makes bread of it for the man, with what little assistance he may give her, she deserves in some measure that one should give her the honor of that invention. See, then, how the Bechuanas have dressed up this fable. Formerly, they say, immense fields of millet covered the earth ; the corn came of itself, without labor, like a universal harvest which had sprung up of itself, and grown of itself, or like the verdure which adorns the plain. At that remote period they allege that men lived on roots and cow dung, while the ox fed on the corn, the virtue of which remained for a very very long time unknown to men ; at length, however, it became known to a woman, thanks to her jealousy. Her husband had a young concubine, whose charms won his heart. He had also an only daughter, for whom he entertained the most tender affection. The wretch was only indifferent to his *great wife;** and she, her passions being roused by the coldness of her husband, conceived the project of poisoning her rival ; so cruel is love when enraged ! One day when she saw her lying on a mat of sorrow, she flew to the river, gathered some heads of millet, crushed them between two stones, cooked them with water, made of them a round and soft loaf, which she gave to the sick woman to eat, saying to her, " The plant which has produced this ball is medicinal, it may be able to cure thee." The man seeing the danger to which she might expose herself, if allowed by him to eat something which they did not know, said to his little wife when they were alone, " Let us eat this bread together my beauty ; if they have cast a fatal lot for thee, and thou must die, I wish also to die with thee." So they ate it, but without sustaining any injury. The jealous woman for a considerable time brought them more of it every day. The husband took it with feigned appearance of gratitude, and went to eat it in secret with the sufferer, until she had

* An expression consecrated by use, which signifies the first wife of a man, his spouse, properly so called, or if one likes it better, the mistress of the house, the *huisvrouw,* according to a dutch term more appropriate than any other that I know.

recovered, when she appeared fresher and more enchanting than before. Upon this, as the tale goes on to say, the baker set about to cook also for herself. And her man,* without, perhaps, loving her the more for it, learned from her from what kind of grain she made such good bread, and the way in which she obtained it. And he, a new Triptolemus, began to cultivate the corn and to live upon it, instead of roots and cow dung. Soon every one wished to learn his art, and they began to imitate his industry, which ended in cow dung falling into complete disrepute amongst all nations.

As a hunting people the Lighoyas do not want talent. It has already been seen that they take a great deal of game in round pits, about six feet deep, which they dig on the banks of pools, or in the paths which lead to them. I know also few animals which they would not also boldly attack with the assagai, with the assistance of their dogs. The game on which they chiefly live are the antelopes, such as gazelles, gnus, and cannas, which abound in their country. It would appear that of all these the gnu renders itself the most formidable by its address, its courage, and the power of its horns. It is for this reason that, in their odes on the animals, the Bechuanas describe it as a warrior :—" The gnu is a man," say they in its praise, " it is a man, we fight together. But we overcome the father of greatness amongst the rocks, and his courage yields to ours."

By the expression "father of greatness" *(ra lebe,)* we must understand an animal of great height, and consequently dangerous. It is often applied to the canna, or cape stag, but still more frequently to the gnu.

The greater part of the wild beasts known amongst the Basutos and the Mantetis, are to be found also in the plains of the Bataungs. There the lion is of a fawn colour, while in the Malutis it is of a darker hue, and has a black mane, from which it is called the black lion. Towards the

---

* *Man*, for husband, is an expression common amongst the ancients (*vir ejus.*) The Africans seldom, if ever, employ any other expression.

Yellow River, but not to the south of it, grisbocks, buffaloes, and some few giraffes, are met with. We no longer find there the hyppopotamus, which formerly abounded in the Caledon, but which has disappeared since the population on its banks has increased. The Lighoyas say that amongst these noble amphibia the male is always longer than the female. In the spring the latter drops her little one among the reeds of the river ; when the calf is about a month old, she begins to take her to the water on her shoulders ; at the age of four months he swims alone. In the summer the hyppopotamus seldom leaves the bed of the river during the day; but it is otherwise in winter. At night he appears particularly furious. They superstitiously allege that he pursues furiously those who mourn for the dead, and will go even two or three miles to catch them and crush them under his feet, and that even though it should be a whole month from the commencement of their mourning. His flesh supplies the people of the land with an insipid food. They assert that his bones contain little marrow. Of his hide they make shields, sandals, whips, bridles, and stirrups.

The usual method of taking him, is to attack him when he is at the surface of the water. They then pierce him with darts, consisting of a short blade of iron flattened, pointed at the end, and well sharpened, with a long shaft of wood for a handle The animal as soon as he is struck plunges to the bottom of the river ; then he reappears, as if to invite a second stroke ; and he sinks and rises in this way many times in succession. Soon his companions, troubled and irritated by the smell of the blood, fall upon him, bite him, and drive him to the shore, where he dies, and becomes the prey of the savages. Thus, at least, have the Lighoyas described to me this hunt, to which I must not forget to add that they repeat with great rapidity the following words before they begin it :

Maghoghubisi a ra molonguaniana patlana a lingopé maghobisi ki maya lé bossiu puu puu puu cubu cubu pépa nguana ré boné kieo tupa é shéu a moghokaré a tlobogania maliba kaoféla sé gu atléla.

That is to say, "The stooping heads, sons of a father with the mouth of a little child, the stooping heads pasture at night. Friends of the deep waters, pooh! pooh!.... Mother of the rivers! Take up thy child, let us see it.... Look at this white wood of the Mogokae, which troubles all the deep holes.... It is going to stab thee."

The hyppopotamus carries its head low. It is mammiferous, and about as large as the elephant; its immense mouth is compared in derision to that of a child. It feeds in general by night, seeking deep and clear water; when it comes up to breathe, it produces a sound which one may almost express by these syllables, *pooh—ooh, pooh—ooh*.

In case of danger the mothers make their escape, carrying their little ones on their back. The Lighoya natives seek these amphibia in all the deep holes, from which they try to drive them by ferreting them out, and by disturbing the waters, in order that they may kill them by means of a strong assegai, with a long white handle brought from the Caledon.

Such, when I analyse it, are the ideas which I find in the short song of the *cubu*, or hyppotamus, quoted above.

The country of the Lighoyas, and in general all that part of the valley of the Orange River which we have traversed, although less rich in the estimation of ornithologists than some other countries of South Africa (as for example Caffraria, properly so called,) possesses nevertheless a considerable variety of birds. Amongst the larger and more common must be mentioned the ostrich; then two species of enormous vultures, of which the one is of a grey slate, the other of an ash color and white under the wings; and a third carnivorous bird, the beak of which is bent from the base, and the wings are prolonged beyond the tail, as in the goss hawk. Under the lower jaw there is a kind of beard formed of stiff hairs like those of the *laemmegeyer*, mentioned by Dumeril. The English of the Cape call it the *golden eagle*, on account of the reddish color of its neck and belly; and the dutch farmers, *lamvanger*, or *lamb seizer*, because it is accustomed to seize, and carry off to its aerie, a lamb or a kid, according as it

may pounce upon the one or the other. I have in my
possession a specimen of this bird, which I intend to send
to the directors of the Paris Missionary Society, and
also a curious little vulture of a very light bay, with
black plumes in the wing, erroneously called *witte kraay*
(white crow) by our neighbours, the farmers. At Paris
any one may verify these notes and complete them
if necessary. I must not neglect to add, with the
view of making the country of which I speak better
known in the particular aspect of it which now engages our attention, that there is no want of spar-
row-hawks, kites, large and small tarsels, and owls.
The common crane is also met with in all the lower
parts ; here and there also the crowned crane ; and the
secretary bird, which the natives call indifferently by a
name which is borrowed from the two long feathers of
its tail, and by another which intimates that it leads the
life of a *hermit*, or *mokheloga* in sesuto, because it is never
found in company with other birds. I have also seen
every where a species of wild turkey, of the size of the
bustard, to which it bears so great a resemblance that in
the colony it is known by that name amongst the english,
but it bears the name of *paauw* (peacock) amongst the
dutch. It is a little larger than the peacock of Europe,
and it is very dainty eating. A number of the other
birds of the country which are good eating, are a pretty
species of hen, very like common poultry, guinea hens,
wild geese, ducks, bats of which there are from six to
nine varieties at least, wood pigeons and turtle doves, partridges, both of the large and of the small sort, two or three
sorts of quails, as many varieties of ibis, to say nothing
of the so-called cape thrushes, wood cocks, larks, and
many other birds, not so well known as these. Amongst
the very small birds, all unhappily devoid of song, there
are several tolerably pretty according to our opinion.
Such are the drongos, commonly called cape fingahs ; the
widows, called also dominicans and red shoulders, the
color of the plumage of the males of which changes regu-

larly once a year ; the fiscal, a kind of *souïmanga*, almost as brilliant as the humming birds. It is of a green plumage, passing into yellow, gold, or some other shade, according to the point of view whence it is seen. The english at the Cape call it the *green laury*, and the natives *tale tale*, which signifies *green green*.

The indicator (*cuculus indicator*) so well known throughout almost the whole of South Africa, is not found, so far as I know, in the Malutis. It is met with among the Lighoyas along the Kei-cop, and it is very common in the country of the Zulas and of the Baperis. This interesting bird is indued with a wonderful instinct for the discovering of the hives, or nests of wild bees, and to lead thither by its peculiar cry the *ratel* (gullo mellivorous) which is very fond of honey, and also the woodpecker, which eats the larva contained in the cells, and even man himself ; but all that with a view to its own interest, according to an observation of Sparrman ; for this author says, " The Indicator is very fond of the honey and eggs of the bee, and knows very well that when a hive is captured there is always some of the honey spilt, which falls to him as his portion ; or that the huntsmen will leave him a part of the booty as a recompense for his services. Nevertheless, adds the swedish traveller, the manner in which this bird communicates to others the discovery he has made is as surprising as it is well adapted to the purpose." Sparrman had observed that when the bees' nest was at a considerable distance the bird in general made long flights, awaiting his hunting companion at each stage, and inviting him anew to follow him ; but that he made shorter flights and repeated his cry more frequently in proportion as he came nearer to the hive.

I also saw with surprise, adds he, what others had previously related to me, that when the bird through impatience has gone too far in advance of his companions, especially if the roughness and inequalities of the ground have prevented them from going on. He flies back again to them, and by redoubled cries which manifest a still greater impatience, he accuses them of being so slow. In fine, when he has arrived at the hive, which may have been constructed in the cleft of a rock, or in the hollow of a tree, or in some hole in the ground, he flutters ·above the place for some seconds, a fact of which I have myself twice had ocular demonstration. That done he alights and rests quietly, most frequently concealed in some neighbouring bush, awaiting the final result, and expecting to receive his share of the booty.*

To these observations which are now very generally known, I will add another less interesting, it is admitted, but quite as well established as the others ;—it is that the Indicator with his constant cry of *cherr, cherr, cherr,* often leads people upon a serpent, or to the den of a panther, or of a lion, so that the natives, notwithstanding their great regard for him, cannot always follow him without fear. One of them in speaking to me of the danger which he found to arise from that circumstance added, with a smile, as a description of a plan not unfrequently adopted by them, that the best means of finding wild honey without danger is, to catch a bee, push a pretty long piece of straw into the anus, and set him at liberty ; one can then easily keep him in sight, and he will not be slow in leading you to the nest.

* See Kay's Travels and Researches in Caffraria, page 368 &c., whence these observations have been taken.

CHAPTER XXII.

On the 28th of April departing from Entikoa after our morning service, at which Makuana and his subjects assisted, we encamped in a Lighoya kraal, called Tlogotlogo (Head Head,) on account of two little round hills commanding the view of it. The inhabitants gathered around the wagon to listen to a religious address from these words of the royal prophet, " O praise the Lord, all ye nations: praise him all ye people." Unhappily our auditors understood very little of the spirituality of the gospel, which was then preached to them for the first time. What convinced me of this was, they alleged that nothing was more precious than a herd of cattle or of sheep. " And your souls ?" we asked,—but it was necessary to explain the term. Their attention being once directed to the subject, I must say, I was pleased with their conversation. One of them said that what we call *the soul* is that which the Bechuanas call *the heart*, and he was probably correct; although they say as we do of a deceased person that he has given up the ghost (*moea*.) A second person said that the soul was something which is found in the heart, and a third maintained that the soul was something diffused through the entrails. So that on the whole it appeared evident to us that these people were not altogether strangers to the doctrine of the existence of the soul. On other occasions we have had incontestable proofs that the natives also knew something of moral evil, of conscience, and to a certain extent of punishment attached to crime by an unknown being, whom they vaguely call by the name of Lord, and of Master of things (*Mongalinto.*) For example, one day when I was with them, one of the Lighoyas proposed to me some rather puzzling questions, such as these, " Our ancestors who died without knowing any thing of the gospel, will they all be lost ?"—a question to which the apostle Paul replies in his epistle to the Romans, " As many as have sinned without law shall also perish without law....." In my turn I desired them to tell me whether the blacks had a conscience. " Yes, all have one," they said in reply. " And what does it say to them ?" I asked. " It is quiet when they do well, and torments them when they sin." "What do you call sin?" " The theft, which is committed trembling, and the murder from which one purifies and re-purifies himself, but which always leaves remorse. To defile the couch of a neighbour is also a thing which we blame, and our parents marry us young to preserve us from evil desires, which insnare men and keep them in constant bondage. Those who curse their father or mother are cursed of all. When it thunders every one trembles ; if there are several together, one asks the other with uneasiness, *Is there any one amongst us who devours the wealth of others?* all then spit on the ground, saying, *We do not devour the wealth of others.* If a thunderbolt strikes and kills one of them, no one complains, none weep ; instead of being grieved all unite in saying that *the Lord is delighted,* (that is to say, he has done right,) with killing that man, and that the thief eats thunderbolts, that is to say, things which draw down upon men such judgments." There can be no doubt, they suppose, that the victim was guilty of some crime, of stealing most probably, a vice from which very few of the Bechuanas are exempt, and that it is on this account that fire from heaven has fallen upon him. From this it would appear that they are not altogether strangers to the idea of an avenging providence. The ener-

getic expression, *a thief who eats thunderbolts*, is so
common amongst them that it has passed into a proverb.
On the 29th, in the morning, we had another religious
service for the benefit of the inhabitants of Tlogotlogo.
At the conclusion of it we presented to them some seed
potatoes, hired one of them as a guide, and resumed our
journey towards the west. After having proceeded about
five miles, we reached a Lighoya kraal, but were unable
to get near the people; they had probably taken us for
enemies, so we passed on the outside. A little further on
four deserted villages presented themselves to our view.
The huts were in good condition; around two of them
the maize and the millet were ripe for the sickle. At
the sight of these fields, beautiful yet sad to look upon, our
guides exclaimed with indignation, The Wicked Pi! this
is the name they generally give to Piet Witvoet. I suppose that seeing the approach of harvest, at which season
the Korannas generally make their devastating incursions,
the inhabitants of the places we found so desolate, rather
than be kept there in continual anxiety, abandoned the
country, and, perhaps, they were wandering in the desert
without either hearth or home, and living on game.
These villages were situated on the north side of a mountain, called Mopororo (cataract.) There we found good
water, green pasturage, and a small forest of mimosas,
the sight of which was most refreshing to us on leaving
the plains of Seghoya, where the eye can scarcely discover any where a bush. The site of Mount Mopororo
seemed to us admirably adapted for the establishment of
a missionary station, and it appears to be the very one
that Makuana had in view when he spoke to us of remov-
ing to the Kei-cop, which is very near. This river, at the
place we crossed it, was about thirty five or forty feet in
breadth, and was more shaded than any that we had seen
on this side of the Orange River. Willows, in particular,
abound there as well as the wild olive tree, and the black
thorn. This part of the country is much frequented by
travelling boers from the Cape, who, finding excellent
herbage, deserted by the natives through their dread of

Lith. de Thierry freres.

IX. **MATEBELE WARRIOR** of the Pacarita tribe (true Kafir type)
Over the forehead a sheep-bladder, worn as amulet—behind the head two crane
wings, attached to the hair with a string—a necklace of red berries—armlets and
belt of glass beads—*Sinku* or buckler of buffalo-skin—tails of wild animals hanging
down from his belt. The position of the warrior has been chosen in order to conceal
his complete nudity.

the Korannas, have there freely pitched their tents, and have even built a good many stone enclosures for their herds.

In the Kei-cop there are found many different kinds of fish, of which the largest is the barbel, a fish generally abounding in the rivers on the western side of South Africa, but strangers in those of the eastern, where, by the way, it is alleged that eels are very common, whilst there is not one to be found on the other side. These facts ap·pear strange, and they well deserve the attention of trav-ellers, to whom I give only an hear-say, that they may verify them if they have the opportunity.

During the 30th of April, and the 1st and 2nd of May, our journey was destitute of any thing remarkable. After crossing the Tikue, abandoning the westerly direction to follow a southern line, we arrived at a considerable branch of the Kei-cop, called Tikuane, which has its source in Mokuatling, or Mekuatling (the Marls,) situated to the west of Buchap. The country on this side is mountain-ous, and well peopled by Lighoyas, Matebeles, and Basutos. But the west is inhabited almost exclusively by gnus, quaggas, and antelopes, of which there are great numbers, as we ourselves have seen. The plains on which such a variety of animals graze are divided by little lakes of fresh water, and are covered with marsh, reeds, and bulrushes. The bugs, unknown further up in the streams of the Malutis where it is colder, infest these lakes, and stagnant water of the valley of the Modder. I may remark, in fine, that both in the high and low countries leeches are very numerous.

On this side of the Tikuane, we found Mokhasi and Puchane, two little kraals, occupied by very poor and wild Bushmen. Further on, arriving at Ralitabane, we again met with some families belonging to that unfortu-nate tribe. They had established themselves on the declivity of a high mountain, in the midst of about a hun-dred Lighoyas. Khomoatsane, the chief of this place related to us how Piet Witvoet had forced him the year

before to remove to this place from Makuana's, and to
his narration, this man, who was in appearance benign,
added, "that he had not a single child left to him, nor
had any of his subjects." We would not at first believe
this, but on examination we found that there were none
but infants in the village ; children from four to twelve
years of age there were none, and the poor people assured us that they had been torn from them by the
Koranna with an armed force. These poor people were
inconsolable. Some of them complained that having
recognised their children with the farmers passing through
the plain, they went in haste to entreat these whites to
restore that which was dearer to them than any thing on
earth besides, but they hastily replied, "Get you gone,
wicked Caffers; these children are ours; we bought them
from the Korannas, and wish only to have to do with
them." Such occurrences are very common amongst the
Lighoyas. Another call for shame on the inhuman ad-
vocates of the most horrible of traffics, carried on as if
men were not the property of God alone!

It is very painful to me to state that the Bushmen of
Ratilabane, and as many of them as I have known on this
side of the Orange River from Philippolis to the Malutis,
have all lost a great part of their children in the manner
described. These unhappy beings live in small isolated
groups, and rarely do they dwell any where but in bushes
and caverns, these being considered the places of greatest
safety. But even there the dutch boers discover them, run
right upon them, fire on the kraal, kidnap the children,
and, when they can, carry off even the adults, and sometimes, with a barbarous refinement on cruelty, tie them, it
is said, to the horse's tail. If unhappily the captives make
any resistance or attempt to run away they are shot. At
all events there remains a sure booty and a more valuable
one in the children.* This practice of depredation by

* That is not to say but that the little Bushmen, when they can, secretly escape from their master ; they do so to return home. Lately I saw two about
seven or eight years of age, who had undertaken the long and dangerous

the wandering farmers or hunters, is so common that the cry of alarm and signal for flight amongst the Bushmen is the following, " *Tuntsi, a sea a nge u kunte,*" " *there is the white man; he is coming to take away our children.*" Tuntsi is employed to designate a white man ; it properly signifies a shooter. It is the onomatopy of the report of a gun, *tuntse.* In ordinary language the whites are called *kho.*

At Ralitabane the millet harvest had been bad, and the herds had been seized by the Korannas, all which, with other misfortunes, had involved the people in great distress. We should have rejoiced to have relieved them had it been in our power, but we had only a little wheat to give them, and a few potatoes, a plant which we would fain hope may in a short time become naturalized in that country for the benefit of the people who inhabit it. Besides this we offered consolation to the natives, and promised to them better days if they would love God and keep his commandments,—according to the gospel promise, which was explained to them, " Seek ye first the kingdom of God and his righteousness, and all these things shall be added unto you."

Pursuing our journey we arrived next at Koba, a new village of the emigrant Lighoyas, who, following the example of their brethren of Ralitabane, had come to seek an asylum in the missionary district of Thaba Unchu. The village is situated on the top of a great mountain, which serves as a rampart, at the foot of which runs from east to west a stream tributary to the Modder. The caravan easily crossed this and, quickening our pace, we soon reached the Wesleyan station of Thaba Unchu.

There the Rev. Mr. Archbell welcomed us as friends and fellow-laborers, which rendered his christian intercourse and his kind attentions to us. as delightful as

journey from Natal to Jammerberg, where their parents lived. During the journey these children lived on roots, and slept in the bushes or under rocks. One day they had the good fortune to find a gnu, which had been killed by the lions, from which they took the more tender parts, such as the lungs, and eat them raw, not knowing how to make a fire, or not daring to do so.

they were welcome. The important institution directed by this faithful servant of Christ is so well known that it is not necessary to say much about it. About a thousand huts made of marsh reeds, and each protected by a railing before it, compose the station. They are dispersed over two large parallel hills, which are separated from each other by a stream of water. Near the top, and looking down upon the town, stand the church and parsonage, also two small buildings, one of which contains a printing press, and the other the forge belonging to the station. It is peopled chiefly by Barolongs, who came in 1834 from the north-west, and submitted to a young chief of an amiable disposition, called Moroko. There are also some Baharutsis to be found there, who are subject to an old morena, who was ruined by Mosolekatsi, in whose neighbourhood he formerly lived. It is painful to look upon him, so much cruelty is there in his countenance. It may be that it is not without reason he has been called *Taona,* or Little Lion.

In the village of the former chief, the only one we visited, we saw an old man who had been blind for some years, and who superstitiously attributed his blindness to the pretended witchcraft of his enemies, and refused to be undeceived. We saw many idle, and others occupied in preparing or sewing furs, for which they procure, from the Basutos, cattle and caffer corn. These furs are very well made, and are much valued in the cape colony, where a single fur of a panther or wild cat of middling size sells for between two and three pounds sterling. The more common ones are made of the skins of fallow deer and other red-haired animals, particularly of jackals, which abound amongst the Lighoyas and higher up towards the Molapo, as they do generally throughout all countries. They are carnivorous animals like the fox, which they resemble in habits and form. The agile and cheerful barolong and batlapi hunters, go with their packs of meagre and little dogs into the deserts at much expense, fatigue and trouble, but always singing this favorite couplet : —

Pukuyue !....
Unketele, unketele,
Ki gu etetse, ki gu etetse,
Ka linao

Hollo ! Jackal !
Pay me a visit, pay me a visit ;
I have paid you a visit, I have paid you a visit,
On my feet.

As soon as they discover one they pursue it armed with a light javelin, which they do not handle without some address, and they animate themselves and their pack by a roaring recital of these words, " Fly little trotter yonder ! Into the river to your burrow, son of a father whose skin is worth a heifer of two springs." Instead of two springs the original is two labours. A labour is a common expression amongst the Bechuanas for a year. I am not aware that they have any other name for summer, which clearly shows that their habits must always have been as much agricultural as pastoral ; yet the tribe of Moroko devote themselves but little to agriculture, excepting that they cultivate a little millet, indian corn, and pumpkin, which work devolves on the women. The young men lead their father's flocks to pasture in the neighbourhood of the town, to which they return every two or three days with leathern bottles full of milk, which they make the pack oxen, called *lipelesa,* carry. This duty is always performed without the assistance of women, but in return it is on them alone falls the work of providing the shepherds with bread and beer ; they make flour of the millet which they carry in earthen pots and baskets on their heads, without ever making use of one beast of burden in any of those numerous journeys which they make. In character, religion, and customs, the Barolongs resemble the other Bechuanas.

Singular to tell an apologue of Confucius has been preserved amongst them. There is blended with it an account of depredations such as are committed in

their country. The following is their version of the tale
of the blind man and the paralytic. " It is said, that
once upon a time a band of black men going in quest of
plunder found their way to a tribe of shepherds, without
making any noise and without baggage; they crept on their
stomachs like serpents, full of cunning, and like these vile
reptiles, each armed with a dart extremely fatal,—the
assagai. The moon was yet young; it had long set, and the
fourth watch of night approached darker than ever, and
not less fatal to the shepherds than usual.* Several herdsmen surprised in their too peaceful sleep were inhumanly
slaughtered, others a little more fortunate succeeded in
flying, dragging after them their wives and children. Rapacious hands pillaged the huts and burnt them, carried
off the flocks from their accustomed sheep folds, to convey
them to their horrible dens. The return of the brigands
according to custom was at a running pace, and marked
by a thousand rejoicings.

" In the morning when the eye of day † illuminated the
scene, there were two wretches seen, the one deprived of
sight, the other without legs. The latter on perceiving
a companion in misfortune, said to him, " You too have
you been left ?" he answered, " Yes, they have left me
without resource, but who are you ?" " A lame man
without resource." The blind man replied, " I was thinking to myself, that if I had eyes I should have followed
those who stole away from danger by flight." " As for
me," rejoined his comrade, " I had eyes to see where
they went, but I cannot move." " As you are blind but
have feet, if I supply you with eyes and you take me upon
your shoulders, would not that be equivalent to a whole
man ?" The proposal being good was accepted, so on
they went together, each confiding in the other. A river
soon interrupted their steps, the lame man said to his comrade, "There is the ford, let us cross there." Further on he

* The attacks are generally made during the first quarter of the moon, and
about three or four o'clock in the morning.

† The Malagasy thus designate the sun (*mazo andro.*) It is an expression
as simple as it is poetical, and therefore I take the liberty to use it.

said again, " There is a precipice ; let us turn aside."
Further on still, he discovered a spring of fresh water,
at which they stopped to drink and to rest a little ; after
which they resumed their journey.

" On their way they arrived at a place where an antelope
was expiring, either wounded by huntsmen with a deadly
dart or brought there by the propitious gods in kindness
to the two travellers. The lame man, on seeing it, said to
his companion, " There is a dead animal, put me on the
ground, we must skin it." Immediately he was put down
he asked his friend for the knife which he had, to cut open
the antelope. But the blind man enquired first, " When
you have flayed it whose will it be, who is its owner ?"
" Mine," answered the lame man, " Does it not belong
to me by good right, since it was I that saw it." The
blind man replied, " But should it not to belong to me ?
who carried you ? tell me !" They disputed a short time
together. At last the blind man asked, " Where is it ?"
The cripple answered, a little piqued, " Go quickly and
flay it, for I do not see it any more, it is hidden from my
sight." After thus jangling with one another for a time,
they set themselves to work to cut it up together,
saying, " Since together we make but one complete body,
one is as good as the other." The animal served them
for provision during the journey, and by short stages they
arrived at the place where their companions were staying.
There is nothing more lovely than mutual assistance."

This pretty fable, as has already been observed, is not
new. It may be read in agreeable verse in Florian. But
if the ground work do not belong to the Bechuanas, both
in its style and in its incidents it is certainly theirs. Besides this they possess some productions of their own,
such as the following, which is very short, and the more
likely to be useful amongst them that they always know
what is right better than they practise it. It relates to a
hyena, generally in this country called a wolf, perhaps,
from its resembling this animal in habits, so that it serves
well as a figure for thieves. But a thief, do what he will,

must meet sooner or later with some more wakeful than
himself, and on this account it is not amiss that they send
the wolf to a Bushman or Moroa. The story may be
rendered in french verse as follows :—

LE LOUP ET LE MOROA.

Un loup, que la faim dévorait,
Sortit au soir, selon son habitude,
Comme tout le monde dormait ;
Il n'allait pas, je crois, sans quelque inquiétude.
Mais qu'advint-il ?—Il grimpa sur le toit
D'un archer moroa, très-prompt et fort adroit,
Qui l'aperçut, comme il voulait descendre
Dans la maison ;
Et lui cria : " Fripon
Si je ne puis te prendre,
Pare ce dard."
Lá fléche siffle, porte, Il était déjà tard
Pour croquer de moutons d'opérer sa retraite ;
Le coup le fit dégringoler
Du haut du faite.
Quel métier plus scabreux qui celui de voler !*

On the 7th of May we quitted Thaba Unchu, and encamped about six leagues to the south of it, in a village of
Basutos, who received us very kindly. It belonged to a
chief who was formerly rich and influential, but the troops
of Mosolekatsi attacked the very summit of Thaba Unchu
where he lived. Mpchuchane (that was his name) was
beaten, despoiled of his flocks, and forced to seek refuge
on the top of Thaba Patsoa, where he afterwards died in
misery. His son Mmpolu, who succeeded him, is at present happy, and he is generally esteemed.

This Mpolu is the sovereign of Thaba Patsoa, one of the
most beautiful mountains of the country, and one of the
best peopled. It presents an imposing aspect, more espe-

*THE WOLF AND THE MOROA.

A wolf famished with hunger, went out in the evening, as was his custom, when every
body was asleep. I believe he did not go without some anxiety. But what happened ?
He mounted the roof of a house belonging to a moroa archer, who was a very active
and cunning man, and who perceived him as he was preparing to descend into the
house. He cried out to the wolf, "Rogue, if I cannot take thee, parry this!" The
arrow hisses ; it strikes. It is now too late for the devourer of sheep to make his retreat,
the stroke has made him tumble from the height. What trade can be more slippery
than that of stealing?

cially to the spectator who is near it. It rises in a plain,
by regular steps, composed of very hard rocks, of a kind
of brown free stone near the base, but higher up they are
softer and of a yellow colour. These immense banks or
shelves of stone form terraces all round the mountain, and
it is on these, at little distances from each other, that
the kraals of the natives are erected to the number of
eight, exclusive of a few huts, which the shepherds of
Moroko have built there. When, from these various
points, one sees a thousand little columns of smoke rise,
expand, and finally lose themselves in the air,—when one
hears the noise of the shepherds mingling with the bleating
of their goats and the lowing of their oxen, one finds in all
this an air of life,—an indescribable feeling of wildness,
which produces a sensation of pleasure, particularly in those
who have still to endure for some time longer the tedious
silence of solitude. The mountain of Thaba Patsoa appeared, judging by the eye, to be rather higher than the
peak of Thaba Unchu, which may be eight hundred and
fifty feet in height. It is also more beautiful in appearance, and, if my memory serves me right, in the form of
a regular table of pentagonal shape. Its sides are very
steep, and the only path by which you can arrive at the top
is so narrow and hidden that the platform makes a perfect
natural fort for the natives, where they found themselves
in greater security than in any other place, when compelled to seek refuge there, with their cattle, from the restless
and rapacious spirit of their neighbours.

On Sunday the 8th, in the morning, Mpolu gathered the
greater part of his people together, and attended worship,
which was celebrated at the foot of the mountain, amongst
the rocks. The assemblage was numerous and attentive.
Our prayers were repeated, sentence after sentence, by the
savages, and our songs of praise they followed as well as
they could The subject of discourse was taken from the
10th chapter of Luke, the 11th verse, "The kingdom of
God is come nigh unto you." A previous conversation
on the nature of sin, and its fatal consequences, had pre-

pared the natives in some measure to understand us by making them feel the necessity of a Saviour. They were all willing to acknowledge themselves guilty before God and their own consciences, except one unbeliever, who pretended to be better than his brethren, because he had been amongst the farmers, and had learned a little of their customs, in which he foolishly made religion to consist. We had also in the assembly a kind of pythoness, who fell into frightful convulsions while hearing us. She cried, laughed, gesticulated, rolled on the ground, and exhibited many apish tricks, until they carried her out of the congregation at our request. When service was concluded she again began her work, and it was not a little amusing to see her. This foolish diviness kept herself apart, standing alone, her two hands raised to heaven and rolling her hideous eyes, in short, putting her whole body into contortion. Now she affected a sullen silence, then rousing herself afresh, in order to get into a fury, she cried out *hae! hae! ha! ho!* and raised a hundred other sharp cries, all very short. At a certain sign which she made, and which the natives only understood, each of them drew near to her, and we did the same. The people said while going, " Now she is about to speak to us."

They stopped about ten feet from the sibyl, which allowed us a glimpse of two red wild eyes and an agitated countenance, covered with perspiration. Suddenly she began to groan, then gave a loud but single cry, then dissembling, she said in a calm and sententious manner, '' Mpolu, thou lovest darkness. (*Long continued silence.*) Thy ways are the ways of darkness. Mpolu, it* says to me that I must say to thee: Where is thy father ?—*He died from starvation.* Mpolu, it says to me that I must say to thee: He is not dead ; he is here in the shade of the wood ; he sees thee, seest thou him, seest thou him ? Mpolu, it says to me that I must say to thee: When thou shalt wash † thyself call thy friends. It says to me

---

* Meaning the oracle, no doubt, but I translate all literally.

† That is to say, when thou shalt purify thyself.

that I must say to thee : When thou shalt wash thyself, sacrifice a red heifer. It says sacrifice also a black sheep." Here Mpolu observed that he had no black sheep, but the oracle replied not, and the pythoness continued in a very calm voice, "Mpolu, it says to me that I must say to thee : Why didst thou formerly complain of the drought? *Hunger devoured us.* It says to me that I must say to thee: Makest thou the corn to grow out of the earth?" Lastly the sorceress added, most likely by recollecton of the sermon she had just heard, "Mpolu, I see two pierced hands. (*Great and long continued silence.*) Why refusest thou to believe the words of the barutis? Why do thy people ask before they will believe, whether the barutis have also seen those hands pierced with nails?"

The scene, though grotesque, was to the natives a very serious thing, and to us it had a kind of mythological interest. In particular the facts which she revealed will be found important. When one lives in the country it is easy to see that all the natives venerate their ancestors, offer to them numerous sacrifices, and look on them as tutular genii, at the same time that they dread their power, sometimes malicious ; that at times they invoke them, while at other times they abjure them. These domestic deities correspond to the *manes* of the ancient pagans. They are called *Merimo* among the Bechuanas, and *Ezetuta* and *Melemo* among the Caffers, whose religion has this peculiarity, that in serpents they see, and also adore, the souls of their forefathers.

The gods of the Africans are, moreover, supposed to enjoy eternal youth, and to be endowed with a wisdom very superior to that of mortals, amongst whom it is easy for them to come when they wish, without the being seen, excepting by the so-called diviners. They live and move about freely in large caverns under ground, the happy possessors of herds of oxen without horns, of a blue color, mixed with red and white spots. From the following imprecation used by the native women, it would appear that there are both great and lesser gods,—" Let the perverse man perish, both here and amongst the very least of the gods."

In fine, these infernal deities, like those of the classic Tartarus, prefer black victims for their sacrifices,

Offre une brebis noire aux noires déités.*

Besides the merimos, a word, I repeat, which is used for the souls separated from the body, for the infernal deities, and for the tutular genii of the deceased, the natives also believe in something which is neither soul nor body, and which is supposed to hold a middle place between them, that is the shades, which they call *lirite*. These are spectres or shades of the dead, which again remind us of the mythological system of the ancients.

It appeared to us that the natives meant, under the denomination of *litutsela*, sometimes to refer to the dead, sometimes to the shades, and sometimes and specially to malignant and restless spirits, other false images of superstition. These fantastic creations of ignorance frequent the banks of rivers, precipices and dark and retired places, where they amuse themselves, like the hobgoblins, by tormenting simple people.

The Zulas told us that their nation acknowledged two principles, the one good, called *Naputsa*, the other evil, called *Kofane*. A legend very current in the south of Africa clearly reveals this doctrine, and we also find in it a presumption in favour of the immortality of the soul, and of the return of the dead to life. Here it is in its simplest form :—

" The Lord (*Morena*) sent in the former times a grey lizard with his message to the world, *Men die....they will be restored to life again.* The camelion set out from his chief and arriving in haste, he said, *Men die....they die for ever.* Then the grey lizard came and cried, The Lord has spoken, saying, *Men die....they shall live again.* But men answered him, the first word is the first ; that which is after is nothing."

* DELILLE's Translation of the Eneiad, Lib. vi.

But with all that, the incredulous mortals in this country have always hated the lively and cunning cameleon, whilst they love the slow but innocent grey lizard.

We do not yet know whether they think heaven is entirely desert, but at all events they have a presentiment that they will be much happier there than they are on earth. This appears evident from their Hymn for the Afflicted, and which is particularly dear to the widows, who are in the habit, when some one dies, of meeting in an open space in the town to sing it in chorus at the same time, beating the ground softly with their feet, and using a kind of tambarine, made of an earthen vessel, covered with the skin of a kid.

The two first verses of this mournful poem are as follows :—

> We are left outside (meaning on the earth)
> We are left for sorrow,
> We are left to despair,
> Which increases our miseries.

> Oh, that there were a refuge in heaven !
> That there were a pot there and fire !
> That there were found a place for me !
> Oh, that I had wings to fly thither !*

The desolate widow adds to these lamentations :—

> O foolish woman that I am,
> When evening comes I open my window,†
> I listen in silence, I watch,
> I fancy that he returns ! (her husband.)

She whose brother has perished in battle, on the other hand, says :—

> If women also went to war,
> I would have gone, I would have thrown darts by his side (her brother's)
> My brother should not have died,
> The son of my mother should rather have returned, he should not have gone half way,
> He should have pretended to have hurt his foot upon a stone.

* The following is another version :—
> Why have I not wings to fly to heaven ?
> Why does there not come down from heaven a twisted rope ?
> I would cling to it, I would mount on high,
> I would go and live there.

† A small opening left at the top of the entrance to the hut.

At the conclusion all the women cry out in a louder
voice :—

> Alas ! are they really gone ?
> Have they left us here ?
> But where are they gone ?
> That they can thence return no more
> To see us again.
> Are they really gone ?
> Is hell insatiable ! !
> Will it never be full ! !

The term corresponding to the word hell in this piece,
is *mosima*, also used by the Baperis as synonymous with
Marimatle. It means a cavern in the earth, a burrow,
and by way of analogy it is used to express the subter-
raneous places of the dead, the infernal regions. We
ought to notice that the expression *to go*, signifies to die.
This use of it is not confined to the Africans. It is well
known that sacred and profane authors employ it also
in this sense. The Saviour predicting his approaching
death, said to his disciples, speaking on this wise, "The
son of man goeth as it is written of him." It is a phrase
which is at once euphonious, and which seems to intimate,
and even to imply, a new existence or another life after
leaving this. To go away, to depart, to go home to their
fathers, as at evening the cattle return to the kraal, is the
most usual way in which the natives express the decease
of a person. They ascribe the death of a young person
to witchcraft; this explains why they lament so bitterly
over premature deaths, instead of rejoicing, as they do
when an old man dies, saying as the Hebrews did, he has
fallen asleep in peace, full of days, and is gathered to his
people.

The depositaries of religion are called *Lingaki*
amongst the Bechuanas, and *Ezinyanka* by the Caffers.
These are men of simple manners like their contrymen,
but very superstitious. They offer sacrifices, circumcise
the young men, administer drugs to the sick, pretend to
make rain, conjure the storms, and predict events by
means of guessing bones, which they always carry with

them, and which they use as charms, so that they are at once priests, sorcerers, and quacks. The study of plants, magic, necromancy, and the interpretation of dreams occupy much of their time; to which they add the knowledge of some moral precepts, and of numerous traditions or legends, which they permit no one to reveal.

On the 9th of May, after our usual morning prayer, the caravan set out from Thaba Patsoa, and not without difficulty crossed the river Patlaletse; the next day we passed Caledon, and on the 11th we arrived safe and sound at Moriah. Our hearts were filled with lively feelings of gratitude towards God for all his care; and the inhabitants of the place appeared to be delighted to see us return. During the last three stages of our journey we saw few villages on the road, and only stopped at that of Leyuetuluri, inhabited by Basutos. On approaching the station we met some bushmen hunters, who sold us one of their bows, some arrows, and a cord made of dried grass, well twisted. The particular use of this cord or line, they told us was to make snares for antelopes, by placing them in defiles and across bogs, into which they try to allure the game, as they kill them more easily there. We have gathered some interesting accounts about these men, and we promised a notice of them, perhaps, we may take the liberty to insert it now, to render complete the different notices we have already given.

CHAPTER XXIII.

THE Bushmen, or men of the bushes, are called in this country *Baroa*, which has the same signification ; but amongst themselves they are called *Khuai*.* The more general name of Hottentot has been given probably from their language, which is harsh, broken, full of monosyl-lables, which are uttered with strong aspirations from the chest and a gutteral articulation as disagreeable as it is difficult. It is as if one heard nothing from them but *hot* and *tot*. So it is not without reason that it has been said of them, that they cluck like turkeys.

This nation is composed of a considerable number of different people, independent of one another, and scat-tered over the whole valley of the Orange, from the embouchure of the river on the shores of the Atlantic to its sources in the Malutis. Some Bushmen are also to be found beyond these mountains on the land of Dingan, and up even to the country of Mosolekatsi, on the north, where ten or twelve years ago many of them became, it is said, the prey of the black cannibals. It is a race of natives frequently met with amongst the Caffers and Bechuanas, with these, however, they have neither sym-pathies nor transactions of any kind. On the contrary, nowhere do they enjoy full freedom, but in the country

---

* This name is also given to a natural apron by which the Hottentots are distinguished from other tribes.

of the Namaquas where they are most numerous. Would not the fact of the dispersion of the race amongst the different tribes of the caffer race warrant us in supposing that it was once sole possessor of all the countries of South Africa, and that the Caffers have taken by conquest from this people what they now inhabit.

The Hottentots, called *Baroas*, resemble the others in almost every respect. They are like them of a yellow brown hue, of moderate height,* lean, and stunted; their head is large, their face large above, but depressed towards the chin, on which in general there is no beard. They have light eyes, but they are small and sunk ; their cheek bones prominent, nose flat, lips thick, hair crisp, but not so thick as that of the Caffer, whose color varies from bronze to jet black, and who are large, well made, and very robust. It is not improbable that these two peoples extend very far up along the western coast of Africa, perhaps, the one by the side of the other, though different in every respect from each other. I have read at least in *l' Histoire des Voyages* † a passage which would lead me to suppose so. " Ca-da-Mosto," it is there said, " was very much surprised to find the difference in the inhabitants so great in so small a place. To the south of the river Senegal they were extremely black, large, well made, and robust....On the other side the men were tawny, thin, and of small stature...." This parallel would be exactly applicable to the two people here, if it were stated that the Caffers are not *extremely* black, but much blacker than the Hottentots, whose color is only tawny, as is well known. In character they are quick, frank, generous, less cruel than the Caffer, but headstrong and vindictive. With a great deal of natural activity they combine extreme indolence ; they are generally sly, and very cunning, independent, and poor

* I have measured a Moroa (singular of Baroa) of ordinary stature ; he stood 4 feet, 4½ inches high.

† Abrégé de l' Histoire des Voyages, tom. I, page 334.

beyond measure, as if they had sworn at the feet of a druid to remain always free, and without possessions.

One of my friends had a young bushman servant, full of spirit, and of great originality. As these characteristics were very seldom seen in the degenerate Hottentots of the colony, it may be said that he had retained the normal character of his people in the desert. His master liked him much, and entrusted him with the keys of his house. Two or three times he even laid a snare for him to try his honesty, but it was to no purpose. Towards strangers, however, the young man was less honest. He would rob them as if it were fun. One day when he was hungry, he went to the drinking place of a *veldcornet*, a kind of country magistrate, squatted behind a bush which would conceal him, and there he waited patiently till evening. When the sheep came to drink, the rogue seized one by the fore legs and held it a little under the water; the shepherd and his flock having gone, he rose, put his prey on his back, and went and regaled his companions with it; for with these he was accustomed to share every thing, even to a pipe of tobacco or a glass of brandy.

Sometimes he would unexpectedly leave the house of his master to go and pass a few days in the fields, living on birds' eggs, the laroa of ants, roots, and game, when he could procure any. On his return home, he would salute his master, and would ask with great glee, when it was the case, how it was that he passed on such a day such and such a place, which he would designate, without seeing him, squatted on an ant hill,—not far from which his master had actually passed, perhaps, seeking him but without perceiving him. If his master should say, scolding him, "But why did you go away so thief-like, instead of telling me first, and asking for your tobacco, and also a skin to cover you at night?" the answer would be, all that was not hottentot. In fine, as this Bushman knew perfectly how to counterfeit the monkey, the jackal, and in general all the beasts of the field, the officers would sometimes, to try him, entreat him to mimic also his master; but he would answer sharply, "No, never; for it is he who gives me my bread." The quarrels of this people are very noisy, they are of daily occurrence, and they are especially common amongst near relatives, although on the other hand it is a virtue amongst them to love one's father. One old woman having fallen dead under the blows of a younger one, the friends of the former collected to avenge her death by beating the other with their clubs. Another time a baroa chief of the neighbourhood set out to hunt with two of his sons and with the people of his kraal. They erected a row of clods at the entrance of an angle formed by the mountains, to which they wished to lead the antelopes, in the expectation that when the animals arrived there they would be terrified at the sight of these little heaps of earth, would go off in single file in another direction, and would fall under the darts of a party of huntsmen placed in concealment according to custom in a ravine by the side. That done Kekhelesi, the chief, went away with two or three men to turn in a herd of gnus, which were feeding at a distance on the plain. Some people remained in ambush near the clods; the rest set off in another direction to seek for game. These last returned soon, driving before them a troop of antelopes. A gnu was killed at the ambuscade. After cutting it up they dug, with a pointed stick, a hole in a white-ant hill, and there as into an oven they put some slices of the flesh, in the midst of burning brushwood. This meat cooked, or at least broiled, it was drawn from the fire, and the whole of it eaten. Then came Kekhelesi, worn out with hunger and fatigue, and a little out of humor at having brought nothing with him. But the sight of a gnu stretched on the ground pacified him a little. His younger son, whom he found there, said to him, laughing, "As for me I have got a belly-full; dost thou see that fire there?" "Yes," answered his father, "and where is the

bit of thy game which thou hast cooked for me?...."
The foolish child turned his back upon his father, a mark
of contempt, and one of the greatest insults in all lands,
and Kekhelesi, very much enraged, let fly a poisoned
arrow at his son, which wounded him slightly. The youth
he returned the shot, but missed. The two had again
bent their bows, when the elder son rushed between them
and separated them. And at the same time he bathed*
the wound of his brother and soothed him. The others
gathered around him also, and tried to soften down his
wrath. And at night the father and the sons, and all the
company of huntsmen chattered away in the kraal as if
nothing unpleasant had happened. It was around a fire,
covered with fries and pots of meat; they had even dug
into the ground, and put there some portions of the game
to broil, a common mode of cooking with them. The
guests tore away at the flesh with their fingers, and they
used a brush, made of gnu hair, by way of a spoon. A
flat stone was their table, and water was their only
beverage.

Supper being over, the women with their children and
the young men set themselves to dance during the first
watches of the night, to the sound of a wretched tam-tam,
made of a small earthen pot, in the form of a quoit, and
covered with the skin of a gazelle, well softened, after
having been stript of its hair.

This is the only amusement known to the Baroas; it is
only practised when they have eaten and are filled, and it
is carried on in the middle of the village by the light of
the moon. The movements consist of irregular jumps; it
is as if one saw a herd of calves leaping, to use a native
comparison. They gambol together till all be fatigued
and covered with perspiration. The thousand cries which
they raise, and the exertions which they make, are so violent that it is not unusual to see some one sink to the

---

* With *Urina*, which is considered by the Baroas a specific for wounds;
when the wound is deep they cut and pare away the flesh.

ground exhausted and covered with blood, which pours from the nostrils ; it is on this account that this dance is called *mokoma*, or the dance of *blood*.

When a man falls thus out of breath in the middle of the ball, the women gather around him, and put two bits of reed across each other on his back. They carefully wipe off the perspiration with ostrich feathers, leaping backwards and forwards across his back. Soon the air revives him ; he rises, and this in general terminates the strange dance ; the employment of the two bits of reed, already mentioned, is the point which to me seems most obscure. I can give no further explanation of it, than that they constantly have recourse to it in cases of severe sickness, and that they say it exerts a salutary influence on the sick person ; I could almost fancy that there may be mixed with it something of religious rite, but I would not push this supposition too far.

The women like these merry makings exceedingly, and they attend them adorned in their best. Their head is always uncovered, sometimes even shaven, but a quantity of the hair is left, and arranged as a round tuft in the crown, like the tails of the Chinese ; and it is always plaistered with ochre, fat, and the powder of an aromatic wood, called *bogo*, a little bag full of which they carry constantly with them for ordinary use. They speckle the face and breast with red and yellow paint and white clay, so as to frighten strangers, who cannot help looking upon them all as so many hags; their forehead is adorned with a narrow band of thread, not very neatly woven, but elegantly covered externally with rings, made from the shell of ostrich eggs. The egg naturally very hard, is first boiled and softened in cold water; they then cut off the shell in small pieces which they polish, and pierce in the form of small rings, of which by their threading them like pearls they make fillets, and bracelets, and girdles, and long aprons, which hang from their middle down to their feet.

The Caffers and the Bechuanas manufacture also

bracelets, and nets of iron, which are very much sought
after by them ; nor do they despise those of bead work, or
earrings and collars of copper. Finally, they adorn
themselves, as do the Orientals, with a lace or cord of
thread, which they pass through the nostril, and tie at the
back of the head. Above their ancles and their wrist
they fasten oblong little bells, made of the skin of the
springbok, well dried, and which by means of small pebbles enclosed in them produce a sound, not very agreeable
to others, but quite to their taste.

The wives and daughters of the Bushmen in the neighbourhood of Bethulie, extract, from the bosjes-spruit,
copper ore, which they burn in the fire, and then by
bruising the ashes between two stones, they obtain a hair
powder, which is very much sought after. They pound also
the copper, and turn it to the same use in some villages in
the neighbourhood of Moriah. They collect it in a ravine at
Thaba Patsoa, a little below Jammersberg, on the Caledon, where they find also asbestos, which the women
amongst the Baroas reduce in like manner to powder, and
put on their hair. As for the men they wear only a small
piece of skin for a girdle, and a very scanty springbok
cloak. But, generally speaking, nothing about the hottentot female strikes me so much as her vanity. This is
the character of woman in all ages and in all lands. The
bible has in many passages depicted it to the life. It had,
however, escaped the attention of the ancients, and the
Africans, so far as I know, have not remarked it any more
than they.

One day I was collecting information in regard to the
Baroas of Impachoane, settled in our neighhourhood; one
of their wives could speak Sesuto well, and consequently
could have been of great assistance to us as an interpreter. But no; not at all. This ugly dame preferred
accusing herself of ignorance, fingering her bead work,
adjusting her little antelope kaross, pirouetting every now
and then before us, and giving herself airs. The natives
call this ill-nature ; but no, it was only levity and display.

The Bushmen do not marry so early in five as the Caffers and Bechuanas, but generally at the age of eighteen or twenty, instead of from thirteen to fifteen. Formerly they were accustomed to give a dowry of cattle to the parents of the bride, but as they have not retained a single head of cattle to themselves, they now give them only copper, or iron, or ornaments, and engage to accompany them every where to procure game for them. It is not seldom that the young man in proof of his agility darts into the plain after the antelopes, and stops not till he has run down one which he carries triumphantly to the feet of his mistress. Sometimes also he engages to wrestle with her for amusement before the public, and if he throws her, she is given to him. But frequently, in such cases, the father and mother of his belle take the staff themselves, and, reaching as far as they can, give him a few random blows, as if to assure themselves that he sincerely loves their daughter. This proof is unquestionably the less agreeable of the two, and they say that it is very common.

One strange custom is, if a woman lose her first infant, and another should be borne by her, she cuts off the end of its little finger and throws it away.* The Basutos have a similar usage, but less barbarous. They shave in such cases the head of the second child, anoint it with some greasy substance, mixed with red ochre, well pounded, and leave at the nape of the neck a very small tuft of hair, which will suffice to remind them of their first misfortune.

The female Baroa herself constructs a fire place of three round stones, fashions, varnishes, and bakes, the few earthenware pots which she is to use, weaves the frail mats of rushes under which her family finds a little shelter from the wind and from the heat of the sun ; she suckles

* One of our converts at Moriah, who grew up amongst the Baroas, assures us that with some amongst them this usage is a destinative mark of caste, and consequently is practised on all their children. Amongst the Tambukis this is also the case. We have at Moriah a Baroa and a Tambuki, both deprived of the end of the little finger on their left hand.

her infants, and decks them with care ; and in fine weather she may be seen going in haste to the fields to gather roots, especially a small white round bulb, of the nature of garlick, and commonly called *uintje* (the *iris eclulis*) which together with the locusts, which she gathers and dries in summer, and the larvae of the termites, and other similar insects, which she takes from the ant hills, constitutes with the game taken by her husband their only subsistence. In general the man cooks for himself, and the wife for herself, but whenever a pot is to be emptied, all the kraal gather round it to lick it clean. They thus go from hut to hut until there remains nothing more in the village to eat.

It is a fact that in winter they have often nothing to eat but the old gnu skins, which they put to steep in water ; they then rub off the hair, boil it on the fire, and then gnaw it if they can, which gives them sore jaws, as one of these poor people once remarked to me. I knew another such miserable being, who was reduced to feed upon caterpillars and earthworms ; not that the blacks would not be generous enough to give them in charity a basketful of millet or of maize, but these Bushmen have a great dread of being captured or shot by the dutch marauders and the Korannas ; and there are critical times at which nothing will induce them to leave their retreat.

The very sight of a white face throws them into an agony of fear. Every time I have gone near them they have raised loud cries, and sought to flee or to conceal themselves, excepting on one occasion, when I found some who knew the missionaries, and the conversation of these, religious in some measure, very agreeably surprised me. Another day I caused myself to be led through another kraal of these Baroas by a basuto chief who lived near them, and possessed their confidence. We found some huts of branches, and three or four cabins of another kind constructed amongst the rocks, with which they might readily be confounded at a distance. All these consisted

of three sticks stuck in the ground, and of two small
mats, of which one served as a screen behind the stakes,
the other as a roof; under the whole of these poor shelters,
there must then have been reposing many wretched creatures; for it might be about eight o'clock at night. I observed that the members of the family, at whose home we
stopped, were laid pellmell, each of them in a little hollow lined with a little straw, and his feet extending
beyond his little kaross, but turned towards a fire of
small wood, which was burning in the middle of this
house, or common chamber. My guide awoke them
gently, quieted by his words the shrieks of fear which
they raised on getting up, and kept them from dispersing
like a flight of starlings, if the comparison may be allowed
me. I announced myself as the white, or missionary of
Moshesh, and this recommendation, joined to the fact that
I spoke Sesuto, a dialect which the chief of the place
then present also understood, had the effect of giving
confidence to all. They asked for tobacco from me, and I
gave them a little, a portion of which was thrust into a
wooden pipe, another portion to the bottom of one made
of a siliceous stone; another by a third party into a gazelle bone. In short, the savages set themselves to smoke,
with a great deal of chattering. The old mamma took
from her neck a bit of some narcotic root, lit it at the fire,
and bringing it near her nose, snuffed in the smoke;
while a younger matron took from her bosom a small
bag of skin, containing hemp seed powder or *daga*, and
poured out a good dose of it into the hollow of her hand,
and there scraped it together with a bit of reed which
she had taken from the lobe of her ear, where she afterwards again replaced it. I must also mention that at one
of the stakes of the hut, I saw a paunch or stomach of an
antelope full of fresh water, which was taken down from
time to time, and passed round the circle that each might
drink his fill. For this purpose all that was necessary
was to introduce the neck of the bottle into the mouth,
and to press the lower part of it, to cause the water to

rise to the opening as might be done with a bladder. I there saw many things which I only knew before by hearsay,—such as the little hollows which the Baroas scrape in the ground, to burrow in at night,—the fact that they sleep with their feet out of the kaross, which is, they assured me, that they may be the more ready to escape in case of alarm. When I asked them why they did not build bush huts like the other natives of the country, their answer was that such huts attached them too much to the spot; that the enemy might burn them all alive in these huts, or kill them in some other way before they could get out ; besides they were not pliable like their own, and they did not know how they could put them aside during the day, to prevent their being seen.

In time of rain they take refuge under a rock, or in the cabins of the Bechuanas in the neighbourhood. They do not remain long in one place, partly on account of the migrations of the game, and partly that no one may know where they are to be found. It is for this last reason also that they go in very small companies, without dogs, without a head of cattle, and with the least noise and bustle possible, and that they sow no kind of grain, or even tobacco, of which they are naturally so extravagantly fond. They complain that the wandering boers persecute them, seizing almost all their children, dishonoring them if they be girls, and sometimes making eunuchs of the lads, as if it were not enough to deprive these poor creatures of their liberty, which man values most, and which belongs only to him and to God. Thus it is that the Bushmen are greatly exasperated. It is not rare to find in the caverns which they frequent, both on this and the other side of the Orange River, drawings of antelopes, painted with ochre and charcoal on the lower walls of the cave ; and in the midst of these innocent playthings, a great fat dutch farmer thrashing his Bushman, and also Bushmen surrounding a farmer to kill him. It is not very long since a dutch emigrant was so murdered in his wagon. Six months before, in the same place, another of these brutal beings having tied his *jong*, or young bushman slave, to the wheel of his wagon, where he was severely flogged for some faults he had committed, sent him then to the chase, whither he went but without bringing back any thing, which procured him another flogging. The next day his master ordered him again to run after the antelopes, and the young man said maliciously without being understood, "If I go to day 1 will kill something, for I will take good aim." In the evening he returned, his hands still empty. The boer on seeing him come, began to threaten him, but he made ready, pulled and stretched him dead on the sand; he then cried : Very well,—threw his gun on the ground, and said to the relatives of the dead man, " Now kill me," which was done on the spot. Such cases of murder are unhappily too frequent, but it is not to my taste to narrate more of them. Let these suffice to show the nature of the bondage of which I speak; the boers do not find their account in it any more than the Hottentots.

In regard to religion the Bushmen are much less superstitious than the blacks, but I do not know exactly what they profess to believe. Those of the mountains say that there is a *Kaang* or *Chief* in the sky, called also *Kue-Akeng-teng, the Man,* that is to say, the *Master of all things.* According to their expression, " one does not see him with the eyes, but knows him with the heart." He is to be worshipped in times of famine and before going to war, and that throughout the whole night, performing the dance of the *mokoma.* All the beasts of the field have marks, which he has given them ; for example, this elan has got from him only the stump of a tail; that a folded ear ; this other, on the contrary, a pierced ear....Kaang causes to live and causes to die ; he gives or refuses rain ; when there is a deficiency of game, the Maccolong say, that *their Lord refuses them beasts.—Kaang ta'ko'ga go si'ko kaa akeng'kuaing.*

One Baroa assured me that amongst his people they
held sacred the blessbok (*antilope pygarga*, Pall.) and
another antelope, the name of which has escaped me at
this moment. There are none of them circumcised excepting those who have a good deal of intercourse with
the Caffers and Bechuanas. Instances of polygamy are
rare, and adultery is less common than amongst the other
natives of the country. Widows find it difficult to get
a second husband, on account, perhaps, of the general
opinion of the natives, that the greater part of the deaths
which occur are rather the effect of witchcraft than of
disease ; but on the other hand great attention is paid to
them in the kraal, where no piece of game is ever eaten
without their having their share.

Amongst the neighbouring tribes a man has no sooner
breathed his last than his relatives wrap him up in his
ordinary cloak, make a large opening in the wall of his
hut, and carry him out that way, for they would consider it
unlucky to carry him out by the door of the living. They
make haste to place the body at the foot of a round hole,
dug under the feet of his herd in the cattle fold, whither
he is lowered ; he is then blessed and revered by the family,
and he is considered one of their gods. These interments
are so precipitate that there are people actually living in
the country, who have been buried in this way, but who
recovering from their lethargy, found means to get out of
their sepulchre. Amongst the Bushmen such scandalous
transactions never occur, because they are in much less
haste. The dead have first the head anointed with red
powder, mixed with melted fat ; then they are coarsely
embalmed, and laid on their side in an oblong pit, whither
the relatives and friends assemble to make their lamentations. They come even from the neighbouring villages
to see and to examine the body, which is then taken out
of the pit; and every one redoubles his cries and his
lamentations. At last they throw into the pit the cabin
of the deceased, and burn it above him. The grave is

then filled with earth to the level of the ground, but without any heap of stones, or appearance of a monument as the blacks have. The funeral over, all the kraal leave the place for a year or two, during which time they never speak of the deceased but with veneration and with tears, as is also the case with the Matebeles.

This respect of the natives for the tombs is an evidence, in our opinion, of a vague but firm belief which they have of the immortality of the soul, and reminds us of their proverbs, which says that *death is only a sleep,—lefu ki boroko.**

With all that, the Bushmen are so debased that they worship an insect of the caterpillar tribe, the *caddisworm.* This hermit, called by them *N'go,* constructs for itself a pretty case of pieces of straw, placed longitudinally, leaving an opening sufficiently large to enable it to put out its head and shoulders when it wishes to seek food ; but in general no other part of the larva is seen but the head and its fore feet, by means of which it attaches itself to leaves, or drags after it the case in which the rest of its body is enclosed, and into which it retires altogether in case of alarm. The Bechuana natives believe that it is very venomous, and are afraid when they meet with it in the grass on which their cattle are browzing ; but the Baroas have made it their God. One of them of whom I asked if he did not pray to his deceased father like the other inhabitants of the land, said No ; adding that his father had taught him otherwise, and had solemnly said before dying, " My son, when thou goest to the chase, seek with great care for the N'go, and from him ask food for thyself and for thy children. Mark, after thy prayer, if he moves his head describing a semicircle (an elbow or angle) which signifies that he has heard thee graciously, and that that very evening thou wilt bring to thy mouth

* This proverb of the natives involuntarily recalls that favorite maxim of the infidels of the eighteenth century, that *death is an eternal sleep.* It is seen by the juxtaposition of the two, that the deists have less correct knowledge on this point than the savages.

a portion of game, which thou shalt hold fast betwixt thy teeth, and shalt cut with thy blade of iron, with thy arm bent, and describing also a semicircle like our god." The prayer is as follows :—

'Kaank ta, ha a ntanga ë? 'Kaang ta, 'gnu a kna a sé'gè. Itanga 'kogu 'koba hu; i'konté, i'kagè, itanga i'kogu 'koba hu; 'kaang ta, 'gnu a kna a sé'gè.

"Lord, is it that thou dost not like me? Lord, lead to me a male gnu. I like much to have my belly filled ; my oldest son, my oldest daughter, like much to have their bellies filled. Lord, bring a male gnu under my darts."

I translate word for word, that every one may the better see how material and gross is this prayer of an idolatrous people, which begins by questioning first the love of his god, and asks then flesh, and only flesh. Besides, the language of the piece is harsh and barbarous beyond expression, but for all that there are cases and inversions, the latter being the natural consequence of the former, which show in the seroa some degree of development, and one somewhat remarkable; this character of the hottentot language is not to be found in the caffer and bechuana tongues, to which besides it presents too little resemblance to permit the supposition that it can have sprung from the same stock as they. The disagrreable clucks of the tongue are only met with in caffer, where they are comparatively rare ; and it is questionable whether they may not have been introduced from the seroa, as well as a number of words apparently the same in the two languages,—such for example as, *I love, itanga* in hottentot, and *itanda* in caffer, to which correspond the sechuana verb *kia* RATA ; by changing the caffer *t* into *r*, and the *d* into *t*, according to the common rule, which leaves only one euphonic letter too much, namely *n*. The clucks are especially found at the recurrence of a letter, which is of a very guttural pronunciation, like the german *g*, which presents great similarity to the *aïn* or *gaïn*, peculiar to the arabic and other oriental languages, as this

horrible aspiration recurs incessantly in the mouth of the
Bushmen, one would feel inclined to say that they bark
rather than speak.

Besides their words are too short to be flowing and
soft, too much loaded with consonants, few in number, I
think, and little varied in form. On the other hand there
are a great many accents, and the meaning of the same
word is altogether different, according to the manner of
pronouncing it. Thus, *N'go* signifies a god ; *kho,* water ;
khô, a white; *khoö,* a strap; *'ko,* a bone ; *'koö,* a tree ;
'kho, great, &c. This reminds one of what has been said
of the chinese, in common with which the hottentot has
also a great many harsh sounds in *ong, ing, ouang, eng.*
The harshness of this language pertains obviously to
its forms ; the people who speak it live under one of the
most temperate climates in the world, and learn to speak
perfectly the sechuana, which is very soft. A case in
point. I knew a Baroa chief, who has composed a poem
in Sesuto ; it begins thus :—

> Raselepe u tlula yuale-ka puri,
> U tlula yuale-ka a poko!

> Raselepe bounded like a kid,
> He bounded like the kid of a goat !

After these general observations, I may be allowed to
insert here a list of hottentot words, and another of
caffer and bechuana words, for those who take an interest
in such discussions. In doing so I will follow three of the
dialects most widely spread over South Africa, namely
the seroa or bushmen, the zula, and the sesuto.

FIRST LIST.

SEROA VOCABULARY.

ENGLISH.	SEROA.
A lamb,	Gneru-kunte,
A needle,	Kègnia,
To add,	Ga kebia,
To go,	Ga kega,
A ring,	Kakane,
A bow,	Secca,
To-day,	Ngomere,
To sit,	Isoania,
Formerly,	Kuue,
An ostrich,	Tuebe,
A baboon,	Mannia,
A staff,	Kibi,
Good and pretty,	Kebese,
Much,	Keoa,
Millet beer,	Ngoang,
A white man,	Khô,
A blessbock, *a species of gazelle*,	Kolingte,
To drink,	Ga kaga,
Scented wood,	Bogo,
Firewood,	Pko,
Good,	Tae,
The mouth,	Gu,
Earrings,	Kekele,
A shield,	Sikoku,
Broth,	Gaba,
A button,	Koatu,
Buttons,	Kokoatu,
Cow dung,	Geng ga kaoga,
An arm,	Kaa,
A sheep,	Gneru,
A camma,	Seka,

ENGLISH.	SEROA.
A canna,	Kong,
A jackal,	Chekalass & koro,
A song,	Koo,
A quiver,	Sebalabala,
A chief, or petty king,	Kaang,
A horse,	Ngangngang,
A dog,	Kuënia,
A pumpkin,	Kakung,
The heart,	Nganantu,
The conscience,	Ngoa,
A bowstring,	Nguème,
To dig,	Ga kaba,
A quagga,	Boriako,
To run,	Ga kalikoa,
A knife,	Kana,
Copper,	Lesenene, kokang,
To-morrow,	Kèbe,
The teeth,	Kentu,
A god,	Ngo,
A servant,	Motaka,
To give,	Ga koa,
To sleep,	Ga küenta,
Hard,	Thaï,
Water,	Kho,
To emigrate,	Ga kakase,
A child,	Akunte,
A wife,	Nga,
The stars,	Koang koang,
A fault,	Mokolu,
A spouse,	Nkèo,
Iron,	Sebeke,
Fire,	Kii,
A girl,	Tubitsoana,
An arrow,	Tloatloa,
Ants,	Jabang,
The cold,	Mokhüele,
The forehead,	Nga,
To smoke,	Ga schu,
A gun,	Khô,
A gnu,	Gnu,
A young gnu,	Ngai,
The knee,	Gnomateng,
The knees,	Ignonomateng,
A millet seed, *literally an eye of* millet,	Tsago-kolo,
Great,	Kho,
Hail,	Kokoso,

ENGLISH.	SEROA.
War, *the same word as fault, wrong, evil*,	Mokolu,
Grass,	Kéhé,
Yesterday,	Itolo,
A Hyppopotamus,	Togu,
Winter,	Mokhüele,
A man,	Kong,
A hut,	Ngeng,
A hyena,	Ohu,
The Korannas,	Teri,
Ugly, bad, and evil,	Komass,
Milk,	Tloang,
Animal sinews, *(serving for thread,)*	Ngueme,
The tongue,	Ngu,
A thong,	Kengnia,
A lion,	Koeng ka oga,
A lioness,	Koeng ka ngte,
Light of day,	Kebe,
The moon,	Kokoro,
A hand,	Kaa,
To eat,	Ga niang,
A skin cloak,	Ngueng,
To walk,	Ga tagagisa,
A club,	Keri,
The Malutis,	Kobane,
Morning,	Kebe,
A mother,	Ngo,
Honey,	Kèo,
Millet,	Kolo,
Marrow,	Süeng,
A mountain,	Komao,
To bite,	Ga tsii,
To die,	Ga ka,
A mat,	Kaakasi,
The nose,	Ngüeng,
No,	Gaa,
A cloud,	Turu,
A bird,	Kui,
The Orange River,	Gariep,
An ostrich egg,	Kibike,
The ears,	Engontu,
Ochre,	Kalass,
Yes,	Ngai,
Bread,	Magobe,
To speak,	Ga kekega,
A poor man,	Mokaboana
A skin,	Togu,

ENGLISH.	SEROA.
To pierce,	Ga koa,
Father,	Haho,
Little,	Nieneko,
The feet,	Nganga,
A stone,	Komao,
The pleura,	Ngoa,
A pipe,	Paga,
Rain,	Chorosi,
Feathers,	Ikui,
A door,	Geng-nganga,
A pot,	Nguaku,
Dust,	Kérushi,
To take,	Ga kia,
Taken,	Kui,
To press,	Ga koga,
The Spring,	Keu,
Beads,	Kii,
To satisfy,	Ga ikoba,
To look,	Ga inga,
To rejoice,	Ga kuia,
To laugh,	Ga kuia,
A river,	Kaba,
A stream,	Kaba nieneko,
A rock,	Komao kho,
Reeds,	Ngongosi,
The sand,	Koba,
An assagai,	Ngualase,
Blood,	Tlauke,
Bleeding at the nose,	Mokoma,
Locusts,	Kuu,
Salt,	Kung kung,
A serpent,	Ngeri,
The sun,	Nguème,
Sleep,	Küenti,
To blow the fire,	Ga sua,
A springbock,	Küe ea
Tobacco,	Kisi,
A bull,	Kuane kaoga,
Termites,	Chuchubi,
Earth,	Koba,
The head,	Nga,
A tortoise,	Ketenia,
To labor,	Ga teriteria,
To kill one,	Kong ka,
A cow,	Kaoga,
True,	Keoa,
A vulture,	Soaisa,

ENGLISH.	SEROA.
The wind,	Koba,
The belly,	Kogu,
Food,	Hôhô,
An old man,	Kobete,
Villain,	Komass,
A village,	Mokhème,
To will not,	Ga koga,
The eyes.	Ntsago.

FAMILIAR PHRASES.

ENGLISH.	SEROA.
I have been walking a long time,	Kuue ntagagisa,
Who are you ?	Ate koa?
Cause the fire to burn,	Sua kii kee,
It is only smoking,	Koba kii kuita,
The rain is coming,	Chorosi kuue a see,
I want to go to sleep,	Itanga ikege küenta,
Be seated,	Soania,
I want to speak to you,	Itanga ikekega,
No, we wish to walk,	Gaa, si tanga ga tagagisa,
Come let us dance together,	A tle a see, si kooke,
I speak the truth,	Ikega keoa,
A small thing,	Chuai e nieneko,
Why do you cry ?	Teng ga tanga khoo?
I have nothing to eat,	Ntloke hô,
I am perishing from hunger,	Ngome kukoa,
See ! The gnus !	Gnu a e e !
Run and turn them,	Akalang gnu a see,
The arrow has struck rightly,	Tloatloa a koang,
The locusts are coming,	Kuu a see,
The locusts are good,	Kuu a tae,
Our tobacco is finished,	Kisi tlo gonga,
We wish to sing,	Se tang se koa kè
One,	Te a ngoa,
Two,	Te ngu,
Three,	Te nguene,
Four,	Te nkeo,
Many things,	Te a gabe.

SECOND LIST.

ZULA AND SESUTO VOCABULARY.

ENGLISH.	ZULA.	SESUTO.
Bees,	Ezinionsi,	Linotsi.
Admirable,	Sebenka,	Tsabegang.
A lamb,	Enfanana,	Koniana.
To go,	Uku ea,	Go ea.
A needle,	Ezungulo,	Lemao.
A friend,	Zala,	Motsuala.
A ring,	Lesale,	Lesale.
To call,	Uku beza,	Go bitsa.
To call to assistance,	Uku memeza,	Go memetsa.
To day,	Namuthla,	Kayenu.
Formerly,	Khante,	Khale.
An ostrich,	Enche,	Mpechè.
To swallow,	Uku meza,	Go metsa.
A staff,	Entumpa,	Tupa.
Good and pretty,	Nthle,	Ntle.
Below,	Saze,	Tlase.
Yonder,	Kua,	Kua.
A shepherd,	Molesa,	Morisa.
A white man,	Molunkue,	Lekhoa.
The white men,	Balunkue,	Makhoa.
An ox,	Enkhomo,	Khomo.
Oxen,	Zenkhomo,	Likhomo.
Wood,	Empaze,	Patsi.
A large shield,	Sethlanko,	Mokoko.
Broth,	Omothlüeze,	Mororo.
An arm,	Mokhono,	Lechogo.
The Bushmen,	Batoa,	Baroa.
A canna or cape elan,	Emponfu,	Pofu.
A song,	Lekhama,	Pina.
To return to the charge,	Uku pentela,	Go petela.

ENGLISH	ZULA.	SESUTO.
A chief or petty king,	Enkhose,	Morèna.
A road,	Enthlela,	Tsela.
The hair,	Lenocle,	Meriri.
A dog,	Encha,	Ncha, Mcha.
The heavens,	Lepezulu,	Legorimo.
To circumcise,	Uku sonka,	Go bulla.
Circumcision,	Lesongo,	Lebullo.
The heart,	Ethlezoe,	Pelu.
To be known,	Uku seoa,	Go tseyoa.
The conscience,	Enfalo,	Lechualo.
To console,	Uku tselesa,	Go tserisa.
To comfort oneself,	Uku iselesa,	Go itserisa.
Region,	Lezoe,	Naga.
To covet,	Uku lakaza,	Go lakatsa.
A horn,	Ponto,	Lenaka.
The body,	Mozempa,	Mele.
A quagga,	Empenze,	Pitsi.
To flow,	Uku rota,	Go rota.
To cause to flow,	Uku roteza,	Go rotetsa.
To run,	Uku kenchema,	Go titima.
A knife,	Mokôa,	Tipa.
To cover,	Uku kuala,	Go kuaela.
To fear,	Uku saba,	Go tsaba.
To cook,	Uku penga,	Go apea,
A cook,	Mopenke,	Mopei.
The thigh,	Moleze,	Serupe.
Copper,	Ezempe-e-mothlope,	Tsepe-e-cheu.
To-morrow,	Uku sasa,	Gosasa.
To cut meat in pieces,	Uku sega,	Go sega.
To put to flight,	Uku kocha,	Go lelekisa.
A soothsayer,	Senoge,	Senoge.
A household god,	Setuta,	Morimo.
The household gods,	Ezetuta,	Merimo Barimo.
To say,	Uku yela,	Go yoetsa.
The fingers,	Ezentumpa,	Meno.
A servant,	Mofongase,	Motlanka.
To sleep,	Uku lala,	Go roabala.
Hard,	Khône,	Thata.
Water,	Amanze,	Metsi.
To crush,	Uku ganta,	Go gata.
To break the head,	Uku kabatela,	Go bata.
To go astray,	Uku lathleka,	Go latlega.
An elephant,	Nthlofu,	Tlou.
A child,	Montuana,	Nguana.
To take away,	Uku tuta,	Go tuta.
To bewitch,	Uku kokula,	Go loïa.
The shoulder,	Thlakute,	Lethlakure.

ENGLISH.	ZULA.	SESUTO.
And,	Na, no,	Le.
The stars,	Zenkuenkueze,	Linaleri.
To do,	Uku eza,	Go etsa.
To be made,	Uku ezoa,	Go etsoa.
Fawn-colored,	Mpofu,	Tsetla.
A woman,	Omofase,	Mosari.
Iron,	Esempe,	Tsepe.
To shut,	Uku fala,	Go kuala.
Thread,	Moento,	Lesika.
A girl,	Entumpe,	Moruetsana.
An arrow,		Mochu.
Fire,	Maione,	Molelo.
A smith,	Lelala,	Lelala.
To make an earthen pot,	Uku bopa,	Go bopa.
Ants,	Zenkuluane,	Linkulana.
A gun,	Sempamo,	Setunia.
A gnu,	Mponkono,	Purumo.
A little gnu,	Mpotunguana,	Purunguana.
The knee,	Entlolo,	Lengole.
To swell,	Uku 'kupela,	Go pipitlela.
A deep pool,	Zenzeba,	Boliba.
War,	'Mpe, (the same word as Evil,)	Ntoa.
Grass,	Oyane,	Boyoang.
Winter,	Bosenka,	Maria.
A man,	Entonta,	Monna.
A young man,	Montuana,	Motlankane.
A hut,	Einthlu,	Intlu.
A hyena,	Empeze,	Piri.
Here,	Neno,	Kuanu.
An island in a river,	Sethlekethleke,	Sethlekethleke.
Day,	Motla,	Motla.
A day,	Motla ope,	Motl'omong.
The Koranas,	Ebekhotu,	Bakhotu.
There,	Kona,	Gona.
Ugly, bad & evil,	'Mpe,	'Mpe.
Milk,	'Mpete,	Lebese.
Milk food,	Mabese,	Mabese.
To dart,	Uku beza,	Go betsa.
A thong,	Mokhèlo,	Lerapo.
The tongue,	Oleme,	Leleme.
Praises,	Ezebonko,	Litoko.
Father of praises,	Bomoka,	Balipoko.
To praise,	Go bonka,	Go boka.
The moon,	Eniaka,	Kueri.
To rise,	Uku ema,	Go ema.
To rise from bed,	Uku funka,	Go choga.

ENGLISH.	ZULA.	SESUTO.
A magician,	Enyanka,	Ngaka.
The hand,	Seanthla,	Seatla.
To eat,	Uku thleoa,	Go ya.
Eaten,	Uku thla,	Go yeoa.
Skin cloak,	Enkubo,	Kubo.
To walk,	Uku gampa,	Go tsamaea.
Marriage,	Zeeo,	Nyalo.
To marry,	Uku lobola,	Go nyala.
The sea,	Leoanthle,	Leoathle.
Mother,	Onionkp, .	Ma.
Honey,	Zinioaze,	Linotsi.
Millet,	Amabele,	Mabele.
Me,	Eme,	Nna.
A heap,	Ngobu,	Kobu.
Mountain,	Enthaba,	Thaba.
To mount,	Uku kuela,	Go nyologa.
Death,	Enkofa,	Lefu.
To die,	Uku nfa,	Go shua.
A mat,	Ole 'khase,	Moseme.
Black,	Nyama,	Nchu.
Food,	Go-'konta,	Go-ya.
A cloud,	Olenfu,	Leru.
Night,	Bosuku,	Bosigo.
A bird,	Enyone,	Nonyana.
Birds,	Zemyone,	Linonyana.
To shade,	Uku tuza,	
The shadow of a person,	Otuze,	Seriti.
The shadow of a cloud,		Lesüeti.
The shadow of a tree,		Moriti.
The ear,	Enthlebe,	Tsèbè.
By,	Ka,	Ka.
To speak,	Uku chumaela,	Go bua.
Every where,	Gon'ke,	Gotle.
To pass,	Uku thlula,	Go feta.
To ford,	Uku selela,	Go tsela.
To pierce,	Uku thlaba,	Go thlaba.
Feather,	Ethlo,	Ntate.
The feet,	Ezenyao,	Mautu.
A stone,	Leye,	Leyoe.
A gunmaker,	Nkhanka,	Khaka.
To sting,	Uku puma,	Gopuma.
To plant,	Uku palula,	Go lema.
Plants,	Mete,	Limela.
Medicinal plants,	Makhôbalo,	Litlare.
The rain,	Enfula,	Pula.
A feather,	Lepape,	Lesiba.
Many,	Banye,	Bangata.
A door,	Monyanko,	Monyako.

ENGLISH.	ZULA.	SESUTO.
A pot,	Empenza	Pitsa.
A hen,	Enkonku,	Khogo.
To take,	Uku thabata,	Go enka.
Near,	Ntutse,	Caofi.
Strife,	Enkhane,	Khang.
To quit,	Uku sia,	Go sia.
Wherewith,	Ka ane,	Ka'ng.
A root,	Monfu,	Motsu.
Of beads,	Bothlalo,	Sefaga.
To satisfy,	Uku suta,	Go khora.
To collect,	Uku bukena,	Go bokella.
To recruit,	Uku bunta,	Go khèta.
The virgin,	Muso,	Muso.
To reign,	Uku buza,	Go busa.
To rejoice,	Uku taba,	Go taba.
To rest one's self,	Uku pumuya,	Go pumula.
A river,	Monfula,	Nuka.
A little river,	Monfulana,	Nukana.
A rock,	Entugu,	Lefika.
Sand,	Mothlaba,	Letlabate.
Blood,	Lekaze,	Mari.
Bleeding of the nose,	Monkola,	Mokola.
A path,	Mosela,	Mila.
To separate,	Uku lamulela,	Go namulela.
A serpent,	Enyonka,	Noga.
The sun,	Lelanka,	Letsatsi.
Sleep,	Botoko,	Boroko.
To go out,	Uku puma,	Go tsoa.
A spring bok,	Esèmpè,	Tsépè.
To be silent,	Uku tula,	Go kutsa.
To keep another silent,	Uku tulisana,	Go kutsisa.
Termites,	Bothloa,	Bothloa.
To fire a gun,	Uka tunyesa,	Go tunya.
The earth,	Pase,	Lefatsi.
Earth or ground,	Mobu,	Mobu.
Head,	Ekanta,	Tlogo.
To kill one,	Uku bolala,	Go bolaea.
To conquer,	Uku kueza,	Go tlula.
Conqueror,	Tekeze,	Motluli.
A vulture,	Lekanko,	Lethlaka.
The wind,	Moea,	Moea.
The belly,	Seso,	Mpa.
Truth,	Sonto,	'Nete.
Meat,	Enyama,	Nama.
An old man,	Lekenkù,	Lekeku.
A town,	Monze,	Motse.
A garrison town,	Lekanta,	
To fly (speaking of birds)	Uku fuka,	Go foka.
Truly,	Tute,	Rure.
The eyes,	Maso,	Mathlo.

ENGLISH.	ZULA.	SESUTO.
An assegai,	Mokonto,	Lerumo.
The Zulas,	Amazulu,	Bakoni, Matebele.

NUMBERS.

One,	Nie,	Ngue.
Two,	Pele,	Peri.
Three,	Tato,	Taru.
Four,	Nne,	Nne.
Five,	Thlano,	Thlano.
Six,	Tatato,	Tselela.
Seven,	Senonia,	Shupa.
Eight,	Tobe-e-meno-e-mele,	Roba-meno-e-le-'mé-ri.
Nine,	Tobe-e-mono-o-mo-nie,	Roba-mono-o-le-'mong.
Ten,	Chume,	Shume.
Eleven,	Chume-le-ne-mofu-'monie,	Shume-le-mochu-'mong.
Twelve,	Chume-le-ne-mefu-'mele	Shume-le-mechu-'méri.
Thirteen,	Chume-le-ne-mefu-'metato,	Shume-le-mechu-'méraru.
Fourteen,	Chume-le-ne-mefu-'mene	Shume-le-mechu-'mene.
Fifteen,	Chume-le-ne-mefu-'méthlano,	Shume-le-mechu-'methlano.
Sixteen,	Chume-le-ne-mefu-'metatato,	Shume-le-mechu-e-tseletseng.
Seventeen,	Chume-le-ne-mefu-e-nonie,	Shume-le-mechu-e-shupileng.
Eighteen,	Chume-le-ne-mefu-e-tobe-meno-e-mele,	Shume-le-mechu-e-robileng-meno-e-le'meri.
Nineteen,	Chume-le-ne-mefu-e-tobe-mono-o-mo-nie,	Shume-le-mechu-e-robileng-mono-o-le-'mong.
Twenty,	Machume-a-mabele,	Mashume-a-maberi.
Thirty,	Machume-a-matato,	Mashume-a-mararu.
Forty,	Machume-a-mane,	Mashume-a-mane.
Fifty,	Machume-a-mathla-no,	Mashume-a-mathla-no.
Sixty.	Machume-a-matatato,	Mashume-a-tselet-seng.
Seventy,	Machume-a-nonie,	Mashume-a-shupi-leng.
Eighty,	Machume-a-tobe-meno-e-mele,	Mnshume-a-robileng-mono-e-le-'méri.
Ninety,	Machume-a-tobe-mono'mong,	Mashume-a-robileng-mono-o-le-'mong.
A hundred,	Ekholu, *the great number*	Lekholu.
A thousand,	Sekete, *the finishing number*,	Sekete.

MONTHS.

January,	Thlolaya,	Perikóng.
February,	Ontaza,	Tlakula.
March,	Mmeza,	Tlakubela.

ENGLISH.	ZULA.	SESUTO.
April,	Mpitloa,	Mesa.
May,	Motekanyone,	Motreganong.
June,	Ofufane,	Pupchane.
July,	Ofufu,	Pupu.
August,	Mpatoe,	Pato.
September,	Otsoetsana,	Logetse.
October,	Nguanazele,	Mpalane.
November,	Uputu'nguana,	Puru'nguana.
December,	Osibathlela,	Tsitoe.

CHAPTER XXIV.

In the different countries of South Africa, included in the colony of the Cape, and bordering on that settlement, we find only two distinct aboriginal people, the Hottentots and the Caffers.

The former, so far as we can judge from analogies of colour and form, belong to the Mongolian race. The varieties of the Hottentot are the Namaquas, the Korannas, and the Bushmen. Formerly they were powerful, rich, and comparatively happy, but the capture of the Cape of Good Hope by Europeans, greatly injured them in these respects. They are now confined almost exclusively to the district of the Orange River, but originally they appear to have occupied all the southern point of the continent. It is well known, for instance, that formerly they were spread over the whole extent of the colony of the Cape, and were to be found on the Fish and Keiskamma Rivers. It is not more than twenty years since they were to be found in great numbers in the country of the Zulas, but having offended one of the chiefs of that people, he avenged himself by destroying them. The old names of Keisthanoma, Keicop, Gariep, and others not less ancient, which have been given to many of the mountains of the country are hottentot. We meet with the drawings of the people in all the caves of South Africa, and the other aborigines call the south *boroang*, the same name which they

give to the Bushmen; while they say that as for themselves, they have come from the north and from the north-
east; and their ordinary manner of expressing themselves,
in speaking of the origin of the different tribes amounts to
this,—" First appeared the Hottentots, then the Caffers,
and then the Bechuanas. The Hottentots adopted as their
weapon the arrow; the Caffer and the Bechuanas, their
masters, took the assagai for theirs."

From this we gather that the Hottentots must have been
the most ancient inhabitants of the land.

The Caffers appear to be a race quite distinct from the
first. They approach nearer to Europeans in the height
of their stature, in the elegance of their form, in the cast
of the skull, and in their intelligence; but their black
skin and crisp locks give them a strong resemblance to
the Negroes. Generally speaking, all the tribes inhabiting the country comprised between 18° 33' lat. S. and
22° lon. E., from Greenwich, and the Ocean are called
Caffers; but in a more restricted sense this designation is
given only to those tribes which go completely naked;
and that of Bechuanas is given to those which cover the
loins with skins of the sheep or the goat, and speak a
language different from that of the others.

This name of Bechuanas, or Bachuanas, although ex-
tensively used now, originated, it is not improbable, in the
mistake of some traveller of a former day, who, having
asked the inhabitants of the country respecting their neighbours, would receive from them this ordinary reply,—*Ba
chuana*, "they are all the same." The fact is that the
natives are not at all accustomed to generalise. It is but
seldom that I have heard the natives of that district extend the designation *Bakoni* to all the Caffers which they
knew; that of *Basuta* to the Bechuanas generally; and
the name of *Baroa* to the whole of the hottentot race, as
is done in the quotation given above, which passes for one
of their traditions. If we would follow the designations
given by the Bushmen, we should call the Hottentots
Khuaï, the Caffers *Tolo*, and the Bechuanas or Basutus

Ku, a word identically the same with *cush,* the cush mentioned in scripture.*

For twenty or thirty years past, the Bechuanas have been the only aborigines found in the western vallies of the Malutis or Blue Mountains, and in the country extending northward from these to the French Mountains. From the mouth of the Lekua to the sources of the Keicop dwell the Bataungs and the Basias, or the numerous and powerful tribe of Lighoyas, as they are otherwise called.

To the south, on the White and the Blue Mountains, were some thousands of Baputis and Bakuenas, commonly called Basutos, and sometimes also Bamonahins, after one of their former kings.

These people, in their poetry and traditions, are often surnamed Batebang, which signifies those from the lower parts, or from the north east, whence they believe that they have all come. In later times they divided themselves into ten small independent states, although acknowledging one principal chief of the country, called Motlume.

---

* To make one general remark on the physical constitution of the Bechuanas and the Caffers. We have found amongst them very few who were feeble or deformed. They are all of a handsome figure, robust, and well made. The testimony of travellers in this respect is unanimous. But, alas! for this national characteristic, – so praised by some who have travelled amongst them,—whence comes it? They make away in one manner or another with the infirm, the deaf, the dumb, and the idiotic ; albinos are thrown to the panther; of twins one is often taken to the woods and left as prey for the leopard ; the suckling who has had the misfortune to lose his mother is, with certain tribes, buried alive by her side ; and with a handful of ashes, or a ladleful of boiling fat, they stifle those who are born blind. One day one of my fellow labourers was at Mafissa, when some young women brought to him a child two years and a half old, which they had just picked up a little above the fountain. The body was covered with bruises occasioned by the blows it had received in falling from rock to rock, the tongue torn by the little teeth was adhering to the roof of the mouth. The mother was called, and being questioned, she excused herself, saying that the child was rickety, and that this had induced her in despair to abandon it to its fate in a retired place, and that the father had killed a goat for the purpose of attracting the hungry hyenas to the spot. In South Africa infanticide is very common but the natives perpetrate it so adroitly, and conceal it so well, that unless one be living in the country, it is almost impossible to discover a case.

He resided at 'Ngolile, in the district of Umpukani; eight
leagues farther towards the north east, were the Bamerabas. The Mafukas spread themselves in the parts adjacent to Intluanachuana. Upon the banks of the Tlotse
lived the Bamokoteris or subjects of Mokachane; in the
district of Kuening, the Bamamotsuanes; at the top of
the same, the Makuakuas. Thaba Bosio and Makoarane
(now Moriah) were occupied by the Baputis; beyond
these on to the Mountains of Storms followed the Bapetlas;
and the plain stretching towards what we now call Beer-
seba and Thaba Unchu, was almost entirely abandoned
to the Baroas, who lived there with ease upon the produce
of the chase; the country there abounding with antelopes
of every kind.

All these hordes, with the exception of the Bushmen,
had the same customs, and spoke the same language.
They were all subject to Monahin, the great grandfather
of Motlume, a chief who, as already stated, exercised at
that time a very great and salutary influence over the
whole country, but more especially in his own kingdom of
Umpukani. His government was that of a prince distinguished for clemency and wisdom, and appeals were
often made to him, when difficult cases arose in the neighbouring provinces. In each of these provinces there reigned
an inferior, but independent chief, who governed his people
as to him seemed best, and who took cognisance of all
their affairs, but they were glad to avail themselves of the
counsel and influence of the king, and the result was an
admirable balance of power, which proved the protection
of the people against despotism and oppression. The
chiefs, moreover, were accustomed to associate with themselves two nobles, who, in the language of the people,
were called his two eyes, or his two arms.

This form of government is almost universal among the
Bechuana tribes. In most of the tribes you will find a
Morena-o-mogolu, a kind of grand seigneur, and two or
three great *tunas*, who are the chief officers of the council.
In the provinces again you will find in each village an

inferior *morena* and two *tunas.* The former always has
his hut simple as the others, but rather more spacious, at
the top of the village, opposite the entrance, and his two
viziers occupy the two other principal quarters, with the
subjects which have been allotted to them, or which they
have succeeded in attaching to themselves. The inferior
morenos have not unfrequently vassals to whom they give
lands on condition of service and fealty. These vassals
mark out to the plebeians the pieces of land which they are
severally allowed to cultivate, and they appoint the pasturage for the different seasons, exactly as the seigneurs,
superior and inferior, do in their respective clans. The
reeds of the marshes used for the construction of their
cabins, belong especially to these chiefs, and no person
dare touch them without their permission. In the season
at which they are cut, each subject is bound to take at least
one bundle of them to his master, and more if they be
required of him, before he dare take any portion of them
to himself. It is then considered that he is bound to
obey that superior with whatever charge he may intrust
him, and in whatever service he may employ him, as for
example, in making a kaross, tending his flocks, cultivating his fields, gathering in his crops, or in going his
errands. In return for such services, the chief is expected
to settle, without any reward, all the disputes of his vassal,
to help him out of any trouble in which he may get involved ; and he gives him, moreover, at one time a present
of a sheep skin cloak, at another, of a quarter of beef;
sometimes he will even give him two or three head of
cattle, and in summer let him have the milk of one or
more cows. And every one being more or less at liberty
to quit his chief and to attach himself to another if he
choose, it generally happens that the power of the chiefs
increase, in proportion as they increase in wealth, and *vice
versa.*

As to the relations of the chiefs between themselves, it
may be said that there is more of fear than love amongst
them. Although the inferior holds his property of the

X. MORIAH MISSION STATION, founded on the 9th July, 1833

A. Village of chief Letsié, future king of the tribe. B. Village of chief Molapo, younger brother of Letsié. C. Village of Taolani, late chief. D. Ewefold of the mission. E. Oxen-pen. F. Springs of the mission. G. Catching pond. H. Thabatélé or high mountain, one of the highest peaks of the Maluti range.

superior, there is very little respect shown by the one party to the other ; and judgments formally pronounced are not unfrequently reversed, and reversed again, till a judgment is pronounced in which all are willing to agree. They are not bound together by any oath of allegiance, nor by any positive law, so that they only give mutual assistance when it is for the advantage of all concerned.*

It belongs only to the chief of the tribe to convoke the others in a national assembly, to discuss and decide the question of peace and war. The others may, indeed, combine against their neighbours without his permission, but not without incurring his displeasure. If any beast of prey, such as a bear or a leopard, be killed on their lands they are bound to carry to him a piece of it ; and when they return from a successful expedition, it is he who appoints to every one his portion, beginning with himself. Rebellious subjects, who under some false pretext, have refused to take the field, are by him despoiled of their lands, if they have any, and these are divided amongst the rest. Such, in a few words, is the spirit of the constitution of these tribes. Such was it also in the days of Motlume.

The natives assure us that at that time they were by no means so poor as now. They were incomparably more numerous, and in general they lived in peace ; not that there were no depredations committed then, but they were rare. On this point, however, they do not trouble themselves to flatter their nation. The old men who still remain in the country, say ingenuously, "What is the history of the lions? wherever you find these animals, there you always find that some innocent antelope falls under their talons, and serves them for food. The timid elan once discovered is watched, surprised, and thrown upon the ground by some one of them. The other. kings

* If they were united by confederations, they would no longer be considered savages ; the desert would become populous, and tranquillity, laws, commerce, and religion, would be established in proportion as civilization took the place of barbarism ; but the social condition of man in a savage state is most wretched.

of the forest then rush to the spot, and soon not a fragment is left. With us, it has been somewhat similar. One
might hear, from time to time, of a petty chief being devoured by those who were stronger than he. But all the
evils then endured were partial and trifling, compared
with those which were not slow to manifest themselves,
when our great morenas began to raise the paw, the one
against the other ; then all our little states flowed with
blood, and our misery was extreme."

Motlume, it appears, had predicted these unprece-
dented calamities ; and it may be interesting to glance at
his individual history, before we attend to that of the
people.

From what was reported after the death of the chief by
Mekoua, his favorite wife, who is still alive, it would
appear that the history of his early life, in common with
the history of the founder of Islamism, had a dash of the
miraculous. Her husband, she says, had at one time
communication with heaven, it was when he was about
the age of thirteen. They had constructed for him in the
fields a wretched cabin, where he passed with his companions the four or five months required for the ceremony of circumcision, to which he had been subjected by
Moniane, his father. One evening at dusk the roof of
his cabin opened of itself, and the place was filled with
light. The young Motlume was then caught up to
heaven, where he saw many different people and nations.
He brought back an honest and prudent heart, and he
never forgot what had been there said to him, " Go,
govern with love ; see always in thy subjects men and
brethren."

This story is now to be found over all the country.
The inhabitants assure us that they have never had a
better king than Motlume. He loved them all indiscriminately, they say, and judged according to the rules of
equity. He was gentle, affable, and easy of access ; he
took particular care of widows and orphans ; these he
collected around him, and considered as his children.

From one thing to another, he was led by his benevolence to purchase wives for those young men who having no resources of their own, attach themselves to princes, depending for every thing on them, and thus becoming their *batlauka,* the service of which is a kind of semi-slavery. This kind of marriage bound the fathers, the mothers, and the offspring to the chief, but at the same time they greatly promoted polygamy and debauchery. The son of Moniane, however, in promoting them, which his immense fortune enabled him to do, viewed them, we must believe, only as a political resource, and an excellent means of extending his influence. By this means he rendered himself at once rich and very popular with the Basutos, as well as with the Zulas, and even in the kraals of the unhappy Bushmen; so that one might justly apply to him that beautiful description which he in some measure realised :—

> Un roi qu'on aime et qu'on révère
> A des sujets en tous climats :
> Il a beau parcourir la terre,
> Il est toujours dans ses Etats.

But, as has been mentioned, that system adopted by a skilful, and at the same time benevolent man, gave a very great importance to a plurality of wives, and greatly extended the evil. Before the time of Motlume, the greatest chiefs of the country kept three or four concubines at the most; now they take sometimes as many as forty. Formerly two or three head of cattle was all that was required by a Basuto to enable him to procure a partner in life, while now the number required is increased to ten, to thirty, or in some cases even to a hundred,—a circumstance favorable only to the rich. But notwithstanding these effects, Motlume was considered by his people to be very chaste. They assure us that he withdrew entirely from his wives when he was of a certain age, in accordance with the religious usage of the wisest of their chiefs; the example, according to the people, having been set to him by Makheta, his brother.

In his temperance he was not less remarkable than in his chastity. He ate little, and drank only water and milk. He seems, moreover, to have preferred the society of children to the society of men, saying, The little ones are better than their elders.

He was a true traveller king. Never, perhaps, had any Basuto visited so many native tribes as he; and he visited them indiscriminately, without fear or danger, such was his character and reputation. In this respect he differed widely from the other chiefs, who seldom visited each other, as much from distrust as from a haughty indifference. They say also that he was every where made most welcome, and that it was customary to consult him, as if he were an oracle. On one occasion, when he happened to be in the neighbourhood of Buta-bute, Moshesh having gone to see him,—Motlume said to him, " My friend, if thou couldst only forget thy country, I would take thee along with me wherever I go. Some day, in all probability, thou wilt be called to govern men. When thou shalt sit in judgment, let thy decisions be just. The law knows no one as a poor man."

At another time, travelling very far to the north, he came amongst a tribe of cannibals, but they did him no harm, alleging as the reason, " that they saw that he was a man of peace;" but Seguaela, the most quarrelsome of his fellow travellers, had nearly fallen a prey to them, and been devoured.

These tribes are well-known to the Basutos under the name of Bamatlabaneng,* and they live, it would appear, very far in the interior. Motlume arrived unexpectedly

---

* The Basutos have many terms descriptive of varieties of colour, and they thus apply that of *matlabane* to signify reddish, from its being the name given to the common brown ox, of which variety the snout and the interior of the ear are reddish. This, however, is not the meaning of the term. Formerly they knew this variety of cattle only by report. But the Zulas have supplied them with these, and, therefore, they called them *matlabane* or oxen from *the east*; and it is probable that finding this variety of oxen common among the natives, whom they visited in the interior, Motlume and his companions called the people on this account the *Bamatlabanang.* Such, at least, is the opinion of the natives.

in one of their villages one day about noon. It was not very hot that day, but nothing was to be seen at first excepting the herds of oxen quietly ruminating in their open folds; and not a sound was to be heard but the troublesome barking of the dogs and the buzzing of the flies.

By degrees, however, the inhabitants of the place came out of their huts; and the chief of the tribe approaching the traveller invited him with his companions to be seated in the shade, and presented to them some human flesh to eat. But the travellers excused themselves, saying that such food was unknown amongst them, and that they dared not touch it. Upon which an ox was immediately slaughtered for their refreshment.

The cannibals put many questions to Motlume, all of which he answered; and they on their part gave him all the information he desired in regard to their small but numerous tribes. They were all, it appeared, black, robust, of ordinary height, and in religion, manners, and language very similar to the Bechuanas. Motlume understood without difficulty all they said. Their country, though dry, was pretty fertile, and the pasturage excellent. Some low mountains run across the country, but the people keep away from these; they prefer the plain, where it is not so cold. They construct their huts of reeds and thatch, and their cattle folds of clods. Their villages are large and circular. They work in iron, of which they make assagais and hoes. As they live under a burning sun, it is their practice to pasture their herds, and to attend to their labours during the night.* About an hour or two after sunset, the women go to the fountains with their pitchers for water; then they set about cooking their pumpkins, and pounding their millet, from which they prepare both bread and beer.

* I accidentally met with the name and history of this people, by mentioning to the Basutos that there are men living at what we call the antipodes, with whom it is day when it is night with us. These, said they, must doubtless be the Bamatlabanang.

In the meantime their husbands go to milk the cows, which are all brown or almost so; then they lead them out to the pasture, and set themselves to cultivate their ground, or to prepare skins, of which they make pendant girdles for the loins, and short cloaks for the shoulders.

These people, according to the concurrent testimony of the other natives of the district, devour the flesh of a corpse, while very often the carcase of an ox which has died is thrown to the vultures, or carelessly covered with earth, on which occasions, no one knows why, they give themselves up to public lamentations. They drink a great deal of sour milk, but their delicacies are made of the flesh of their own kind. Their long crisp hair is besmeared with human fat, and their bodies with red ochre. They purchase their wives with oxen, and at the celebration of the marriage, as is done also among the Matlekas, they slay the brother of the bride, or failing such, her sister. Of one of these people, Masefako, it is told, that having no brother, she saw herself on the marriage of her younger sister exposed to the operation of this dreadful law. They selected a darkish evening to go to strangle her, according to custom, in the cattle fold. Obedient to the commands of the executioners, she entered, but she glided stealthily to the other side of the cattle, and so managed to escape. All that night she ran like a maniac in despair. The next day a few wild roots, and a little water repaired her exhausted strength, and she continued her route. After having cleared several extensive wildernesses, and passed safe and sound through many tribes of unknown Caffers, she arrived at last among the Lighoyas, where she married, had three children, and afterwards died a natural death in the neighbourhood of Racebatane.* Such, with the exception of the last mentioned illustrative and corroborative fact, was the information brought back by Motlume from among

* Caleb, one of the members of the church under my care, who knew Masefako for many years, assured me, that all these particulars are perfectly correct.

the Bamatlabaneng with whom he considered it prudent not to remain more than three days.

Amongst the questions which chiefly occupied this philosophic king, was, "Where can the end of the world be?"

In regard to disputes, I have never heard of his having any, excepting one which he had with his own father respecting a gazelle. In all the villages which he visited, he would settle the differences of the people when they desired him; and he entered into treaties of alliance with the chiefs, recommending them to cultivate peace; a subject on which he would say with great glee, "It pays better to fight the corn, than to whet the spear!"

Several of his maxims are still preserved amongst the people, such as the following connected with natural theology:—"There is in heaven a powerful Being, who hath created all things; nothing warrants me to believe that any of these things which I see could create itself. Do you ever see any thing create itself now?" "Conscience is the faithful monitor of man; she invariably shows him what is his duty. If he does well, she smiles upon him; if he does evil, she torments him. This inward guide takes us under her guidance when we leave the womb, and she accompanies us to the entrance of the tomb."

Motlume believed in the immortality of the soul, he said often, "Oh the vanity of every thing! Every thing passes swiftly, and I also, I pass away; but it is to go to rejoin my ancestors!" He reached a great age, but he could not give up his travels. In the course of one of his journeys he was seized with inflammation in the kidneys, a disease to which he was subject. His son Letela, who accompanied him, put him then a-stride on a sumpter ox, putting two branches of a tree under his arm-pits to sustain him, and conducted him to his hut at 'Ngolile, where he lived only a few days. Before he expired he said to those who stood around him, "My friends, it was in my heart to bring up my children in some place where they would be out of the way of war, and with this view

I intended to remove my cabin to the top of Kheme, opposite Makoarane; but my sickness renders it now impossible. After my death a cloud of red dust (awful wars)
will come out of the east, and devour our tribe. The
father will eat his own child. Farewell, I now go to the
dwelling place of our fathers."

This chief died generally regretted, but being an old
man there was no great demonstration of grief. Throughout the country his memory is every where revered;
and in the sacrifices offered to the dead, he is never
forgotten by the Basutos. Those in particular who live
in the plains, and who are supported in part by the
chase, are accustomed in times of great scarcity to
gather themselves together in some convenient place, to
call upon him and others of their gods for help. In these
superstitious ceremonies the *lingaka*, or priests, and the
people cut themselves with small knives in token of their
grief. They lie down among the ashes, and rising they
utter most piercing cries. They go through religious
dances, in which every one takes a part; they make
great lamentations; they groan and sing the most melancholy airs, until every one is exhausted by these wailings,
which last the whole day, and are often continued also
throughout the night. In concluding these pagan ceremonies, they pray thus to their gods, addressing always
those of the latest apotheosis first:

> We too are of a race divine,
> And yet we famish !
> Oh ye gods of the last creation, pray all to the more ancient;
> Intercede for us with 'Nkopane-Matunia ;
> Oh ! intercede for us with Motlume-Matsie, &c.*

The next day they spread themselves over the plain,

---

* Ki le nguana a Morimo, ka ota!
Morimo o mocha, kapela oa rhale ;
Rapela 'Nkopane-Matunia ;
Rapela Motlume-Matsie, &c. &c.
'Nkopane was the elder brother of Motlume, who at his circumcision took
the name of Matunia, as Motlume took that of Matsie.

running from one side to another to their snares and
their traps, hoping that the prayers of the evening
before may have been heard and accepted, and answered by those to whom they were addressed; but alas!
the *baalim*,*—when did they ever grant the requests
of their worshippers?

To bring this notice to a conclusion, Motlume appears
to have been a man comparatively virtuous, wise, and
something more than ordinary. His life, in spite of the
defects which may be remarked, recalls, and in some
measure illustrates, what Paul says to the Romans:—
" When the Gentiles, which have not the law, (the
written law,) do by nature the things contained in the
law, these, having not the law, are a law unto themselves;
which show the work of the law written in their hearts."

It seems as if God, in mercy to the pagan nations, raised
up in the midst of them, from time to time, such lights as
he, for the sake of the natural law, and consequently for
the benefit of those whom it is designed to enlighten and
to rule. Moshesh, the present king of the Basutos, considers it a high honor to be compared to Motlume,
whom he is ardently desirous of emulating in several particulars. On the other hand his people also wish, as
under the old regime, to be governed with affection, and
according to the rules of justice,—rules which are well
known in the country, much better, I must acknowledge,
than I could at first have believed or imagined. How
wonderful is the Lord in all his ways. Every day I see
more clearly that God hath put into the heart of all the

---

* This hebrew word corresponds exactly with the sechuana word *barimo*,
the derivation of which the missionaries have been unable to ascertain, but
which presents some analogies to the hebrew word equally striking with
the resemblance of the rites described above to those described in 1st Kings
xviii, 26—29. These analogies appear more striking when it is considered
that *r* and *l* are used indifferently in Sechuana, and that words in this language
very rarely terminate in a consonant, and never in *m*. Remove the euphonic *o*,
and substitute for the medial *r*, its interchangeable letter *l*, and you have a word
the resemblance of which to Baalim, the hebrew plural of Baal, must be apparent to all.

Africans an incorruptible witness to their conduct, a just judge of their actions, a guide as safe as benevolent,—a *shepherd*, as they themselves express it, always faithful and always good. They know full well how to distinguish between the equitable and the unjust, to discern between the true and the false, the pure and the impure; and they appear skilful casuists in matters of good and evil.

War, to which they are addicted, is never called any thing among them but *'mpe*, which signifies *ugly* and *evil*.* Unchastity, a vice deeply rooted in their hearts, bears no other than the defamatory designation of *boniatsi* or *blame*. The greater part of their maxims are excellent, as are also some of their laws. In their disputes, and in the management of their affairs in general, they display an admirable discernment. I once heard a Basuto say, on an unjust judgment being pronounced, " The judge is powerful, therefore we must be silent; if he were weak we should all cry out about his injustice !" In conclusion, I believe there is not one among them who could not faithfully subscribe that avowal of a celebrated heathen :

> *Video meliora proboque,*
> *Deteriora sequor.*

The death of Motlume occurred in 1818 or 1819. Some time before, the king had been called to lament the death of his son Koiane, the legitimate heir to the crown. As this interesting young man was tending the flocks of his father in the neighbourhood of 'Ngolile, the shepherds of his uncle Morosi came upon him unexpectedly, picked a quarrel with him respecting the pasturage, and killed him. His brother Letela would in all probability have taken his place, if he had only had as much of talent, or even ambition, as he has of natural kindness; but he has always been content, since the death of his father, to follow the fortune of his younger brother Moyakisane, who, though we cannot say that he is deficient in talent, has never been able to inspire the natives with confidence.

* *'Mpe*, moral evil ; *botluku*, physical evil.

Indeed, a man so superior as Motlume could not, it seems, be replaced. A short time before his death, he himself demanded with disquietude, of his brother Makheta, the only influential person who remained near him, " To whom then can we now look? To whom can we now intrust the guardianship of our children, of our people, and of our customs?"

CHAPTER XXV.

MAKONIANE AND MOSHESH.

In this general destitution of influential chiefs, there might have been seen amongst the Bamokoteris, a younger branch of the family of Monachin, one young man who gave promise of becoming at no distant period a ruler of distinction,—Moshesh, a man at once ambitious, intelligent and brave.

He and his friend Makoniane, whose military talents will probably never be surpassed amongst his countrymen, subsequently founded a new dynasty, which has proved no less remarkable than that of Motlume. Many circumstances combined to favor their design, and having the courage to take advantage of these, they needed nothing more to enable them to effect wonders amongst a barbarous people.

Makoniane was born at Makosa, on the Tlotse. His father 'Ntseke, seeing him to be of a weakly constitution, suspected that some of the sorcerers of the place were exercising their influence to prevent his growth, and sent him to a friend in the neighbourhood, who was willing to undertake his early training.

When about thirteen years of age, he returned to his father's house. It was on the occasion of the circumcision of Moshesh. Mokachane, the *morena*, or chief of Makosa and of the whole district of the Tlotse, having appointed a day for the circumcision of his son, caused

proclamation of his design to be made throughout the
district by a military herald, requiring the parents of all
lads of the prescribed age to bring them forward to be
circumcised at the same time. Makoniane was one of
these. He was circumcised, and thus in common with
the rest of the party, he was declared a *man*, the subject
and future soldier of Moshesh, according to the national
mode of enlistment.*

Shortly after this he was sent to take charge of a
number of calves belonging to the village; of these he
was robbed, and he returned to the village mortified and
ashamed. Mokachane was enraged, and insisted that he
should be put to death for his negligence, and his father
'Ntseke gave his consent; but Pete, the father of Mochachane interposed, and said, "No, the calves have been
carried away by Makara's people; but who is to blame?
You lately made a marauding incursion upon them; and
they have taken their revenge. Let the child live. When
he is grown he will do as they have now done." It was
agreed to, he got a beating, nothing more. The only thing
he did wrong, they said, was, that having been told to
drive his herd in one direction, he had driven them in
another.

When he was of the age of eighteen or twenty, he was
sent by Moshesh to Makara's village, to recover, if possible, the cattle he had formerly lost. Rejoicing in the
confidence reposed in him by his chief, he set off at night
in high spirits, armed with his buckler and a simple club,
and accompanied by his two friends, Galegala and Ramachosa. In the fields they encountered five or six of
Makara's subjects, who were on their way to plunder
Makosa. At their head was Chama, who was the first
to give the challenge, "Who are you?" "And you,—
Who are you? Where are you going?" was the retort
of Makoniane, who, without waiting a reply, threw himself upon Chama, and with one blow of his club laid him

* I believe I have already remarked that the ceremony of circumcision is
with the Bechuanas as much a civil as a religious rite.

lifeless at his feet. At the same moment one of the
enemy struck Galegala, who fell to the ground, dangerously wounded. The same man then ran at Makoniane,
who at first pretended to flee, but wheeling suddenly
round, and running against his new adversary at full
speed, he hurled him to the ground, but without killing
him. They fight like fiends in the dark,—their wrath
alone animates them,—the darkness favors the confusion,
—the air is rent with cries, which no one hears, except it
be the malignant spirits which such a combat could
amuse or interest.

At length the soldiers of Makara were allowed to
return to their homes, leading away their wounded comrade, while Makoniane and Ramachosa assisted Galegala
to a neighbouring hut. There Makoniane kept watch,
while his friend ran to Makosa, with intelligence of their
nocturnal conflict.

Mochachane, Moshesh, and the father of Galegala, on
receiving information of what had occurred, set out at
once, and towards midnight they reached the spot where
the conflict occurred. Galegala's father cut off the head
and the two arms of the unfortunate Chama; the others
took up the wounded man, and they returned together to
Makosa.

Makoniane at the entrance of the village was welcomed
with savage *bravos*. He and his two companions went
and took their seats in the court of the men, a circular
uncovered enclosure of reeds in which the chiefs and the
soldiers usually spend their time. It was a doleful day
in the village of Makara, one marked by public lamentations; but in the village of Mokachane the people gave
themselves up to all manner of rejoicings, while the
priests, in accordance with the ancient usages of the
people, were engaged in superstitious rites for the purification of Makoniane and his companions in the fight.

First, there was a general hunt of the cattle, which were
collected together in the fields by the youths. The men
in the meantime having suspended the head and arms of

Chama immediately above the entrance of the *lesaka*, a circular enclosure of stakes or of stone, erected in the centre of caffer and bechuana villages for the protection of cattle; the oxen, cows, and calves came on in a crowd, urged forwards by the youthful herds, who kept shouting behind them, and waving their long plumes of white feathers. The cattle were thus forced to pass and repass again and again under the dangling hands of the murdered warrior, before the cows were relieved of their milk. This kind of hunt, which is of frequent occurrence, is designed to teach the cattle that they should betake themselves to the fold whenever there is any danger of their being taken by the enemy ; and they are made to pass under the cold hand, and the lifeless eye, of the stranger, that they may learn to suffer no eye to smile upon them, but the eye of their rightful owner, and no hand to touch them but the hand of their master.

While this was going on at *the fold*, at the court of the men were to be seen superstitious observances without number, one following on the heels of the other, as if it was designed that they should be interminable,—all, the consequence of the remorse which follows crime, and the attempts of man to allay it, and to heal a wounded conscience. From this fact alone we may learn something of importance, and we, therefore, proceed to detail the ceremonies.

Moshesh, on his return from the scene of the fight, in accordance with the religious observances of his countrymen, called Mobe, the priest of war, and brought to him a fine black ox, which being examined and pronounced suitable, had its designation *como*, ox, formally changed to that of *peku*, or victim of expiation. Mochachane then stabbed it to the heart with his javelin, and so slew it. It was then skinned and cut up by 'Ntseke ; and Mobe cut off the tip of the tongue, one of the eyes, a small piece from the hamstring, and another from the principal tendon of the shoulder. These he mixed up with certain herbs which he had brought with him in his

priest's horn, and which were supposed to be possessed of
peculiar virtues. He then fried the mixture with great
care, while the cooks set on the fire a potful of meat,
taken from other parts of the victim. Returning to the
carcase a second time, Mobe cut off a portion of the
pleura, which he dipt first into the sacred fry which he
was preparing, and then put into the common pot in
which they were cooking for Makoniane, and the rest of
the men. He next emptied the gall bladder into a large
vessel of pure water taken from a running stream, and
with the mixture he washed and rewashed the bodies of
the marauders, all excepting the head. He also introduced into all the joints of their limbs a little of the fry
he had made, and cutting a slit in the gall bladder, he
passed it on to the wrist of Makoniane ; and lastly he
took the large gut, introduced into it a good portion of
the sacred fry, and bound it round the neck of the soldier.
What remained in the pan was then carefully pounded
and put into Makoniane's horn for daily use if he chose,
or, if he preferred, for some future occasion when he
might again think of going on a plundering expedition.

Fule, the mother of the young warrior, then came up
to him, holding in her hand a sharp blade, with which
she shaved his head and the heads of his two companions.

That being done, Makoniane dipped his finger into a
mixture of chalk and water, and with this he marked one
of his temples as a sign of triumph, and his friends hastened to congratulate him, saying, " See, he is purified !
See, his time of mourning is over !" They then poured
out the potful of meat. Fule brought beer, into which
her son put some of the powder of purification which he
had received. The three marauders then seated themselves on the ground, and ate and drank. Mobe, the
chiefs, the rest of the men, and some old matrons did the
same. As for the young women they are never admitted
to such feasts, lest they should be defiled. When all
had eaten to the full, Mobe quietly returned, driving
before him a black heifer which Mochachane had given

XI. BASUTO WARRIOR

Lith. de Thierry freres.

him as a fee, and the soldiers got up a war dance. Mokoniane and his two friends remained in the court of the men all night, and not till the morning were they permitted to go and again see their youthful companions and the children.

These particulars he himself supplied to me, and he accompanied them with the following explanations, which are not more curious than necessary to a proper understanding of the rites.

" If they cut off and purify the tongue of the victim, it is with the view," said he, " of procuring from the family, or tutelary, gods that they will prevent the enemy from injuring them; and by the other portions which they cut from the carcase they intimate their desire that the sinews of the hands and feet of their enemy may fail them in battle, and that the eye of their enemy may never dare to cast a covetous glance upon their cattle.

" The gall, continued he, represents the anguish of death. That anguish the murderer shares; it seems to cleave to him as if it were a part of himself; but may not even it be washed away by the water of purification?

" The pleura of the animal is the symbol of conscience, and, therefore, is it so carefully purified.

" The large gut is not worn simply as an ornament; being worn round the neck day and night, it constantly reminds the murderer of the expiation which has been made for his crime, and so disperses frightful dreams and melancholy thoughts of death, through which the warrior might otherwise become deranged, or even die of remorse. With the same view the mother shaves away the hair, that a new crop may grow, while all that was old and defiled, having disappeared is forgotten."

Such is the purification practised by the Caffers and Bechuanas after their fights. We must not suppose, then, on hearing the interminable stories of marauding expeditions, that these people know nothing of the upbraidings of conscience. Too well do they know what is right and what is wrong to escape the condemnation of

conscience, and their ablutions and their expiatory sacrifices are, like their depredations, without number.

After this successful debut, Mokoniane was not slow,
at the instigation of his morena, to betake himself to the
pasture grounds of a petty chief in the neighbourhood,
called Peo. Two of his friends and his uncle accompanied him. On perceiving the strangers, the herdsmen
raised the alarm, which, rising from the plains to the
mountains, was soon spread over all the heights. In an
instant every man seized his assagai and flew to the plain.
One of the flocks had already been carried off. In confusion and disorder they ran upon Makoniane, they attacked him, he defended himself and put the whole to
flight. Arrived at Makosa, the thirty or forty oxen
which had been captured were divided amongst the three
plunderers, and Pete, Mokachane, Moshesh, his brother
Ralisaoane, and Fule. The chiefs of the town, by
receiving part of the booty, became security for the safety
of the robbers, whose crime, moreover, they endeavoured
to extenuate by quoting a favorite maxim of theirs, to the
effect that robbery does only a partial injury to a village,
it is pillage which ruins it.

Some time after this, a prince of the Bamokoteris,
called Magao, threw himself on the cattle of Motake, and
captured them with the assistance of Makoniane.*

It was then that Moshesh also began his career of plunder. Taking Makoniane as his champion he went forth with
him and his troops to take first a herd of three hundred
cattle at Maquai; then one of two hundred at 'Ntisane;
then another of seven hundred at Molagilane. Crossing

---

* In that country depredations are committed very much as they were in the
days of Job, so much so that the language of the natives, and their plans of
attack, correspond exactly with what is said in Job i, v. 15 and 17 :—"And the
Sabeans fell upon them and took them away; yea, they have slain the servants
with the edge of the sword; and I only am escaped alone to tell thee.
While he was yet speaking there came also another and said, The Chaldeans
made out three bands and fell upon the camels, and have carried them away,
yea, and slain the servants with the edge of the sword; and I only am
escaped alone to tell thee."

the Caledon he threw himself on the Lighoyas of **Mabula,**
a town situated between Thaba Unchu and **Mekuatling,**
put to the sword ten or twelve herdsmen, and carried off
about a thousand head of cattle.

In all these incursions, and in many similar expeditions,
Makoniane rendered himself celebrated for his hardiness,
his ferocity, and his courage. He carried off the cattle
with wonderful dexterity, and became formidable at once
to the herdsmen, the soldiers, and the chiefs of his foes.
" He glides," said his friends in his praise, " he glides into
the fold like a fish in the water. He roars like a hyæna,
and like it tears the prey. The bravest are speared to
death by his lance ; the strongest are crushed to death by
his club, with his vigorous hand he lays hold on the thigh
of the swiftest of foot ; and he hurls them to the ground.
He rains stones on the heads of his enemies, and burning
torches on their habitations."

This celebrity of Makoniane gave hope and joy to the
heart of Moshesh. " Thou art my right hand," said he
to his friend. " Together we will found a new empire.
Let us first render ourselves popular by mighty deeds, and
afterwards we will speak of peace and clemency. In the
disputes of others let us always put ourselves on the side
of the strongest. If we would become rich in men and
cattle, we cannot help making enemies ; but they will not
roar for ever. Motlume has carried out to a great extent the important system of polygamy, we must go
beyond even him in this. He considered that it often
was better to entreat enemies than to fight them ;—this too
we must follow out when necessary. And as a regard for
the poor, for widows and for orphans, is every where considered by the tribes to be a sacred duty, we must care
for them also."

It was, so far as can be ascertained, towards the end of
1821, or the beginning of 1822, that Moshesh and Moka-
niane thus laid their plans, and attempted to estimate the
difficulty as well as the glory of establishing the new

basuto empire, of which they had just laid the foundation
by their numerous successful incursions upon the neighbouring districts. About the same time serious distur-
bances began to arise beyond the mountains. One of the
most influential of the zula princes, called Mosolekatsi,
was attacked by Sekognana, and obliged to remove with
his subjects away to the north. In the course of his
journey he destroyed many tribes, as for example, those
of the Makhoras and of the Makhatlas. This formidable
inkhosi ruined also a powerful chief of the Lighoyas,
called Rankokoto, who was living on the banks of the Enta.
The natives allege that a short time before an eclipse of
the sun had presaged these misfortunes and those which
followed.

The country of Chaka being thus greatly disturbed,
two other powerful chiefs of the tribe, Pacarita and Matuane were obliged to leave it, the one fleeing before the
other, and both before the wrath of their inkhosi, whom
it appears they had offended. Pakarita approaching the
Malutis, frightened the Mantetis, who were then living at
Thaba Unchu, on the sources of the Namagari. These
abandoning their villages, went along the mountains, dis-
placing in turn a colony of Zulas, called Matsetses,* who,
sought an asylum on the heights beyond the Komokuane,
while the enemy pushed on more to the south, away to
the Stormberg, whence he directed his course upon
Boteta, (opposite Beersheba,) and thence, by a retrograde
march, upon Mekuatling. But there he was met by the
troops of Pacarita, which attacked him, overcame him,
and forced him to return to the home he had left, with
great loss of men, of cattle, and of baggage.

This invasion of the country by the Mantetis and the
Matluibis, or the subjects of Pacarita, augured little good
to the Basutos. The first, it is true, did them no harm except in passing ; but the others established themselves in
the district of Umpukani, and thence they surrounded them

* Called Amazizi by Thomson.

in all their little states, and ruined them one after another, without their ever dreaming of combining to oppose the common foe.

Makheta came down from 'Ngolite to the country on the other side of Thaba Bosio; the other chiefs on the contrary fled towards the west, where they were despoiled by the Korannas; the more prudent sought safety in the mountains, but there also war soon raged as it had done in the plains. They quarrelled amongst themselves, and it ended in their eating one another's flesh.

Mosutuane, one of the chiefs of the Bamokoteris, who had received the Matsetses, with apparent hospitality, destroyed them, when they least expected.

Makoniane also was sent under some false pretext to sack and pillage the Mafukas.

CHAPTER XXVI.

MOSHESH, who now found himself comparatively rich, left his father at Leinchuaneng, whither he had gone to seek a refuge, and went to found a new settlement at Butabute. At the same time he sent two officers to Pacarita with the following message :—" Our master has no more corn ; wilt thou give him some? Wilt thou allow his subjects to mingle freely with thine. He sends thee two oxen as a present, and in proof of his sincerity."

The reply was : — " Take two sacks of corn, present them in my name to Moshesh. Tell him that his message was welcome. Of his two oxen one has been received. Explain to him that the other was taken from you by my soldiers ; and that they slaughtered it without my knowledge. They are ferocious and insubordinate men. You need not be surprised if they maltreat those of your tribe who come to purchase corn, or to hire themselves to me for bread ; nevertheless, come, buy and live. I dread Matuane, perhaps he will yet force me some day to go and hire myself to your master for bread, and if he do, I will do so."

Matuane was, indeed, at the gate a month or two after this, the news of his having entered the country spread every where, carrying terror to every heart. Moshesh hearing that this formidable zula inkhosi had sent a detachment of soldiers against Letulu, a basuto prince, settled in the neighbourhood of Butabute immediately sent Coho, with another distinguished officer, to present ten cattle to the royal invader, and to implore his clemency. Coho met the troops on their way to Letulu. The soldiers seized the cattle and said to the messengers, "Return quickly, and tell your master that this very night he will be attacked by a body of soldiers, similar to what you see." The information was in some measure well meant. Many a savage voice cried, "Hamstring the messengers, and leave them!" But the chief said, "No, according to the custom of our people the person of an ambassador is safe whatever be his message ; and our customs permit that we should sometimes give timely warning to those whom we mean to attack." They then offered refreshments to the deputies, and left them at liberty to return to Butabute.

That very night Letulu was ruined. Moshesh armed all his people, and he stationed twelve of them as sentinels below the village. These poor soldiers fell asleep. Towards day break an unusual noise awoke them. It was occasioned by the approach of the Zulas. They fled. The enemy entered Butabute, carried off betwixt two and three thousand head of cattle, and departed with their rich booty. They only lost three men ; and on the side of the Basutos, only one was slain.* Tsueniane, a young prince of the tribe, disappeared however, no one knew how ; nor has it since been discovered what became of him.

These events occurred in 1823. Defeated by Matuane, Pacarita, the inkhosi of the Matluibes, had just invaded the country of the Lighoyas. There he completed the work of extermination, which had been begun a short time before by the fierce Mantetis. The tribe of Makuane that year lost almost the whole of their cattle, and in their

---

* I find that, in general, the wars of the natives are mere skirmishes. Their system of pillage is pretty well arranged, but they have neither the skill nor the courage necessary for a decisive battle, otherwise the whole of Africa would long ere now have become an immense desert in the most absolute sense of the word. But Providence, careful of the most savage tribes, has caused even their ignorance to subserve their preservation.

destitution they became partly cannibals. Their chiefs then
dispersed ; some emigrated to the colony of the Cape,
others took up their abode among the Griquas. Amongst
those who joined themselves to the latter, we may mention the name of Molitsane, who saw himself almost
entirely ruined, although his power before these calamities
befel his people was such that one would have said it was
equal to that of Mosolekatsi. But nothing was more
common at that time amongst these tribes than such re-
verses.   Take one other example, the case of Pacarita
himself. After having proved so formidable to the Bamonahins and to the Bataungs, this prince, as if possessed
by the demon of war, determined to try his strength with
Matuane, but he in one single day utterly destroyed him.
The battle took place on the banks of the Mogokare (the
Caledon.)   Pacarita and his principal captains were slain,
their immense herds of cattle were seized, and the greater
part of his subjects—men, women, and children—were put
to the sword.

Of the family of the unfortunate chief of the Matluibes
there survived only Setenane and Pake, two of his sons,
and with them one or two thousand of his subjects,
who at the recommendation of their chief placed themselves under the protection of Moshesh, and settled in the
district of Mekuatling, where they have remained to the
present time.

Strengthened by their assistance, Moshesh succeeded at
length in driving the Mantetis from Butabute, where he
established himself again, not, however, at the foot of the
mountain as before, but on the elevated and extensive
table land which forms its summit.

In the month of January following, 1824, just as the
Basutos were beginning to gather in the sweet reed, and
to entertain the hope of a harvest, who should appear
again, but the enemy so lately expelled! The chief of
Butabute immediatly sent an ox, together with this message to Sekoniela, "Spare my millet, and let us fight for
the cattle." The millet, however, was not spared the more

for that, and as for the cattle, spear in hand they contended
for them for two whole months.

The Mantetis took their station at the foot of the mountain, where they encamped, and every morning when the
Basutos went down to water their herds, with a troop of
soldiers at their head, and the cattle behind, under charge
of the herdsmen, there was a battle between the two parties. While this was going on the cattle were drinking,
eating a mouthful of grass, and regaining the summit of
the mountain, where they were pretty well off for herbage,
but they had little water.

Let it suffice to say, that, from time to time, the enemy
carried off some ten or twelve head of cattle, that two or
three hundred were removed to Leinchuaneng, and that
a considerable number died from exhaustion Towards the
end of the siege the misery on the top of Butabute was
so great, that the people were fain to eat their dogs, their
sandals, and their old skin cloaks. Still they continued
to sing their war songs. To these bravadoes the enemy
below replied with war dances ; and morning after morning
the basuto herds found the drinking places filled with
earth and cow dung. Greatly annoyed with such a state
of things, Moshesh cried one day to the Mantetis, " Flee,
or this very night I will cause you to be devoured by the
Matebeles." He had, indeed, already called those of
Sepeka to his assistance, who fell upon the enemy that
night, and put them to flight.

Sepeka himself lost a good many people. On the side
of the Batlokuas, the old queen 'Ntloku was slain. Her
grandson Sekoniela, having bewailed her, marched upon
Metabing, to attack the Bamerabas, who at first defended
themselves courageously. They had had the precaution
to fix in the ground, on all roads leading to their town,
sharp pieces of iron and of bone, which greatly impeded
the enemy, and did them no little harm. After some
days of perseverance, however, these succeeded in reaching the town and in pillaging the besieged. These they
compelled to flee to the Malutis, and they took possession

of their dwellings, whence they have never since been expelled.

As for the Bamokoteris, they went down to Thaba Bosio, where it appears they arrived about the beginning of June 1824. None, the chief of the Baputis, whom they found settled there, made them welcome, and received from them assurances of peace. The immigrants seeing that the town of the Baputis was built at the foot of the mountain, began theirs at the summit. Moshesh recommended his subjects to respect the Baputis, and to give themselves but little to the cultivation of the fields that year, as it was his intention to remove in the following year to the Kheme. At the same time he issued orders that the corn which his people might require in the meantime should be legitimately procured ; but his brother Ralisaoane stood up against this plan, objecting that if it were followed, the poor would be in want of bread ; and he was not slow to attack None. Makoniane, however, was sent, and he dispersed the aggressors ; but scarcely had he returned to the mountain when he saw them again advancing to the attack. He hastened down once more, but when he got near he found that the Baputis were in the act of fleeing. " Ho, ho, cried the warrior, this alters the case. I will now have bread to eat as well as the others." He then joined Ralisoane instead of fighting him, and together they finished what he had begun.

In the evening None returned to the village, and found it pillaged ; but he entrenched himself and his cattle amongst the rocks. At the same time he sent Limo to call a band of Manquanes, or the subjects of Matuane, to his assistance. These came, but only with the design of despoiling the Baputis of their cattle. Being inferior, however, in number to those whom they intended to pillage, they were repulsed by None.

Three months rolled on, and this chief was again attacked by Ralisaoane, who seized part of his cattle, and compelled him to vacate the place, and go to live further up amongst the mountains. On this occasion Moshesh joined his brother for the sake of the booty, of which he took a goodly portion.

The ruin of None was afterwards completed by Makheta, the brother of Motlume, in whose neighbourhood he had sought a refuge.

He, in his turn, saw himself attacked by the Bamokoteris, who despoiled him of a great part of his wealth, and made him a prisoner. But Moshesh wishing to show himself possessed of more clemency than the other chiefs, set him at liberty, paying over at the same time five head of cattle to the soldier who had captured and brought him to Bosio.

The unfortunate brother of Motlume, humbled and ashamed, returned to the district of Thaba Cheu. He had still one herd of cattle. These he led out himself to pasture, partly to make himself certain of his possession, and partly from disgust at the society of men whom he hated, and with whom he wished to have no further intercourse.

The first care of Moshesh, after having made himself master of Thaba Bosio, was again to seek the favor of Matuane, whose near neighhourhood he greatly disliked. This foreign inkhosi was then settled at Seniutung, on this side of Umpukani, from which position he did no little mischief to the petty chiefs who still reigned in the country. Moshesh employed every means in his power to secure his good graces. He sent him, for example, considerable presents, thereby professing to be only his humble vassal. One of the wives of the zula king having visited the mountain of Bosio, she was received with great deference. Moshesh himself put a collar of copper round her neck, adorned both her arms with bracelets, gave her ochre powder and perfumes for her toilet, and when she went away presented to her a beautiful cow, " in order my sister," said he to her, " that thy children may also drink of my milk, and that from the white cream of this milk, thou, their mother, mayest procure for thyself a

befitting ointment, wherewith to anoint thy locks, thy
hands, and thy feet, according to the usage of princeses."

Some time after, a friendly inhabitant of Seniutung came
to inform Moshesh of the approach of Moselane, one of
the captains of Matuane, who had been sent at the head of
an army against Bosio.

Immediately all the inferior chiefs of the town were
summoned by a herald to the court of the men. Their
morena said to them, "My friends, to-morrow we shall
have to fight. Every one must help himself. Hitherto I
have said of the Manquanes,—Perhaps they wish to settle
in the country, let us cultivate their friendship. But these
men are our enemies. Go, sharpen your assegais, scour
your bucklers, and let each of you to-night keep a close
look out on the approach to your respective kraals. If at
daybreak the enemy attack us, let us defend ourselves
boldly. They say that he is powerful,—but, is that to say
that he is invincible?"

Immediately the Basutos set about getting ready their
weapons; each of them put on his calf skin buskins, his
small leather cuiras, and his gorget of polished copper.
On their head, there waved bunches of light feathers, or
of the fur of the ant-eater disposed in curls; and from their
shoulders hung a light mantle, made of leopard or panther
skin. In the left hand every soldier took a square buckler,
a club, and a long black plume, made of bamboo, covered
with ostrich feathers; in the right hand each of them held
two or three assegais.

They passed the night at their appointed posts, but when
the sun had risen, seeing no enemy appeared, these military
herdsmen cried out, "A false alarm! Let us lay down our
arms in the court of the men, and go milk our cows!"

They were too hasty; an hour or two passed, and the
Manquanes appeared at the pass of Tupa Kubu. To look
at them, they were all tall and robust men, they were
naked, but girdles of skin, with the hair upon it, hung like
the tails of wild beasts from their loins, their breasts

were covered with false hair; and a pad of otter skin protected their ebony forehead, lending to their large eyes
the color of blood, and giving to them a most terrific appearance; their heads were adorned with crane's feathers,
the emblem of victory; they carried on their left arm a
large long oval shield, which covered almost the whole of
their person; in their right hand they carried a short but
stout assegai.

So soon as they had cleared the Putiatsana, the army of
Moselane parted into two equal bodies, of which one
marched against the kraal of Mokachane, the other against
that of Moshesh. This chief was to be attacked first.
He descended in haste from the top of his mountain.
Arrived below, he placed behind him a herd of cattle, as if
to defy the Manquanes, who had come solely in the spirit
of plunder.

Afterwards dividing his troops into three bands, he put
that of Malelo, or the battalion of FIRE, in the foreground,
although the weakest and the least inured to war. On
the left of that he stationed the corps of Likaloas, composed of tried soldiers, and commanded by Makoniane.
Moshesh placing himself at the head of the Matlamas,
formed with them the right wing of the army.

These arrangements made, the Manquanes, who were
near enough to have observed them, came up at a running
pace, arranged in different ranks, but forming one body.
The Malelo immediately advanced at a running pace to
meet them. At thirty paces distant a matebele champion,
all at once detached himself from his regiment, threw himself precipitately amongst the Basutos, broke their ranks,
carried off one of their bucklers, which he tossed in the
air, crying *What's that?* and with one blow of his shield he
laid Taolani prostrate. Moshesh coming up immediately
to the assistance of the Malelos, threw himself upon the
intrepid champion, struck his immense buckler from his
arm, and with one blow of his spear laid him dead at his
feet. The whole of his troops then fall upon the enemy;—

the attack is repulsed. The Likaloa come up and second it. The enemy in turn fall back. The Basutos pursue them.... Suddenly they wheel round, raising frightful cries of *hi zi! hi!* The Basutos immediatly throw their javelins, stones, clubs,—defeat them, put them to flight, and the Manquanes fall under a shower of arrows, or throw themselves into the ravines of the mountain, or drown themselves in the river. Those who conceal themselves in the bush or behind the rocks are dragged out, and torn to pieces on the spot by the Matlamas.

While this was going on, the Likaloas had been sent against the right wing of the army of Moselane, which they encountered below the kraal of Mokachane, where for half an hour Ralisaoane and Pushuli had been defending themselves boldly, although without any hope of victory. Makoniane falling on the Manquanes, filled them with terror ; they immediately turned back, keeping up a running fight, and retreated towards Bokate, after having lost some ten men, and slain only two or three Basutos.

On the evening of that day, as honorable as important for the tribe of Moshesh, the triumphant inhabitants of Bosio began their war dances.

They gathered together for this purpose on the public place situated in the centre of the town. The greater part of the men were armed, and decked with their military ornaments. They divided themselves into two equal battalions, and took their stations in two opposite ranges, three hundred paces distant. The women, with tambourins, formed an outer circle around them. A shrill cry was raised, and the two battalions advanced towards each other at a smart running pace, keeping time, and stamping violently with their feet. All at once they stopped. An intrepid warrior detached himself from one of the companies, advanced, threatened the enemy, defied him, pretended to attack him, and returned to his place. Both parties then shook their bucklers, brandished their spears, and raised many a cry of defiance and of triumph. After which they returned to their original position again to go through the same manœuvres. In their songs of triumph they said :

" Matuane is deceived by Moselane : he is deceived by the nobles of Seniutung. How *?* The foreign inkhosi made himself a vassal ultimately to destroy him !

" ...... Father of Tillage (Moshesh) tell how thou canst break the clods in a field of millet ; tell how thou didst break the heads of the army of the enemy.

" The assegai has devoured the son of Kabekoe; it hath torn the flesh of the fierce Umpepang.

" The son of an old man hath rushed against the son of a prince.

" A servant complains that the quaggas have entered the field of Kuetse.

" He says that a male quagga having been wounded, hath been left behind by the troop; that his strength is gone. He staggers, ready to fall lifeless amongst the green ears...."

This triumphal song has not been preserved entire in the memory of the Basutos. The above is but the beginning of it, but we see from it with what derision the conquerors jeer at Matuane. He had undertaken an imprudent and a disastrous war. His counsellors had deceived him ; his first captain had failed him, and he himself had broken faith, and that with a valiant man, called by a double metaphor, *the father of tillage*, by which it was intimated that he was a true leveller of enemies' heads.

The recital of the battle follows.

First falls the fierce Umpepang; this noble son of Kabekoe has been trampled in the dust by the son of a chief yet more noble and brave, that of the old Moka-chane.

One of the fields of millet, scarcely yet in ear, had been traversed by the Manquanes, who are compared in the song to those herds of quaggas with their speckled skins, and savage and unsociable habits, which in that country sometimes run through the fields of the natives when they are pursued.   But one of the enemy was wounded and left there by his troop.   The song relates the fact· The other allusions probably relate to similar incidents.

CHAPTER XXVII.

SETTLEMENT OF MISSIONARIES.

AFTER the battle of Bosio, the Manquanes made preparations again to attack the Bamokoteris; but Chaka, without knowing any thing of it, disconcerted their plan. One dark night his troops, when they were least expected, entered Seniutung, seized numerous herds of cattle, set fire to the town, and forced the inhabitants to flee to the southward towards Thaba Cheu.

Moshesh, taking advantage of their disorder, despatched Makaniane and his troops in pursuit. They surprised them in the pass of Lipatoa, surrounded them, and at last compelled them to seek safety still further to the south, leaving behind them a booty of some hundred cattle.

Matuane then entered the country of the Tambukis, but alarmed by the approach of so formidable an enemy, Faku, the chief of that tribe, had implored assistance from the government of the Cape colony, which was granted for the benefit of Caffraria, which had been for some time in a very disturbed state. Attacked in July and August 1828, by a body of british troops and of boors, the Manquanes saw themselves forced to abandon the banks of the Umtata, and to return to their own country, after losing some hundreds of men, and five or six thousand head of cattle.[*]

[*] Compare Mr. Kay.

Their defeat, in which the other natives rejoiced, is narrated by them in a manner which is very original. "The whites," say they, "did not seize the enemy as we do, by the body, but they thundered from afar. The fire of their artillery is to men, what the conflagrations of August are to the dry pasturage. Whither can one flee from the lightning of their musket? where can one conceal himself from the thunder vomited forth by their awful cannon? Their bullets were at first taken by the Manquanes for polished pebbles.* Mantuane caused his soldiers to conceal themselves behind the thickest trunks of the forest, that they might be in safety,—but it was in vain. They skulked amongst the rocks, but still it was in vain. They threw themselves into the river, but even there a sudden death reached them;—it raged every where, like the death vomited forth by the tempest. Then the Matebeles reduced to despair, sought safety in flight, but the bombs of the enemy set fire to the grass beneath their feet, and they knew not how to escape the general conflagration, which was soon spread over the whole country. The next day the Amatembus saw nothing in the fields but dead bodies, on which ravenous vultures were making their repast." It is said also, that some tender infants were seen tugging at the stiffening breasts of their mothers, from whom they demanded, by their dying groans, those attentions which they never before had asked for in vain.

To these heart-rending details one scarcely knows how to add others. But it remains to be told that those who had been wounded in the battle, and those whose feet had been injured by the burning of the grass, were left behind to the mercy of the tigers and the hyænas. Many mothers, in their precipitate flight, dropt and lost the child from their back. Others maddened, and in despair, threw theirs into the river, or into the dens of the wild

---

* We were informed by a british soldier, that when the first bomb fell in the camp of the Manquanes, they gathered around it in astonishment, not having the least expectation of the explosion which followed.

beasts, and who can doubt but some who could not find it in their heart to do so, sat down by the side of theirs, having no strength to carry them further, having no bread with which to feed them, but willing, at least, to die with them?....Hunger raged to such a degree amongst the Manquanes, that they did not hesitate to attack one another, and make a repast on human flesh.

As for their unfortunate chief, there remained for him no other resource, after such misfortunes, but to go in his confusion and despair to Dingan (the successor of Chaka) of whom he implored clemency,—as if a zula inkhosi could show clemency! This time, however, the deceitful emperor, assuming an air of compassion, assigned to the suppliant and his surviving subjects a corner of the country, and even entrusted them with two or three herds of cattle to tend as his vassals. Some time after this he called Matuane to Mokokutlufe. He obeyed the summons, but not without some sad forebodings. As soon as he arrived, two executioners laid violent hands upon him. To them he said, " Let me alone ; am I a bird to fly away to heaven? I know that I am going to meet my death." Dingan first caused them to goudge his eyes, then they forced pieces of wood up his nostrils. At this horrid spectacle the crowd of sycophants cried out, " It thunders in the place where Chaka dwells. It rains at Chaka's town. We all know Chaka. But why should they say that it thunders, or that it rains at the home of Matuane? Is there any where any other chief but Chaka?"

Matuane expired in torments. The Zulas immediately tore out his entrails, and emptying the gall bladder they inflated it, and hung it as an amulet on the head dress of their bloody prince, while a regiment of soldiers was sent to massacre all the Manquanes, men and women, old men and children.*

* Without wishing to anticipate events, I may here remark that Divine Providence mercifully preserved, in the general massacre of the Manquanes, one poor Basuto and his wife, who had hired themselves to them for their food. He

Thus perished this little nation as rapacious and ferocious as that of the Matluibis, and ultimately no less unfortunate. Their history, and that of the african tribes
in general, may be summed up in these three words of a
modern historian: *Qui vit de pillage, ne vit pas long-
temps*;—a robber's life is short.

The common proverb of the natives themselves is,
that the spirit of plunder is their greatest curse, and the
cause of their destruction. At the time of these sad calamities, the history of which we have attempted to retrace,
it was customary to say to the chief after having ruined
him, and that even to the most innocent among them, as
for example None:—*Go now, and live on human flesh.*

Cannibals were to be found every where. No one
could travel in safety. No one dared trust his neighbour.
On the other hand, the wild beasts multiplied greatly,
and pursued people even to the doors of their houses into
which the people were accustomed to enter backwards,
as if it were necessary even there to use every precaution
against their attacks. It has happened oftener than once
that a Basuto having gone out of his hut at night has
been carried off to some neighbouring wood by the hyænas, there to be devoured. His cries would naturally
cause his relatives to hasten to his help, but soon his cries
would cease, and the relatives would hasten to regain
their huts.

The chiefs, for all that, continued to prey upon one
another. Disturbed by the Bamokoteris, Makheta
imprudently resolved to call the Korannas to his as-

---

received a deep wound on the right side, which laid him amongst the dying,
unable to move from pain. The Zulas went away; he rose, sought for his
partner in life, and found her also dangerously wounded, and lying amongst the
bodies of the dead. He took her and set out with her for their native
country, which they at length succeeded in reaching, having, it may be said,
dragged themselves thither. Some years later the gospel was preached to that
tribe; this unfortunate African was *the first* to believe; and from that time he
has experienced its life. His wife also is a convert, and their happy children
daily attend the school at Bosio. The one parent is called Daniel 'Ntlaloe and
the other Umpule.

sistance. They went together and plundered the former, who took revenge for this by murdering the brother of Motlume. Then Moyakesane openly complained, and threatened the Basutos that he would have recourse to the expedient of his uncle, at the same time taking better precautions than he. They entrusted their cattle to him to keep, as much to appease him as in consequence of a promise which he gave to lead these herds with great care, and in all safety, to pasture on the banks of the Orange River. But the Korannas discovered him there, and went and took from him the whole.

Nine times in succession did these brigands pillage the Basutos, who in their turn took from them their horses and guns, but without being able to turn these to any account. They could neither understand, the use nor the mechanism of the captured arms; and they broke down the guns, and all the iron of the saddles and bridles to make hoes of the material.

It appears that the Korannas arrived only in companies of eight or ten at a time, and these often not well selected. One of them, having been thrown from a skittish horse, was found by some of the Basutos alone in the midst of the fields. The unfortunate man was a cripple, who could hardly drag himself along with the help of a wooden leg. He implored mercy, but it was in vain. Never could such vagabonds have done the mischief they have in those districts, if it had not been that they alone of all the tribes were acquainted with the use of fire arms. After having ruined many of the smaller basuto chiefs, they went to attack them ; these met them below Merabing, and overcame them notwithstanding all their boasting. It is related, that during an unsuccessful attempt made by Piet Witvoet, to secure the herds belonging to that town, one young woman on hearing of the death of her husband, who had been killed, ran in a state of distraction to the field of battle, threw her infant to the bottom of the mountain, and cast herself after it, at the same place in which the father had fallen.

The superstitious natives, in speaking at that time of

the evils with which they had been deluged, were accustomed to say, that the sorcerers by their enchantments had sown death throughout the country. For three years in succession the corn was destroyed by drought, or hail, or locusts. In 1831 Mosolekatse sent his troops to attack, one after the other, the Lighoyas, the Mantetis, and the Basutos. Divided into five small battalions, they laid siege to the five posts of Bosio. But the inhabitants of the town overwhelmed them with stones and showers of darts. The chief of the Matebeles, filled with indignation, set fire to the millet growing at the foot of the mountain, and cried to the natives as he was going away, "You calves; you are still little and lean. They must fatten you, and I will come for you next year." It is said that the furious general, with his own hand, stript the soldiers of their plumes. As to what more Mosolekatse did to them no one knows; only it is avowed that this formidable inkhosi, like the Chakas, sent out his troops to ravage or to fight on horrible conditions; and that their life, as in the case of Regulus at Carthage, depended on the success of the expedition.

In spite of his numerous and powerful enemies, Moshesh, during these calamitous times, maintained his position, aggrandised himself, and, more fortunate than any other chief of the country, even acquired a great reputation for wisdom and glory. Besides the oxen which he seized in the country itself, and those which he held of his father, he undertook two military expeditions against the Tambuquis, from whom he carried away many herds. The natives, seeing him comparatively rich, attached themselves to him. He recommended those of them who were emigrating by hundreds into the Cape colony and to Natal, to return after a time to their native country.*

Having heard in 1832 that there were missionaries, he

---

* Thompson relates that in the space of about two years (probably in 1827 and 1828) upwards of a thousand fugitives, the greater part of them in a state of extreme destitution, sought refuge in the colony,—a circumstance without a parallel in the previous history of the Cape.

took steps to procure one to settle amongst his people, and the providence of God supplied him with three in the course of the following year. About the same time peace took up its abode in the dwellings of the Bamoko-teris, and it has reigned there ever since. Their chief has succeeded in gathering around him thousands of natives, whom the calamities of the times had dispersed. He is every day becoming more enlightened and enriched, as are also his subjects; some of whom have received the gospel in faith and in love.

Amongst these is to be found the fierce and impetuous Makoniane, who now, gentle as a lamb, simple and docile as a child, said lately to one of the missionaries, under a feeling of his wretchedness by nature, and of his blessed-ness as a servant of God, " Evil may see itself personified in me. I have committed all kinds of crimes. My bloody hand hath slain no less than forty herdsmen, whose only crime was the possession of cattle, and this, without men-tioning those whom I have only wounded, or the canni-bals with their long detestable locks, whom I have exter-minated. I who had, in some measure, reduced them to the frightful alternative of dying of hunger, or of eating their children and their wives.

" Often, when my instructor has preached to an assem-bly of hearers, I imagined that he was relating to them my crimes. Often would I fain have stopped him. He seemed to be going a little too far. The word of his mouth, which he called the word of God, exposed my nakedness, and showed as in the light of day the plagues of my soul. Truly, I have a heart of clay; I am a worm which trails itself along,—a vile insect which attempts to exalt itself,—a particle of dust driven of the wind; I live, and yet I was ignorant of Him for whom I ought to live, the author of my life, the father of my salvation. Oh, that the Lord in his mercy should have revealed himself to me!

" Messengers of God, but for you we would have been as the Matluibis....Do not regret your native land. On no account return thither. Oh, never leave us. Forget, if you can, that you have brothers and sisters at home. God hath sent you to our aid. You have brought us peace. You have brought us life. Lately I counted my years by the number of my wars; since you have come hither I count them by the number of my harvests. The fountain of bread would have been dried up in this country but for you; there remained for us only the water from the rock, which was plentiful and always good, but we were afraid to stoop to drink it, and our wives dared not go to fill their pitchers from fear of the enemy; the sight of an antelope, the cry of a bird, the appearance of a bush filled them with fear. I foolishly believed that there were no men in the world but Basutos and Caffers : the Baroas having been destroyed by the assegai, or inhumanly consumed amidst the reeds and flags of the marshes where they thought to have found a refuge. I did not think that there was a place in the world where another question was entertained than that of war; and yet at that very time there were whites,—whites who are the friends of peace, who carry it to the pagan nations, who preach it, who cultivate it, and by daily fervent prayer implore it from heaven.

"When I saw you for the first time, I said to myself, These men have guns; they will teach us the use of them; and they will fight for us. When you told us to kneel on the ground and pray to Jehovah, I said in my heart, No, I must see him first. That is the reason why I looked at you through my fingers. The wisdom of the beasts of the field—such was mine. The foundation of your house excited a smile in me. Those of the church at Bosio when they were dug, made me wickedly to suppose that you were going to conceal powder with the design of destroying us all in one day. It was this which taught me that I carried within me a wounded conscience, and an accuser, which would leave me no peace.

"Am I indeed a man ?....Yes, I am ! I am a man ! and a christian, since I have found health for my soul in the gospel of Christ. But by nature? By nature I am a wild beast. No, rather let me say, I am one of those beasts of the field which lie down and which rise up, without even knowing what they do; which graze where-ever they find pasture, but without thinking where they will be able to rest at night; which die as they have lived, and are immediately devoured by the birds of prey, from the rocks of the valley. The gospel alone has made me know what I am, and what I ought to be, my greatness, my nothingness, my duty towards God, my duty towards men. This gospel speaks to me. It seeks me out when I wander. It calls me back to myself. The pain which I suffer through sin leads me to comprehend, to love, and to praise. Jesus is my Saviour. That is what I believe, what I feel, what I love to hear, what my heart keeps repeating. It makes itself manifest even to Makoniane!"

APPENDIX.

Place of Observation.	Date.	Time of day.	Thermometer.			
			Reaumur.		Fahrenheit.	
			Sun.	Shade.	Sun.	Shade.
Thaba Bosio.	Feb. 14	8 a.m.	25	15	89	65
		Noon.	29	22	98	82
		4 p.m.	29	22	98	82
——	15	6 a.m.		12		59
		Noon.		21		80
		8 p.m.		17		70
Penane (sources of the Saule.)	16	7 a.m.		15		65
		½ p. 1 p.m		16		68
		4 p.m.		15		65
Konguana (above Kuening.)	17	7 a.m.		18		72
		Noon.		24		86
		4 p.m.		19		74
		10 p.m.		16½		69
Pororo (S. E. of Makosane.)	18	6 a.m.		15		65
		8 a.m.	22		82	
		1 p.m.	72			
Mokokuane (above Butabute.)	19	7 a.m.		15		65
		Noon.	26		91	
		8 p.m.		12		59
Game (S. E. of Intluana-Chuana.)	20	Sunrise.		10		65
		Noon.	30	17	100	70
		9 p.m.		15		65
20 miles south of Intluana-Chuana.	21	Sunrise.		7		48
		Noon.	29	15	98	65
		Sunset.		7		48
		9 p.m.		5		43
Cavern du Dimanche (S. W. of Mont-aux-Sources.)	22	Sunrise.		2		37
		Noon.	23		84	
		9 p.m.		7		48
——	23	Sunrise.		4		41
		Noon.	29	17	98	70
		4 p.m.	17½			71
		Sun set.		12		59
		9 p.m.		10		55
Port des Louanges (14 miles south of Mont-aux-Sources.)	24	Sunrise.		5		43
		½ p. 1 p.m.		19		74
		Sunset.		11½		58
		9 p. m.		10		55
——	25	Sunrise.		6		45
		1 p.m.	25		89	
		4 p.m.	10		55	
		Sunset.		10		55
		9 p.m.		7		48
Game.	26	Sunrise.		4		41
		Noon.	27		91	
		Sunset.		14		63
		9 p.m.		12		59

State of the.Heavens.

In the morning, thick fog; at noon, clear sky; at 4 p.m. cloudy to the E. and N. E.; and at 9 p.m. sky covered with clouds.

At 6 a.m. sky covered to the E. and N. E.; 1 noon, every where covered; 8 p.m. rain.

At 7 a.m. sky covered with light clóuds at great height; 1 p.m. heavy rain; 4 p.m. changeable.

Sky obscured all day; at midnight, rain.

At 6 a.m. cloudy; remainder of day, clear sky; towards evening, sky obscured.

Cloudless sky.

At sun rise, serene sky; noon, clouds to the N. and E.; afternoon, heavy rain; at 9 p.m. rain ceased.

At sun rise, light clouds scattered over the sky; at noon, clear sky; at sun set, light clouds to the E. and N.; at 9 p.m., clouds coming from the E. and N. W.

At sun rise, light clouds in the S. E. and N. W.; at noon, light clouds in the E. and N., and a light wind from the N.; at 9 p.m., sky dappled with small clouds.

At sun rise, light clouds above the mountains; at 4 p.m. clear sky; at 9 p.m. clear sky.—N.B. The temperature of this day was taken in the Caverne du Dimanche.

At sun rise, light clouds above the mountain; at 1 p.m. thick clouds to the E.; in the evening, clear sky.

At sun rise, light clouds; 1 p.m., clear sky; 4 p.m., cloudy to N. E., wind N. E. very strong; 5 p.m., storm accompanied with rain and hail; sun set, thick clouds to the N.; at 9 p.m., sky covered to the N., clear to the S.

Morning, clear sky; at noon, light clouds to the N. and W.; sun set, sky covered to the E.; at 9 p.m., sky clear.

Place of Observation.	Date.	Time of day.	Reaumur.		Fahrenheit.	
			Sun.	Shade.	Sun.	Shade.
Game.	27	Sun rise.		10		55
		Noon.	23		84	
		10 p.m.		18		72
Merabing.	28	9 a.m.	25		89	
		Noon.	30	19	100	74
		6 p.m.		19		74
		9 p.m.		16		68
Mekuatling.	29	9 a.m.	24		86	
		Noon.		27		91
		9 p.m.		14		63
——	Mar. 1	10 a.m.		12		59
		Noon.		13		61
		4 p.m.		17		70
		9 p.m.		16		68
Thaba Bosio.	2	8 a.m.	20	12½	77	60
		Noon.	24		86	
		9 p.m.		17		70

State of the Heavens.

Sunrise, cloudy on the top of the mountains and along the rivers; noon, storm with claps of thunder to the N. and W. ; 10 p.m., sky very clear.

9 a.m., a mist along the vallies ; noon, sky covered to the N. E. ; 6 p.m., storm in the N. E., sky covered with high and light clouds.

9 a.m., sky sprinkled with bright and piled clouds ; noon, thick clouds to the N. W. and S. E., wind from the S. W. ; between 3 and 4 p.m., rain with claps of thunder ; 6 p.m., sky clear.

Morning, storm, cold rain ; noon, fine weather.

8 a.m., light clouds to the E. ; all the rest of the day, cloudy.

SEASONS OF THE YEAR.

MALUTIS.		EUROPE.
	SPRING.	
September.		March.
October.		April.
November.		May.
	SUMMER.	
December.		June.
January.		July.
February.		August.
	AUTUMN.	
March.		September.
April.		October.
May.		November.
	WINTER.	
June.		December.
July.		January.
August.		February.

INDEX